Peter Lassen

Legendary Truths

Peter Lassen & His Gold Rush Trail
In
Fact & Fable

KEN JOHNSTON

Cover Design: Antelope Design
Cover Photo: Ken Johnston

Quotes from George R. Stewart used by permission of
University of Nebraska Press, Lincoln, Nebraska

J. Goldsborough Bruff drawings used by
permission of Huntington Library, San Marino, California

We offer other great books in a variety
of genres including some award winning Novels, Mysteries, Western History
titles, Gardening, Cooking, Personal & Spiritual Growth and Books for Kids.
We offer traditional "Tree-Books," E-Books, and downloadable Audio Books.
Visit our website at PronghornPress.org
Read the Publisher's Blog, Sign Up for Our Newsletter
and Join Us on Facebook!

Support a Small Press!

www.pronghornpress.org

"We find few historians who have been diligent enough in their search for truth; it is their common method to take on trust what they help distribute to the public; by which means a falsehood once received from a famed writer becomes traditional to posterity."
—John Dryden (1631-1700), English poet

Table of Contents

Preface ... ix

Prologue ... xvii

Part 1

Peter Lassen the Early Years

Part 2

Gold Rush 1849

Part 3

Lassen's Gold Rush Trail and Alternate Routes

Part 4

Lassen 1849 and Beyond

Preface

All peoples have a myth, and as Americans we love our legends but often loath our history. Many of us prefer to view our past more as a heroic parable than as a complicated and contentious record of the human experience. Few epochs in the history of the United States have achieved a status as legendary as the creation of a continental nation... The story of the overland trails that brought more than half a million new settlers to the American West between 1840 and 1870 is central to this beloved tradition. Like all legends, it is a powerful mix of fact and fable.

—Will Bagley

In 1970, after my service during the Vietnam War, I exchanged my Navy officer's uniform for a Ranger uniform and moved to Northern California where I had the good fortune to be employed as a National Park Service Ranger Naturalist/Interpreter for eight summers at Lassen Volcanic National Park. In addition to being one of the jewels in the National Park system, the park has the distinction of having a historically active volcano; geothermal springs and pools; spectacular scenery with mountain lakes, cascading streams, and melodious waterfalls; a rich legacy of Indian cultures; and a historically important segment of the Nobles Emigrant Trail running through it.

In addition to leading nature walks, guiding backcountry hikes, working in the museum, and giving evening campfire programs, I spent four summers developing and doing a Living History Program interpreting the Nobles and Lassen Trails. The program traced their development from the beginnings of the Oregon Trail to the branching off the California Trail and its evolvement into a trail system that brought emigrants to California over Walker Pass into Southern California, and over Stephen's Pass, which was popularly called Donner's Pass because of the Donner Tragedy that occurred there in 1846. The Donner Party had followed the Truckee Route west of where Reno, Nevada now stands on their way over the high Sierras to Sutter's Fort, where Sacramento, California is now located.

Shortly after the discovery of gold in California in 1848, a Mormon company returning to Salt Lake pioneered a new route over the Sierras to the south of the Donner/Truckee Route in order to avoid the difficulties encountered by the Donner Party. The Mormon Route* continued, passing south of Lake Tahoe and following up the Carson River to where it joined the Truckee Route east of where Reno now stands and followed the California Trial up the Humboldt River. Both of these routes were equally steep and treacherous for wagons to cross. In 1848, in order to avoid the steepness of these routes, Peter Lassen pioneered a new route that branched north off the established California Trail along the Humboldt River near where Winnemucca, Nevada is now located.

Lassen Trail crossed the Black Rock Desert, which was equally as foreboding and difficult as the Forty Mile Desert the other routes crossed, but it avoided the steep, rocky ascents of the other two trails. Lassen Trail continued around the east and then south sides of the base of Lassen Peak and entered the Sacramento Valley north of present day Chico, California. It then went directly to Lassen's Rancho on the Sacramento River.

During the Gold Rush of 1849, twenty-five to thirty thousand gold

---

* The Mormon Route later became known as the Mormon/Carson Route because it followed the Carson River.

seekers, who soon came to be called the Argonauts, after the classic Greek tales of Jason and the Argonauts (seekers of the Golden Fleece), rushed to California following the established trails of the Truckee Route over Donner Pass and the Mormon/Carson Route farther south. About a third (8,000 to 9,000) of the 49ers came over the Lassen Trail. Although easier to travel, it was longer than the other routes and detoured as far north as Goose Lake in southeast Oregon before turning south to California.

The distance of this northern route was greatly shortened in 1852 when William Nobles pioneered a shortcut from Black Rock Desert that went more directly west toward the base of Lassen Peak and traversed the area that would later become Lassen National Park.

In addition to researching the history of the trails and passing on the

Author, Living History Program, Lassen National Park

information to park visitors at the Pioneer Program, my job as a Park Ranger was to portray the conditions that the emigrants encountered on the trails on their way to California. For the presentation, I used horses for transportation, and hitched oxen to a covered wagon and pulled it to a campsite, where women in pioneer dress mixed the dough used in cooking Dutch oven biscuits while telling children's stories to younger visitors. As the biscuits were baking, I recounted the development of the California trail system, including the Lassen and Nobles Trails, and the experiences of the emigrants traveling those trails to the adult visitors. The program was very successful and is still presented to visitors each summer at the park.

While I researched the history of the trails, I continually encountered historic discrepancies and contradictions, especially about the character and ability of Peter Lassen, for whom the trail and the park were named. Whereas his friends and contemporaries, including prominent pioneers and military officers sought his company, advice, and guidance, others, including some disillusioned, trail worn Argonauts and even some historians, denounced him and his achievements.

My curiosity was piqued. I began to research journals, diaries, manuscripts, newspaper articles, recorded recollections, books, and graduate dissertations located in libraries of colleges, museums, and historical societies across the country—from the Beinecke Library at Yale University in Connecticut, to the Bancroft Library at the University of California in Berkeley. I continued to collect information and record various quotes and anecdotes, searching records in as diverse locations as: The National Frontier Trails Museum in Independence, Missouri, Chariton County Court House Records and Lassen's farm in Missouri, The California Trail Interpretive Center in Elko, Nevada, and the Lassen Historical Museum in Susanville, California.

I have ridden my mountain bike over the Lassen Trail from Lassen's Meadows (now Rye Patch Reservoir) on the Humboldt River, through the Black Rock Desert and High Rock Canyon (in present day Nevada), down the Pit River, around Lassen Peak, and down the ridge between Mill and Deer Creeks to Vina, California, where Lassen's Rancho was located. In addition, I have traveled sections of the trail many times in four-wheel drive vehicles, on horseback, and on a motorcycle.

In doing so, I became aware of and joined the Oregon/California Trails Association (OCTA) and Trails West, Inc.—both outstanding organizations that promote trail protection and mapping. Both organizations have meetings, conventions, campouts, and work sessions where historians and trail enthusiasts gather to preserve, to learn, and to share information about the various trails.

In traveling the trails and doing the research and writing, I have encountered many obstacles and difficulties, as did my predecessors with their wagons and oxen. However, I have also had the help of family, friends, and competent librarians and historians, who have helped me compile my research into a book that I hope will dispel some of the discrepancies and contradictions abounding in the Lassen legacy.

Author at Lassen's Meadows with bike packed for ride over the Lassen Trail

First and foremost, I must thank Jo Massey for accompanying me on many of my research trips, and for her editing skills in weeding out run-on sentences, checking spelling, punctuation, and all those obstacles that confront an author on his journey to completing a book. She also researched proper format and footnote usage, and any mistakes that may remain should be attributed to me, as I'm sure she found the path to completion both rocky and difficult.

The librarians and staff at many libraries were very helpful in locating journals and manuscripts. The staff at the California State Historical Library in Sacramento provided a wealth of information on innumerable visits, as did the staff at the Bancroft Library. Especially helpful were Anne Hiller Clark and Barbara Ditman at the Shaw Historical Library at Oregon Institute of Technology in Klamath Falls, Oregon. Anne Hiller Clark introduced me to the Lassen Thread (see Bibliography), which presented many current opinions and sources of more current thoughts on the legacy of Peter Lassen.

I would like to thank Zellamae Miles (Great-granddaughter of Isaac Roop), Bob Middleton, and Tony Jonas, all docents at the Lassen Historical Museum in Susanville, California for their help in making such items as Peter Lassen's pipe and other items available for photographing. Also, Tim Purdy of Susanville, was helpful in providing anecdotal history on Lassen as recorded and passed down from the local inhabitants in the area since Lassen's time.

Peggy McGuckian and Kathryn Ataman, archaeologists for the Bureau of Land Management in Winnemucca, Nevada were very helpful in providing historical information about events and persons associated with the recovery of Peter Lassen's rifle, which was apparently the only item taken after his murder—information that sheds some circumstantial insight into who Lassen's murderer may have been. In addition, they shared documented forensic evidence from recently excavated remains of Edward Clapper, who was also killed at the Lassen Murder Site near Black Rock.

I would also like to express my deepest appreciation to trail historians, authors, and editors including: Will Bagley, Bob Black, Don Buck, Bob Clark, Tom Hunt, Dr. Jack and Patricia Fletcher, and Richard Silva for the time they spent reading the manuscript, and for their comments and suggestions for improvement. I must admit that in some cases, where opinions may have varied, I stubbornly stuck to my interpretation of the material available, but in all fairness, I have tried to present the facts so that the reader may form his or her own conclusions.

And finally, as we reach the end of the trail, I extend my gratitude to Annette Chaudet, of Pronghorn Press for completing the journey and leading us to our destination.

Kenneth L. Johnston
Klamath Falls, Oregon

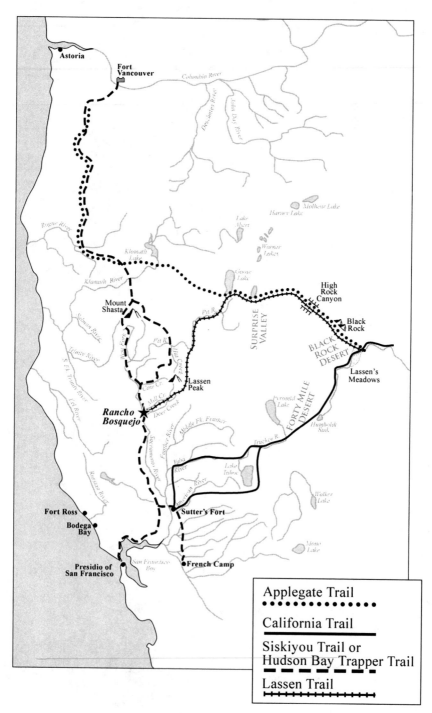

Astoria

Fort Vancouver

Columbia River

Des Chutes River

John Day River

Rogue River

Klamath Lake

Klamath River

Mount Shasta

Salmon River

West Fork

Trinity River

Pit R.

S. Fk. Trinity River

Eel River

Cow Cr.

Mill Cr.

Hat Creek

Lassen Peak

Deer Creek

Rancho Bosquejo

Russian River

Fort Ross

Bodega Bay

Presidio of San Francisco

San Francisco Bay

Sutter's Fort

French Camp

Sacramento River

American River

Feather River

Middle Fk. Feather

Yuba River

Bear River

Lake Tahoe

Truckee R.

Pit R.

SURPRISE VALLEY

Goose Lake

Lake Abert

Warner Lakes

Harney Lake

Malheur Lake

High Rock Canyon

Black Rock

BLACK ROCK DESERT

Lassen's Meadows

Pyramid Lake

FORTY MILE DESERT

Humboldt Sink

Walker Lake

Mono Lake

Applegate Trail
•••••••••••

California Trail
————

Siskiyou Trail or
Hudson Bay Trapper Trail
– – – – –

Lassen Trail
—+—+—+—+—

Prologue

Truth is always paradoxical.—Confucius

The search for truth implies a duty. One must not conceal
any part of what one has recognized to be true.

—Albert Einstein

The legends and legacy of Peter Lassen have captured people's imaginations and interests in a surprising array of ways that have prompted both admiration and derisive criticism. He is remembered for his instrumental role in the development of California, and his name has been attached to more geologic and geographic features in California and Nevada than any other California pioneer except, perhaps, John C. Fremont or Kit Carson. They include a mountain, a national park, a national forest, a county in California, a college, a high school, post offices, creeks, the USS Lassen AE-3 (a World War II Liberty ship),[1] and innumerable businesses and landmarks. But perhaps the most important and controversial toponym is the Lassen Trail, an emigration route into California used during the Gold Rush era, which he helped develop.

Although longer than some of the previously popular routes of the California Trail, the Lassen Trail avoided the steep and extremely difficult ascents to Carson Pass and, especially, the infamous Donner Pass. It was shorter than the Walker Pass route. Although the Black Rock Desert, which the Lassen Trail crossed following the previously established Applegate route, was as daunting as the desert stretches encountered by other trails after they reached the Humboldt Sink, the important fact is that the Lassen Trail provided an alternate and perhaps safer route for the final hordes of 49ers flocking to California in 1849. It may well have saved the lives of many emigrants because of overgrazed conditions and hardships they would have encountered had they followed the Carson and Truckee routes late in the season.

The earlier Argonauts of the year had crossed the Carson and Truckee routes depleting their resources, and rumors abounded about the conditions to be encountered on those trails. Due to the availability of feed for the oxen, lower elevations, and less difficult passes for the estimated 8,000 emigrants who chose the combined Applegate and Lassen routes, a Donner-like tragedy was averted. Even so, stragglers were caught on the trail in "blinding snowstorms," and rescue parties were sent to aid them. But the conditions and snow depths they encountered were far less severe than what the Donners had experienced three years earlier on the Donner Pass.

Major Daniel Rucker, who was placed in charge of the 1849 government relief parties sent out on the incoming trails, reported:

> *Although the distance is much greater than by the old routes, and some of the emigrants were longer in getting in, I cannot but think it a fortunate circumstance they did so, for the loss of property would have been greater on the old trail as the grass would have been eaten off long before they could have arrived.[2]*

Technically, the Lassen Trail began at Goose Lake, where it branched off from the Applegate Trail.* Often the route from Lassen's Meadows

---

* The Applegate Trail branched off the California Trail at (what was later called) Lassen's Meadows and went past Goose Lake on its way to Oregon. It is recognized by Trails West (an organization located in Reno, Nevada, that preserves and marks historical trails) guides and markers that the Lassen Trail officially began at Davis Creek near Goose Lake. Some referred to the route from Lassen's Meadows to Goose

to Goose Lake was referred to as the Applegate/Lassen Route or Trail, because for this part of the route they were the same. This section contained some of the worst difficulties and hardships of the entire journey. The Applegate Trail went to Oregon, whereas, emigrants going to California generally referred to this part of their journey as the Lassen Cutoff, or sometimes the Cherokee Cutoff. Ironically, the blame and/or credit for the hardships encountered on this section by the emigrants of 1849 was not attributed to Applegate* or the "Cherokee," but to Lassen, who had been the first wagonmaster to lead a wagon train over the route to California in 1848. Even though often blamed for the hardships, Peter Lassen was also given credit and was honored by later having the route named for him.

As a member of the Stockton Party, Lassen had personally witnessed the grisly remains of hardship, starvation, death, and cannibalism at the Donner camp on his trip from California east to Missouri in 1847. Lassen, along with other members of the party, recognized the advantages of a new northern route, and he chose to lead his train over it to his ranch in the Sacramento Valley. It is true that he and his train suffered the same hardships of the arduous journey that others also suffered on the other trails. However, he had previously been over part of the route in 1846 and had had close association with other western explorers, route finders, and guides including: Joseph Chiles, Kit Carson, John C. Fremont, John J. Myers, Milton McGee, Benoni Hudspeth, and Hudson's Bay trappers. These men, who had experience and information about the route and its advantages, undoubtedly shared their knowledge freely with Lassen.

It is obvious that when he chose this route in 1848, he could not possibly have had the clairvoyance to foresee the hordes of Argonauts in 1849 that would follow McGee, Hudspeth and Myers, when they turned off the main trail to follow his tracks through the mountains. It is ironic that he was both honored for developing the route, and at the same time subjected to aspersion and opprobrium for developing a "shortcut" that was not a shortcut. The trail was derisively called the "Greenhorn Trail," the "Lassen Horn Route," and the "Lassen Death

---

Lake as the Applegate/Lassen Trail or the Lassen/Applegate, but it was Jesse Applegate with Levi Scott who opened it in 1846.

* The Applegate Trail, although named for Jesse Applegate, was co-pioneered by him and Levi Scott in 1846.

Trail" by "greenhorns"* who took his trail and who suffered hardships that were common to all the trails that year.

George Stewart, in his history of the development of the California Trail, included a chapter on the Lassen Trail where he wrote, "A generation later it became legend, and old men of Lassen County were telling tales. But the stories have a ring of truth about them, at least of that legendary truth which sometimes comes closer to basic reality than mere history can."[3] Stewart and other historical authors have stuck to their "legendary truths." Harold Curran in reference to *Fearful Crossing* wrote, "The stories weren't always the same but that doesn't matter—imagination is the soul of legend."[4] John Ford, in reference to *The Man Who Shot Liberty Valance*, said, "When the myth takes over the shadows of the truth, you print the myth." In the stage play *Man of La Mancha*, written by Dale Wasserman, Don Quixote said, "Facts are the enemy of truth." Mark Twain advised, "Get your facts first, and then you can distort them as much as you please."

Osborne Russell, a trapper, noted this tendency to embellish the truth in his journal:

> *I am fully aware of the numerous statements which have been given to travelers in a jocular manner by hunters and traders among the Rocky Mountains merely to hear themselves talk or according to the Mountaineers expression give them a long yarn or "Fish Story" to put in their journals, and I have frequently seen "Fish Stories" published with the original very much enlarged which had not at first the slightest ground for truth to rest upon. It is utterly impossible for a person who is merely traveling thro, or even residing one or two years in the Rock Mountains to give an accurate description of the Country or its Inhabitants.[5]*

Fortunately, many of the emigrants on the trails west and on the Lassen Trail kept journals or diaries, adhering to the dictum that "a life worth living is a life worth documenting." Men like John C. Fremont, John Bidwell, Joseph Goldsborough Bruff, Alonzo Delano, Israel Lord,

---

* George R. Stewart mentioned that '49 could well be called "The Year of the Greenhorn" because many of emigrants, especially the latecomers who took the trail were "city-dwellers" and "definitely men of a soft generation, far removed from the frontier."

and many other early Californians and emigrants recorded their daily experiences and observations, and these have been preserved in libraries and historical archives for us to research today. It is this rich resource, which has caused modern historians, including the author of this book, to investigate the "legendary truths" and to ferret out the facts.

It is too bad that others, including Peter Lassen and more of his close associates, didn't leave written documentation of their travels, thoughts, and dealings, since this lack has provided opportunity for the myths and fables to proliferate.

George Orwell once wrote, "A writer writes in order to convert history, to set the record straight." That is why it is time to look at the "legends" and myths surrounding Peter Lassen's life and the development of the Lassen Trail. Many books and articles that have been written about Lassen and his trail perpetuate the myths and legends about him, but many manuscripts of pioneer journals still exist from people who knew him. It is from these writings that the facts about Lassen's travels and activities are drawn, and these facts are causing historians to question the "legends."

It is the intent of this author to present the story of Peter Lassen as the facts reveal, and to point out the sources of misinformation, myth, and rumors that have served to unjustifiably denigrate the integrity of one of Northern California's most prominent pioneers—a mountain man and explorer, who led a colorful and adventurous life and who earned the confidence and respect of his contemporaries.

PART 1

Peter Lassen
Early Years

LEGENDARY TRUTHS

1829–1838
Denmark to Missouri

*As scarce as truth is, the supply has always
been in excess of the demand.*—Josh Billings

Peter Lassen's name has been variously spelled as Lawson, Larsen,
Lassin, and Lasson at different times and places in his life. He was born
on October 31, 1800, in Farum, about fifteen miles from Copenhagen,
Denmark, to parents who were reportedly farm laborers. His father
was Lars Nielsen. According to Danish tradition, Peter took his last
name in honor of his father's first name and should have therefore
been called Larson (Lars' son). His mother was Johanne Sophie
Westergaard, the daughter of Peder Oluf Westergaard, a schoolmaster
in Norre Herlev, Denmark.

Little is known of Peter's early life, but his nephew several
generations removed, a man named René Weybye Lassen of Denmark,
has done much research in the early records of Denmark, his home
country, and in America. While doing research in California, he
stayed at Bruce Barron's Lassen OX Shoe Ranch in Manton, where
he became familiar with the western landscape known to Peter Lassen.
In the words of Bruce Barron, René Lassen's research and book were
written to "...shine a light on many unknown facets of history that

have reflected on the life of this pioneer trailblazer."[1]

Peter's parents were married in Norre Herlev in 1799. Living in near poverty, they moved from farm to farm following available work. Their first son, Johan, was born a year before Peter, their second child. Their third child, Stine, was born in 1803 and died the same year. Their fourth was also a son, born in 1804 and he, too, soon passed away. Times were tough, but Peter thrived and grew, and his parents moved to Hilleröd when he was about nine years old.

It was in Hilleröd that his older brother died at the age of twelve. His parents had another son, named Christian, and later a daughter, named Karen Marie. However, there are no further records of those siblings.

Peter learned the blacksmith trade as a youth and his actual apprenticeship was under his uncle, Christian Nielsen. Throughout his life, he practiced this trade, interspersed with other pursuits. Wanting independence, he moved to Copenhagen in 1823 and was enrolled in the conscription register, but at sixty-two and a half inches, he was too short to be accepted as a soldier. Despite his diminutive stature, we can deduce that he possessed the strength needed to perform the heavy labor required of a blacksmith.

In order to become a master blacksmith, he had to be enrolled in the civic guard of Copenhagen. He sent his application to the king with a reference from Mr. Sigersted, his employer.[2]

> *That—journeyman blacksmith Peter Lassen Farum, who is working for me, and for the last two years has been in my employment—is an extremely competent journeyman of his profession, and has always shown very good conduct and behavior—that, is hereby certified on request, Copenhagen, 15 March 1827.*
> *—P. Sigersted, Master Blacksmith.*
> *Dronningens Tvergade no.335*

The application tells us that Peter had blue eyes and brown hair, and from later drawings, we know his facial features and prominent nose. He later received permission to join the guard, and the way was opened for him to become a master blacksmith, a distinction he attained on August 25, 1827.[3]

Lassen moved into his own apartment and started an independent business, but times were difficult and the economy was depressed in

Copenhagen. His father had passed away, leaving him responsible for his mother's welfare. Soon after, in March of 1829, Peter's grandfather died, leaving his inheritance to Peter's mother. Fischer, in his dissertation, speculates that this inheritance made her financially able to take care of herself. This freed Peter of his filial responsibility,[4] so he requested an exit permit from the King to emigrate to the "new established Danish Colony in America."[5] However, according to René Lassen, there was no record of a Danish community in America ever having existed. Perhaps this was merely a legal ploy to gain permission to emigrate.

Some writers claim that Lassen emigrated to America in 1829.[6] Stewart, in *The California Trail,* wrote, "… Peter Lassen was born a Dane, and had grown up to become a blacksmith. But wanderlust smote him. In '19, himself aged nineteen, he went to the United States…"[7] However, his application to the King was dated September 30, 1830. The Danish newspaper, *Helsingors Avis,** of October 12, 1830 reported that "On October 10, the following three persons were emigrating: master smith Larsen, carpenter Olsen, and master carpenter Holst—all bound for Boston."[8]

It isn't known how long Lassen remained in Boston or how long he stayed on the eastern seaboard, but he later moved to St. Louis and then to Keytesville, Missouri. Keytesville was named for James Keyte, who arrived in 1830. Keyte built a log cabin on the banks of the Muscle River (a tributary of the Missouri), where he established a small business, a post office, and later a water mill where Lassen may have worked. The *History of Howard and Chariton Counties*[9] said, "The original blacksmith was Peter Lassin, a Dane." However, it isn't clear from the history whether Lassen was the "original blacksmith" of the mill, or the community at large, or both.

Lassen purchased a tract of land, which he farmed, in the fertile bottomlands of the Missouri River, "…being the northwest quarter of section twenty eight of township fifty three north of the base line range no. nineteen west of five principal meridian situated in Chariton County state of Missouri containing one hundred and sixty acres more or less together with all and singular the rights liberties priviliges hereditaments appurtenances thereunto belonging or in anywise appertaining."[10]

---

* Local newspaper published in Elsinore, Denmark, at the time of Lassen's leaving.

Lassen purchased this land from M. Eiler for the sum of $250 on March 14, 1837, and farmed the land while working at his blacksmith trade. It was several miles from the Keyte's mill; however, according to Swartzlow, "The blacksmith shop was located at what later became

Keyte's Mill in Keytesville, Missouri.
Courtesy of General Price Museum, Keytesville, Missouri.

the town of Keytesville." Lassen later built a sawmill in California, perhaps using mill knowledge and experience gained in Keytesville.

On February 18, 1842, after he had moved to California, he sold half of the quarter section for $300—"the south half of the northwest quarter of section twenty eight, township fifty three and range nineteen, containing eighty acres be the same more or less." The land sale was recorded and signed by Henry W. Allin, attorney in fact for Peter Lassin [sic].[11] When or if he sold the other half isn't known, and there apparently is no record of communication between Lassen and his attorney.

LEGENDARY TRUTHS

Lassen became a member of the local Masonic Lodge, Warren Lodge No. 74, Keytesville, and it was in Missouri where he made many friends and acquaintances who would later play a part in California's history. He also met John Sutter, who left for Oregon on his way to California in 1838, and who would later help Lassen enter California and get established. Many of Chariton County's documents were lost in a fire and it is impossible to verify early records, but Lassen was reported to have been a member of the local militia and may have been the one who organized the militia of "seventy-five men and had them ready for duty in 1838."[12]

Missouri, at that time, was filling with people following the American frontier and learning by experience how to live in and tame the wilderness. The popular Leatherstocking novels by James Fennimore Cooper were piquing people's interest in the mysterious lands farther to the west. Washington Irving's three western narratives, *A Tour of the Prairies, Astoria,* and *The Adventures of Captain Bonneville,* written in quick succession in 1835-1837, held readers spellbound as they vicariously experienced adventures in the unfamiliar, far-off lands. The lure of adventure, the promise of more "elbow room" in a "land of opportunity" on a continent "allotted by providence," the descriptions of fantastic natural features, and the abounding rumors of the fertile agricultural lands and healthful benefits of "salubrious zephyrs" in California were fomenting a drive of expansionism that would later be called "manifest destiny." People in the East wanted to "see the Elephant!"—a nebulous term that later was used during the 1840s to describe the journey, the opportunities, and the hardships associated with such an undertaking.

In 1836 while Lassen was still in Missouri, Dr. Marcus Whitman and his wife Narcissa, along with Rev. Henry H. Spalding and his wife, Eliza, followed a route that would later be known as the Oregon Trail, to Fort Vancouver. The Whitmans set up a mission for the Cayuse Indians at Waiilatpu near Walla Walla, while the Spaldings started a mission for the Nez Pierce Indians, east and slightly north of Walla Walla at Lapwai in Idaho. The two wives were the first women to cross the continental divide, a courageous act that opened the minds of others to the possibility of taking their families west. It was an important event in the development of travel that opened the West. A great epic of western migration was about to begin,* and Lassen was in the right place at the right time to have his penchant for wanderlust re-activated—or re-awakened.

That penchant would lead to a life of exploration and adventure, fame, elusive fortune, and one that would end in mystery.

---

* The Panic of 1837 caused a depression in the United States, and as the value of the dollar sank to five cents, many people began to look more seriously at the opportunities the West could provide.

LEGENDARY TRUTHS

1839–1845
Moving West to Oregon

Legends die hard. They survive as truth rarely does.

—Helen Hayes

In the spring of 1839, Lassen's wanderlust caused him to join an emigrant party of twelve men and two women emigrating from Missouri to Oregon. Included in the group were the wives of Rev. J. S. Griffin and Asahel Munger, missionaries. Others in the party included J. Wright, William Geiger, and Dr. J. S. Wislizenus. At the more favored "jumping-off point" of Westport,[*] on the Missouri River, they joined with two other parties. One party was from St. Louis including D. G. Johnson, Charles Klein, David D. Dutton, and William Wiggins, whose destination was California. The other group of nine men "in the service of the Fur Company of Saint Louis (Chouteau, Pratt & Co.), an amalgamation of the American Fur Company and the Rocky Mountain Fur Company" under the leadership of Moses "Black" Harris. They were to bring merchandise to the annual fur rendezvous to be held at Green River.[1]

---

[*] Westport became the "jumping-off point" of choice, because it was farther west than Independence and had a more convenient port. In addition, those departing from Westport avoided the necessity of fording the Blue River—a difficult crossing.

Unfortunately, Peter Lassen never kept a journal, or at least one hasn't surfaced; so the writings of some of the members of the party, including Wislizenus and the reminiscences of Wiggins and Munger, give us some idea of the adventures and happenings Lassen experienced with the party on the trail. Journals of other travelers of the time painted verbal portraits of the conditions on the trail and the places they saw. It is also important to note that on this journey with mountain men and trappers, Lassen was exposed to skills and techniques of western travel that he would later use as a wagonmaster, trail developer, and guide.

An interesting account of the party's travels was also given in the Saturday, April 6, 1878, San Jose, California paper, *The Pioneer*. It was attributed to the "pen of Williams of Monterey" and was excerpted from an earlier edition of the *San Francisco Examiner*. Swartzlow, in her book, *Peter Lassen, Northern California's Trail Blazer,* believed that Williams and Wiggins were probably the same person as their writing styles were quite similar.

Both made references to the pronunciation and the mispronunciation of place names, and their writings sounded remarkably alike, but the question remains that they may have been different men. A discussion of Wiggins in a later chapter, will point out that he wrote a letter* to Thomas Larkin, the U.S. Consul, denouncing John Sutter and making accusations against Peter Lassen, asking Larkin to report it to the Governor of California, Manual Micheltorena. In contrasting opinion, Williams, in his reminiscences, highly praised John Sutter and his hospitality and contributions to the development of California.

If they were indeed different people, as these differences of opinion seem to indicate, then Williams was one of the un-named members of the party, but his colorful descriptions add significantly to our understanding of the party's journey.

It was on May 4, 1839, that they met at Sapling Grove, about eight miles west of Westport, Missouri. The party consisted of twenty-seven persons in all, a heterogeneous mixture of mountain men, trappers, missionaries, a medical doctor, a blacksmith, and other adventurers. The fur company goods were loaded onto four two-wheeled carts, each of which carried 800-900 pounds, and other effects were packed on the

---

* Written in "Sagante" (variously spelled: Sayante, Lagante, or Layante. Author's note: These are probably all misspellings of Zayante, where Peter Lassen built the first water powered mill in California.)

LEGENDARY TRUTHS

fifty to sixty pack mules and horses.

The daily routine was established soon after their start, and according to Wislizenus, "At dawn, the leader rouses the camp with an inharmonious: 'Get up! Get up! Get up!' Every one rises. The first care is for the animals. They are loosed from their pickets and allowed an hour for grazing. Meanwhile we prepare our breakfast, strike our tents, and prepare for the start." The carts went first, followed by the pack animals, which were led during the first days of the journey, but were later left free to follow.

A noon rest of from one to two hours was usually observed. The animals were turned loose to graze. They were hobbled and they dragged a long rope fastened around their necks or to their halters, to ease their re-capture.

Later in the afternoon, campsites were chosen with the requisites of water, grass, and wood for the fire. Supper was eaten and the weary travelers sprawled by the campfire, whiling away the evening with chatter and smoking. They had seven tents, which they shared, and slept wrapped up in blankets.

On the fifth day, they reached the Kansas River, where they began to see the Kaw or Kansas Indians and their villages, and were visited by them. Wislizenus described the men as having heads shaved so, that on top, only a long lock remained, or else the sides were shaved leaving a helmet-shaped comb in the middle.

The company marched two days along the Blue River, "without following its windings...Round about, to the horizon, one sees nothing but grass and sky; no bush, no creek relieves the eye from the wearying prospect...only an antelope at times flits by."[2]

William Wiggins, on the other hand wrote in his reminiscences that after leaving the departure point at Sapling Grove:

> *...nothing of import occurred until we reached the buffalo on the Platte. Just at this juncture everything in the way of groceries and breadstuffs gave out, when the party fell back on nature's larder, which at that time was bountifully stored. ...Thenceforth the bill of fare consisted of buffalo, deer, elk, antelope, cat-fish, sucker, trout, salmon, duck, pheasant, sage fowl, beaver, hare, horse, grizzly bear, badger, and dog. In short, the party preyed upon every animal that would support life, from the buffalo down to the*

ground-squirrel, asking no questions for consciences sake. As minimum understanding seems to prevail in regard to the last animal alluded to, a particular description of it may not be uninteresting.[3]

It is perhaps somewhat larger than the ground squirrel of California, is subterranean and gregarious in its habits, living in "villages," and from a supposed resemblance in the feet as well as in the spinal termination to that of the canine family it is in popular language known simply as the prairie-dog. But in the imposing technology of the mountain graduate it is styled the "canus prairie cuss," because its "cussed holes" so often cause the hunter to be unhorsed when engaged in the chase.[4]

David Dutton also noted, "At this part of our journey, we were surrounded by game in great plenty, wild horses, elk, deer, bear and mountain sheep being the most numerous."[5]

Buffalo were so plentiful that it was a common thing to see hundreds or thousands, so many that Dutton said, "They were very numerous and in making our way to the crossing of the Platte, we were many times obliged to wait for them to pass."[6] Wiggins added, "on one occasion, had the camp not halted, should have been trampled down."[7]

Buffalo were killed not only for their meat, but also for hides. Dutton described a hunt:

The excitement and pleasure of killing buffalo in the chase exceeds all rural sports I ever engaged in. It is attended with dangers unaccustomed to the chase, for as the animal is shot, he whirls and makes a last and deadly plunge at the horse and rider to avoid which the trained horse with the rapidity of thought, sheers off without being reined and thus escapes the threatened danger. He still pursues, himself and horse excited to the highest degree; they run side by side till the blood pours from his mouth; he bellows and plunges to the earth, weltering in gore and the hunter is left to gaze with astonishment upon that which has been sport to him but death to the buffalo.[8]

In these reminiscences, Dutton indicated that he and Lassen rode mules on the trail, but used horses when hunting buffalo.

LEGENDARY TRUTHS

Buffalo hides were used to make bullboats, which were employed in carrying the packs of the Fur Company across the Platte. At one point, they were used to cross the river:

> ...in order to avoid a large band of Sioux who confronted us; for, though professedly friendly, they were treacherous then as now. They came into our camp in large numbers, were quite impudent, and stole every small article they could lay their hands on. Had they known of the alcohol in the mule carts of the Fur Company, a difficulty would have been unavoidable.[9]

Wislizenus wrote:

> The wolves followed promptly after the hunters, and howled for us all night long. Such nocturnal music is so common in this wilderness, especially in the buffalo country, that I finally regretted missing it, and found a sort of enjoyment in the long-drawn wails of these beasts, which run through all the minor chords.[10]

Many rainstorms were encountered, and one day they had to stay in camp nearly all day due to the downpour. Williams said that, "before leaving the Platte we were visited by one of those terrible hailstorms not uncommon in that section, and, nearly half an hour after the storm was over the writer picked up a hail-stone half the size of a hen's egg."[11]

Daily tasks became routine—if not boring—and the plains seemed unending, monotonous, and flat as they followed along the Platte River, or Nebraska as it was earlier called. The valley was from one to two miles wide; the river itself was wide and shallow, up to 2,200 yards wide and three to six feet deep, as measured a few miles below Grand Island. However, in differing years and seasons, the river depth was sometimes less than a foot deep, but the sandy bottom could be treacherous with quicksand, and was better avoided. In addition, the banks of the river were devoid of the cottonwoods and willows that now line its banks, so buffalo chips were used to fuel their fires.

As they proceeded up the Platte, Wislizenus mentioned Chimney Rock and other formations, which Lassen would later pass again and use as landmarks as he led wagons west in 1848.

Some were perfect cones; others flat round tops; others, owing to their crenulated projections, resembled fortresses; others old castles, porticos, etc. Most of them were sparsly covered with pine and cedar. The scenery has obvious resemblance to several places in Saxon Switzerland.[12]

In this vast, flat land, the rocky profiles provided a welcome visual change from the endless, treeless expanses of the prairies. But more noticeable than these rock formations, was Scotts Bluff in western Nebraska. Lassen and his colleagues must have marveled at the enchantments of its scenery, cliffs, and spires that were later described as "Buttresses and barbican, bastion, demilune and guardhouse, tower, turret and donjon-keep, all are there; on one place parapets and battlement still stand upon the crumbling wall of a fortalise like the giant ruins of Chateau Gaillard...." (Richard Burton, 1860).[13]

In 1841, Rufus Sage wrote in his journal, "I could die here... certain of being not far from heaven."

Having two-wheeled carts and pack animals probably enabled them to traverse the sandy and sometimes muddy soils of the prairies and the steep hills with greater ease than the later emigrants with wagons would experience. Also, their expertise at packing and handling their animals alleviated the need to undergo and record some of the hardships later emigrants would describe. No mention was made by Lassen's colleagues of the steep descent on Windlass Hill as they moved downward into Ash Hollow, but one later pioneer wrote, "I don't know the angle of our descent, but there are those who go so far as to say that it hangs just past the vertical."

Beyond Scotts Bluff, they came to "Laramies Fork," which had earlier been described by Captain Bonneville as "a clear and beautiful stream, rising in the west-southwest, maintaining an average width of twenty yards, and winding through broad meadows abounding in currants and gooseberries, and adorned with groves and clumps of trees."[14]

It was here, too, that Fort William had been established by Mr. Robert Campbell (a former trapper for the Rocky Mountain Fur Company), to support the fur trade. It was named Fort William in honor of William Sublette, but that name was later changed to Fort Laramie in honor of a French trapper, who had been killed by Indians nearby. It was in possession of Piggi, Pappin, and Jaudron when the Lassen Party visited

LEGENDARY TRUTHS

it. Wislizenus reported that it was an excellent site for trade with the Indians and noted that they had traveled 775 miles from Missouri.[15]

Only a few miles up the Platte River (Nebraska River) from Fort Laramie, they came to Register Cliffs—sandstone formations that bordered the south side of the river and towered above inviting camping places. Here innumerable travelers rested, recruited their animals, and recorded their signatures and the dates of their visits, before they entered that wild and broken tract of the Crow country called the Black Hills. Weather and erosion have erased many of the original inscriptions, and later visitors have damaged some of the earlier names. However, there is no record of Lassen's party recording their visit.

In the Black Hills, their journey probably became similar to Captain Bonneville's earlier experiences:

> *...toilsome in the extreme. Rugged steeps and deep ravines incessantly obstructed their progress, so that a great part of the day was spent in the painful toil of digging through banks, filling up ravines, forcing the wagons up the most forbidding ascents, or swinging them with ropes down the face of dangerous precipices. The shoes of their horses were worn out, and their feet injured by the rugged and stony roads. The travelers were annoyed also by frequent but brief storms, which would come hurrying over the hills, or through the mountain defiles, rage with great fury for a short time, and then pass off, leaving everything calm and serene again.*[16]

Perhaps the toils of the earlier parties had made the going easier for Lassen's party, and Lassen, being a blacksmith, could have tended to the shoe problem.

As elevation was being gained as they approached the Continental Divide, the dry, rarified air began to take its effect on the woodwork of the carts and, later, emigrant wagons. The wood shrank, the felloes loosened, and the iron tires fell off the wheels. To correct this problem, a band of wood was fastened around the outside of the felloes, the iron rim heated red hot to expand it. It was replaced around the repaired wheel, and then cooled to shrink tightly in place.

The Platte River (Nebraska), in its passage through the Black Hills here:

...is confined to a much narrower channel than that which it flows in the plains below; but it is deeper and clearer, and rushes with a stronger current. The scenery, also, is more varied and beautiful. Sometimes it glides rapidly but smoothly through a picturesque valley, between wooded banks; then impetuously through narrow defiles, roaring and foaming down rocks and rapids, until it is again soothed to rest in some peaceful valley.[17]

Indian sightings were commonplace in the country of the Kaw and Sioux, and the Indians visited the train both out of curiosity and with hopes to trade. In doing so, they caused some concern at times, but also provided subject matter for describing their colorful customs and clothing. The Indians remained friendly, and it wasn't until they entered the Crow country that Wislizenus said the party became more cautious, because they were "a treacherous hostile Indian tribe, equally proficient in stealing and scalping."

West of the Black Hills the party with Lassen left the Platte (Nebraska) River and traveled over plains of loose sand to the Sweetwater River, which at that time was reported to be a stream of some twenty yards breadth, and four or five feet deep. It flowed between low banks over a sandy soil forming one of the forks of the Platte.

The soil was light and sandy; the country much diversified. Frequently the plains were studded with isolated blocks of rock, sometimes in the shape of a half globe, and from three to four hundred feet high. These singular masses had occasionally a very imposing, and even sublime appearance rising from the midst of a savage and lonely landscape. [18]

As they entered the gradually ascending South Pass, which made passage through the Rocky Mountain barrier possible for wagons, they could see the Wind River Mountains to the north. Here Wislizenus marveled at the scenic beauty of the snow-covered summits and speculated on the height of some of the peaks. "It is said that one of these peaks was measured 'geometrically and barometrically on behalf of the Hudson's Bay Company, and that it is 25,000 feet high.'"

He added "...it may well be that they do not seem to the eye as high as they actually are; yet such an assumption as to their height, which would put them in a class with the Himalayas, can scarcely be correct."[19] Gannett Peak is actually the highest mountain in the range at 13,804 feet.

As the party was nearing the Green River, scouts were sent out to find the location of that year's rendezvous, and when they returned, fur rendezvous agents accompanied them:

> These agents were accompanied by their Indian wives and a lot of dogs. The two squaws, quite passable as to their features, appeared in highest state. Their red blankets, with the silk kerchiefs on their heads, and their gaudy embroideries, gave them quite an Oriental appearance. Like themselves, their horses were bedight with embroideries, beads, corals, ribbons, and little bells. The bells were hung about in such number that when riding in their neighborhood, one might think one's self in the midst of Turkish music. The squaws, however, behaved most properly. They took care of the horses, pitched a tent, and were alert for every word of their wedded lords.[20]

The party arrived at the rendezvous site on July 6, and Wislizenus, in describing the area wrote:

> In the vicinity grew willows, cedars and some birches (quickenasp). During all this time we had only very few pleasant days, but rain and storm almost daily. The region of rain now behind us; and —to use the words of our leader— the country where the wind reigns is before us.
>
> I visited many tents, partly out of curiosity, partly to barter for rifles, and sought to make myself intelligible in the language of sign as far as possible...A pound of beaver skins is usually paid for with four dollars worth of goods; but the goods themselves are sold at enormous prices, so-called mountain prices. A pint of meal, for instance, costs from half a dollar to a dollar; a pint of coffee-beans, cocoa beans or sugar, two dollars each; a pint of diluted alcohol (the only spirituous liquor to be had), four dollars; a piece of chewing tobacco of the commonest sort, which is usually smoked, Indian fashion, mixed with herbs, one to two dollars. Guns and ammunition, bear traps, blankets, kerchiefs, and gaudy finery for the squaws, are also sold at enormous profit.[21]

Wislizenus also described the daily activities of the trappers and of their Indian women sitting in front of their tents searching through the scalps of their men and picking lice, which they placed between their teeth, biting and swallowing them.

During their stay at the Green River Fur Rendezvous, the party including Lassen was disappointed in not being able to get a guide to show them the way to California.* They decided to go on to Oregon, leaving Green River on July 10. The party consisted of the original party plus Captain Francis Ermatinger, the agent of the Hudson's Bay Company at Fort Hall, about a dozen of his men, some trappers going back to trap, and several hundred Indians, chiefly Flatheads, on their return to their home across the mountains.[22]

The party continued on to Fort Hall, which lay on the left bank of the Snake River between Portneuf Creek and Blackfoot Creek and was the most southern fort of the English. Ermatinger and another clerk, Mr. Walker, were generous hosts to the party. It was at this time that Klein, Dr. Wislizenus, and his German companion, after resting and recruiting their livestock for eight days, decided to return to the States, thus reducing the original party from Missouri to five.

For information on the remaining party and Peter Lassen from Fort Hall onward, we have to rely on the narratives of Williams and/ or Wiggins.

"Williams" wrote that at Fort Hall, they were equally unable to procure a guide to California, but upon hearing of a settlement on the "Wallamut River," now called the Willamette, they decided to proceed.

William Wiggins, in his reminiscences of their journey, said that when they reached Fort Hall the party finally joined a group of trappers in the employ of the American Fur Company, who were making their annual trip to Oregon. From Fort Hall, the party increased in size, and included twenty-seven trappers. They traveled to The Dalles, then by boat to Fort Vancouver and from there to Camponit (Champoeg)—that is now called Oregon City—where they spent the winter.

René Lassen, in *Uncle Peter*, also wrote the party joined twenty-

---

* At this time, in 1839, only a very few mountain men or trappers had crossed the deserts and mountains to enter California. It would be another two years, 1841, before the Bartleson/Bidwell Party would attempt to take wagons to California. They would succeed in getting across the mountains, but would have to abandon their wagons on the way.

seven trappers at the fort and proceeded to Oregon, and he noted that Klein and Wislizenus returned to the States after reaching Fort Hall.

In Swartzlow's *Trail Blazer,* the writer (Williams or Wiggins[*]) differs in his description of their arrival at Fort Hall:

> *...so that our party was reduced to five—Johnson going ahead and leaving for the Sandwich Islands. On arriving at the Dalles Mission, the other four getting employment, the writer (Williams) proceeded across the Cascade Mountains with their horses, accompanied by Indian guides, and on the 21st of September reached the Wal-lam-ut river—not Wal-lam-ette or Willamette, as the modern corruption has it...*[23]

Williams arrived at the Willamette on September 21, and wintered near the present day site of Oregon City.

René Lassen wrote that the party went from The Dalles to Fort Vancouver by boat and then to Camponit (Champoeg). "Williams" spelled it "Chimponic," and he described it as consisting of some half dozen houses populated by a cosmopolitan group of:

> *...every possible shade of color as well as of admixture. The white settlement was made up for the most part of sailors, many of them runaways and free trappers; and these with a sprinkling of missionaries, a very few gamblers, adventurers, reformed preachers and other refugees from civilization made up the tout ensemble of that interesting community.*[24]

They wanted to continue to California following the well-established trappers' trail[†] up the Willamette, across the mountains, and into the

---

[*]   Williams or Wiggins—see explanation of name confusion on page 10

[†]   This trail, used by Hudson Bay's trappers, ran all the way from Fort Vancouver, up the Willamette River, passed through the Umpqua River and Rogue River areas, and over the Siskiyou Mountains to the Sacramento Valley. It then passed the place where Lassen's rancho would later be located and Sutter's Fort. From Sutter's Fort, it went west to San Francisco, but trappers also followed the trail south to French Camp, and farther to the Kern River. In the 1820s, the trail followed Indian routes east of Mount Shasta, up the Hat Creek drainage and west over the mountains between Burney and Magee Peaks, then down Cow Creek to the Sacramento River. In the 1830s, cattle drives opened the route north to the headwaters of the Sacramento River, west of Mount Shasta to the Siskiyou Mountains. Today, it essentially follows Interstate 5 and

Sacramento Valley. But, since a sufficient company could not be raised to safely cross Indian country in the mountains and enter California overland, and the lateness of season threatened to block their way with snow, they had to wait in Oregon until the next spring, when they arranged passage on the *Lausanne,* a ship from England carrying missionaries to Oregon.*

The *Lausanne* was planning to touch California on its return voyage, and in company with a number of his emigrant friends, including William Wiggins, David Dutton, John Stevens and John Wright, Lassen took the small vessel, captained by Josiah Spaulding, to Bodega, California. "Williams" said, "My three companions from Missouri got on board, but the writer not having a dollar, saw no hope to get away." He then, as a last resort, was able to borrow $60 for the passage.

"Williams" said the ship sailed on July 3 embarking on what was to become a dangerous and exciting voyage. According to René Lassen, the ship would nearly be wrecked at Tongue Point on the southern banks of the river by a violent storm, and having survived the storm, it would later strike a rock at the mouth of the Columbia.[25] It took three weeks to overcome these difficulties and to sail the ninety miles to the mouth of the Columbia. Then it took another thirteen days to sail south to Punta Russe de la Bodega (now called Bodega Bay) in California:

> *Here a dilemma arose of quite a threatening character. The Mexican Commandant sent a squad of soldiers to prevent our landing, and as most of us were out of money the Captain refused to take us any further; so that to appearances were placed in the position of the ancient Britons, who when surrounded by a powerful Roman army, exclaimed, 'These Romans drive us to the sea—the sea beats us back upon them, so that we have no alternative but to be drowned in the waves or to perish by the sword.* '[26]

---

is known as the Siskiyou Trail, but in Northern California, highway signs still call it the "Old Oregon Trail" or the Oregon California Trail.

* The writer (Wiggins or Williams) said the *Lausanne* arrived with missionaries from Nero, England, but Swartzlow, in *Lassen, His Life and Legacy,* said the ship arrived, bringing Methodist missionaries from New York.

LEGENDARY TRUTHS

Just at this crisis, however, the Russian Governor arrived, and ordered the soldiers to leave, be shot down or go to prison; like prudent men they 'dusted.' Still several passengers left on the vessel—so that of their original party, Peter Lassen and the writer were all that remained.[27]

California at the time was under Mexican rule, and the authorities were suspicious of any Americans trying to enter the country. According to Mexican law, it was illegal to enter California, except with permission received via the customs officials stationed at Monterey. The Mexican authorities refused to allow them to stay in Bodega. So in a letter signed by Peter Lassen, William Wiggins, David Dutton, John Stevens and John Wright on July 25, 1840, written to the American Consul of California, they asked for passports. They described their predicament of not having funds to proceed farther, of being refused entry into California by General Vallejo, and they threatened to take up arms to defend themselves as they traveled into California, if relief was not forthcoming.

An interesting side note is that Swartzlow questioned the authenticity of the letter stating that: "It is doubtful that they received a reply, for there was no United States Consul in California at the time of their arrival, but the content of the letter is quite typical of the characteristic spirit of those pioneers."[28]

After months of frontier hardships and wilderness living, followed by a dangerous voyage, and an unwelcoming Mexican government, they were now given a glimpse of Russian aristocracy: the music of Mozart, played by Princess Helena, was coming out of the Rottsheff's house. The guests were served French wine, and outside the stockade, rose gardens were blooming.[29]

The Russian Governor (known to our party only as Don Alexandro) invited us—six in number—to Fort Ross, where we were most kindly received—good quarters were provided for us—meals were also sent to us and an abundance of liquors and cigars, and a servant to wait on us, and the Governor told us to stop on his premises a year if we liked.[30]

On July 26, the ship left Bodega Bay and sailed to Yerba Buena (later called San Francisco) without them. Lassen and his compatriots, having been invited to stay with the Russians at Fort Ross, remained there until a few days later, when they allegedly received permission from General Vallejo to stay in California.* They purchased horses from the Russians and proceeded to Captain Sutter's ranch, at New Helvetia, which would later become Sutter's Fort. Wiggins wrote that they arrived there in the middle of August 1840, after spending twelve days on a circuitous route to avoid the authorities, indicating that they probably had never received permission.

Two weeks after their arrival at New Helvetia, Sutter took Lassen and William Wiggins to Yerba Buena (San Francisco) in a sailboat. Wiggins wrote in a report that there were about six houses there at the time. From Yerba Buena, Lassen and Wiggins went to San Jose, which at the time had about five hundred inhabitants and offered more opportunity for work. Lassen worked as a blacksmith and general repairman until he built what was reported to be the first sawmill to operate in California in 1841.

Some sources say that Lassen bought land to build the sawmill on the Zayante Rancho† near the site of the present village of Fulton, in Santa Cruz County, California, where a sign still marks the site.

After cutting some 50,000 board feet of lumber, he sold the mill to Isaac Graham for one hundred mules. Interestingly, Jorgensen wrote that Lassen received one hundred donkeys for the mill (this is after being translated into Danish and back into English—the way "legendary truths" arise!).[31] At the time, it was illegal for foreigners to own land in California, and some sources say that Isaac Graham may have already owned the land and just paid Lassen for building and operating the mill.

Lassen intended to return to Missouri with the mules, but failed to interest enough men to form a company, and he abandoned the trip. By 1842, Lassen was working for Sutter. In his spare time, it was said that he "was hunting with the Indians; that he was catching wild horses—

---

* According to René Weybye Lassen, General Vallejo sent permission, but according to Swartzlow in *Lassen, His Life and Legacy,* the party entered California illegally and had to take a circuitous route to avoid Mexican authorities, therefore agreeing with the *Reminiscences of William Wiggins.*

† Joseph Majors, a Mexican citizen, applied for the land grant that awarded him the Zayante and adjoining San Augustine Rancho. Majors procured the land for a syndicate of men, who declined to become Mexican citizens—a requirement for owning land in the Mexican territory.

and that his blacksmith house was a rendezvous for all who wanted to be visiting, white as well as colored."[32] He then built a new cabin sixteen miles south on the Consumnes River.[33]

An unmarried Dutchman named A. Sargent, whom Lassen had met in Sacramento City, moved to the cabin and lived with him as

Site of the first water powered sawmill in California, built by Peter Lassen on Zayante Creek in 1841. *Photo by Ken Johnston*

a housekeeper. One Swedish traveler, G. M. Waseurtz, who came to America in 1842 or 1843, and who visited Lassen's place on the Consumnes River, later wrote, "An old Hollander a sargent live with him and make butter chees and bread so with the venison and milk they live really comfortable both have their Indian squas but in the adjacent

Indian camp and never residing with them."

This indicated that the two men each had an Indian woman who kept the house for them, leaving the cooking to the Dutchman. These women lived in the camp of their tribe and came in each morning to carry out their chores.[34] This is the only written record that could be construed to indicate Lassen ever had female companionship, but there are hints of this in the "legendary tales." *

Waseurtz also described Lassen as "A Danish blacksmith who led a nomadic life, moving his blacksmith shop and small stock of cattle, horses and mules about the rich prairys." He continued:

> *He is a most extraordinary and industrious men (sic) hospitable and kind to everybody also to Indians who dot on him when in the afternoon he leave off his blacksmt. work he saddle his horse rides about with his rifle and kill some deer or some antelope Indians are always ther on the lookout and receive for carrying home the half of the flesh the skins he dry for sale. His cattle are so tame that only striking in a certain way with his hammer on the small side of the anvil they come up about the cottage or temporary shade regular as soldiers called at orderly.[35]*

Lassen was also described as always being at work repairing firearms for the hunters and agricultural implements for the farmers. He was industrious, hospitable, kind, and able to get along well with the Indians.[36] He earned a reputation during this time for making fine saddles, beautiful bridles, and furniture, and showed the pride of a craftsman in his work.

For instance, Jorgenson wrote that while Lassen was employed by Sutter he built furniture to completely furnish the mansion of a Don Anionis Sunois (possibly Don Antonio Suñol), a wealthy landowner.[37]

In the summer of 1843, while working for Sutter, Lassen was appointed as a member of a posse, along with John Bidwell, James Burheim, and some others, to retrieve two horses stolen from Sutter's

---

* Such tales are rife in the Susanville area. The *Nataqua News* said, "If memory serves me well, I believe it was said that Peter Lassen had a local Indian woman as his common-law wife, and when anyone asked her... name , she replied, 'Me Nataqua.'" When Bruff and Lassen were on a prospecting trip in the mountains, Bruff wrote on August 10, 1850, "Lassen's squaws went out to dig roots."

ranch. They pursued a party of emigrants who were traveling up the Sacramento Valley following the Hudson Bay Company trappers trail on their way to Oregon. The emigrants were overtaken at Red Bluff, and the stolen animals recovered.

The northern end of the Sacramento Valley was unsettled then, and Lassen was greatly pleased with the country. Both he and Bidwell had been so taken by the beauty of the northern Sacramento Valley that they later returned and settled there.

While returning south with the recovered horses, it is said that they met one of the grizzly bears that were then common in the area. Some of the men started their horses in pursuit trying to get close enough to kill the bear, which they finally succeeded in doing. However, when they returned, Lassen was very angry, because the newly recovered horses and some of their own nearly got away while the men were killing the bear.[38]

When they passed the confluence of the Sacramento River and Deer Creek, Lassen saw rich grasslands interspersed with towering oaks and the snow covered peaks of the Cascade Mountains in the background, one of which would later bear his name. He was so impressed with the beauty of the land that later, after returning to Sutter's, he would request this place as a land grant from the Mexican Government. However, in order to do so, he would have to become a naturalized citizen.

Continuing south from Deer Creek and nearing Sutter's Buttes, Lassen was in the lead, when an amusing incident occurred, which Bidwell recorded. It gives us an interesting insight into Peter Lassen's character. This apparently "tongue-in-cheek" comment by Bidwell would later give historians justification for the legendary truth that Peter Lassen "always got lost."

I have already mentioned Peter Lassen as being of our party. Peter was a singular man, very industrious, very ingenious, and very fond of pioneering—in fact, of the latter stubbornly so. He had great confidence in his own power as a woodsman, but, strangely enough, he always got lost. As we passed Butte Mountain going south, our route of course lay between the Sacramento and Feather Rivers. The point we wished to reach that night was Sutter's Hock Farm, on Feather River. Night had overtaken us when some fifteen miles from it. Peter Lassen insisted on keeping the lead. Our Indian vaquero, however, who knew there country well in that vicinity, pointed to the eastward as the way we should go. Lassen, however, could not be persuaded to diverge to the east, and finally at midnight we concluded to tell him we must go to the east or we would leave him. But this had no effect on Lassen; he kept on to the south, while we, following the Indian, came to the farm. The only place Lassen could reach was the intervening tule marsh. Now if you have any curiosity to observe a man's humor after being in a tule swamp full of mosquitoes all night, you ought to have seen Peter Lassen. The next morning, when he came to camp at Hock Farm, he was so mad he would not speak to any of us; would not travel in the same path, but kept a hundred yards to either side of us all day. I think he never forgot or forgave us.

Still he was a man possessed of many good qualities. He was always obliging in camp. He was a good cook and would do any and everything necessary to the comfort of the camp, even to the making of coffee, provided those traveling with him would pretend to assist. If they did not offer to aid him, they became the target for the best style of grumbling that any man born in Denmark is capable of inventing....

Considering the area and the prominence of the Buttes in the landscape, with the Feather River to the east, and the Sacramento River to the west, it would be unlikely that anyone would truly get lost (as in not knowing where one was and where one wanted to go). However, it would be easy to get into areas of difficult going, so that the most direct way might not be the quickest or best. As Lassen arrived the following morning at his desired destination, one would have to conclude that he did indeed know the way, even though it wasn't the best way. Modern adventurers have a saying for this sort of dilemma: "All who wander are not lost." Or as Chris Parmeter so astutely advised, "Keep your powder dry and your eyes on the horizon and you'll know that 'lost' is, by and large, just a state of mind."[39]

Later, when they had arrived at Sutter's Fort with the retrieved horses, on October 11, 1843, Lassen applied for both his citizenship papers and the grant of land he wanted. The application requesting the land grant was titled, *"Bosquejo del terreno solicitado por Pedro Lawson,"* which translates as "wooded land requested by Peter Lassen." [40]

LEGENDARY TRUTHS

Lassen was given permission to occupy the land while waiting for the paperwork to be approved, so he returned to Deer Creek. Bidwell later wrote in his reminiscences, "Peter Lassen started in the fall of 1843 to take possession of the ranch selected on Deer Creek, but did not get there, the rains detaining him in the Butte Mountains in what is now Sutter County till January or February 1844."

When Lassen finally arrived, he began building his rancho, utilizing Indian labor to construct an adobe cabin, a blacksmith shop, a corral, and other buildings, including a store where, when completed and stocked, he would sell food, tools, whiskey and "other necessities." Joseph Goldsborough Bruff later sketched these buildings as having shingled roofs. Later, in 1849, Lassen had workers cutting shingles in the mountains to the east of his ranch between Mill Creek and Deer Creek. Did the shingles on his buildings also come from the same area?[*]

Isadore Meyerowitz (variously spelled Meyrowitz, Miroitz, Myrovitz), a Russian emigrant, helped move Lassen's cattle from the Consumnes. He spent some time on the rancho, but due to its remoteness and loneliness, he didn't stay long. They remained friends, though, and would later prospect and travel together into Indian Valley. [41]

It was shortly after Lassen moved from his cabin on the Consumnes to Deer Creek that his housekeeper, Mr. Sargent, also left, leaving Lassen by himself—the only white man around, alone among the Indian tribes with only his herd of cattle, horses, and mules.[42] During the summer, he farmed and trapped beaver and otter, selling the skins, which brought three to four dollars a pound.

The Hudson Bay Company Trappers Trail (Siskiyou Trail) extended from Fort Vancouver in Washington south to Sutter's Fort and passed by Lassen's rancho. The trail was well established, and from Lassen's it followed the Sacramento River north to Cow Creek near the present site of Redding. It then followed Cow Creek northeast into the mountains, crossing into the Hat Creek drainage just north of Lassen Peak and

---

[*] When Lassen returned with Bruff to Bruff's Camp on April 20, 1850, they loaded three wagons with shingles that some of Lassen's men had cut the previous year (summer of 1849). Did Lassen get shingles for his cabin and other buildings from this same area in 1844? If so, then he would have known the ridge to take to his rancho between Mill and Deer Creeks before he led wagons down it in 1848! Perhaps this is how Lassen became familiar with the ridge between Deer and Mill Creeks, and when he guided wagons to his ranch in 1848, he advised them to stay on the ridge and not to go down to the creeks, indicating that he had previous knowledge of the terrain.

south of Burney Peak. It later crossed the Pit River (often spelled "Pitt" in many journals) near Fall River, going north on the east side of Mount Shasta, then west and north through the Rogue River area into the Willamette Valley and on to Fort Vancouver.

Occasionally travelers on the trail would stop at Lassen's, and he soon gained a reputation for his hospitality as he welcomed all visitors. Lassen's rancho and trading post was soon to become the northernmost settlement in California.

One group that camped near Lassen's rancho was reported in *Hutchings' Magazine*, in an article that said:

> In the fall of 1844, a circumstance occurred which ought to be associated with the history of this State, and which is this: 'Some whites visited the neighborhood of Mr. Lassen's residence, for the purpose of trapping beaver, with whom was an Oregon half breed named Baptiste Chereux, who, while camping with his company on Clear Creek, found a piece of gold, in weight about half an ounce, but thinking it some kind of brass metal, kept it in his shot pouch, never dreaming that it was gold. After the gold was discovered at Coloma, this man returned to the same spot on Clear Creek, and discovered a very rich lead.'* [43]

The lump reportedly weighed half an ounce, and gold was then worth sixteen dollars per ounce. Both Jorgensen and René Lassen in their books on Peter Lassen gave a different date for Chereux's discovery, stating it as being in "the autumn of 1845," but they didn't list their sources. [44] If this was true, then it is ironic that gold was first discovered on Lassen's rancho, and Lassen later lost his ranch while he was off looking for gold.

Speculation about the truth of this story leads one to wonder if Hutchings meant Deer Creek, as some rumors claim, rather than Clear Creek and to wonder about the geologic possibility of gold being likely in the area. It is highly unlikely, considering the density of gold and the weight of a piece that size, that it could have been carried or washed down the Sacramento River that far, and the smaller streams near

---

* Did Hutchings mean "Deer Creek," which was on Lassen's property rather than "Clear Creek"? It is more likely that Chereux's discovery was on "Clear Creek" north and west of Red Bluff where Pierson B. Reading later discovered gold in 1848.

LEGENDARY TRUTHS

Lassen's rancho came from out of the Cascade mountains, which are volcanic in origin and therefore not a likely source of gold.

Sutter by this time had built a sizeable fort, establishing himself as a prominent Mexican citizen in northern California, and he was a personal friend of the Mexican governor, Micheltorena. It was with Sutter's help that Lassen and several others finally received their land grants. Lassen received his citizenship papers, which were signed by Micheltorena on July 25, 1844, in Monterey. He later received his grant of *Rancho Bosquejo* from the governor on December 26, 1844. It was a grant of five square leagues—over 22,000 acres—at Deer Creek, where the present town of Vina is located, about twenty miles north of Chico.

Likewise, with Sutter's influence, Pierson B. Reading was granted Rancho Buena Ventura, which is located near the present site of Redding, California, but his grant was dated December 4, 1844, preceding Lassen's grant by about three weeks. Reading had entered California with the Joseph Chiles' pack train in 1843 on the northern route, entering the Sacramento Valley on the trappers trail that came by Lassen's rancho. His route had also crossed some of the same country the Lassen Trail would later cross.

In the Chico area, to the south of Lassen's *Bosquejo*, several other land grants were given in 1844. Included in these was Rancho Del Arroyo Chico, totaling 22,000 acres, which was granted to William Dickey. He later sold to John Bidwell, who had been an employee of Sutter and was a friend of Lassen. Bidwell, after striking gold on the Feather River, acquired Arroyo Chico in two separate purchases in 1849 and 1851.

California was entering into a time of political unrest and the Mexican government was concerned over the numbers of emigrants arriving from the States. Russia still held Fort Ross in the north, and the British were keeping close watch for an opportunity to access the territory.

On New Year's Day, 1845, just six days after his land grant had been approved, Lassen marched as a rifleman with Sutter's force toward Mount Diablo. With him were old Caleb Greenwood, the legendary mountain man; his two sons, John and Britton; Michael Laframboise, former leader of Hudson's Bay Company trapping parties in California; Isaac Graham, the fiery focus of an international incident of 1841

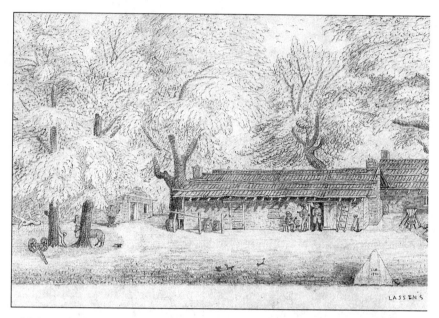

LASSEN'S

which rocked California,* Ezekiel Merritt, destined to be a leader in the Bear Flag Revolt; and Moses Carson, Kit Carson's brother; and 80 others.[45] It was a disastrous campaign for Sutter, who joined forces with Micheltorena, and they met with defeat at San Fernando. Both Sutter and Micheltorena were captured and later released.

Lassen returned to Sutter's on April 1, 1845, and shortly thereafter, he took possession of *Bosquejo:*

> *Except for the Indians who helped him care for the stock, he was alone during the first years. He trapped beaver and otter and sold the skins for three or four dollars per pound; he fertilized the soil where already wild oats grew five feet tall; he planted cotton and started a vineyard with roots he brought from southern California. He saw the potential for growing grapes and was reputedly the first to make wine in this region—later to become famous for its quality product.* [46]

---

* In 1840, Graham began agitating for a Texas-style revolution against the Mexican Government in California. He was arrested, and with other prisoners was sent by ship to San Blas for deportation back to their home countries. Concern over their mistreatment caused British and American diplomats to pressure Mexican President Anastasio Bustamante to release them and return them to California.

LEGENDARY TRUTHS

J. Goldsborough Bruff, *Lassen's Rancho.* This item is reproduced by permission of The Huntington Library, San Marino, California.

Utilizing Indian labor he continued building his rancho, and he worked with William C. Moon and Ezekiel Merrit quarrying and fashioning whetstones from the stones found at Stone Creek. In the fall the three men left Lassen's rancho on a boat and floated downriver as far as Sutter's Fort, and possibly to Yerba Buena, peddling the whetstones. Later on October 31, his 45th birthday, he left Sutter's Fort with one hundred sheep and returned to *Bosquejo.*

In only a few years from leaving Denmark, Lassen was beginning to experience the "American Dream" of becoming successful through initiative and hard work. His rancho was prospering, and his herds and flocks were growing. The men who were, and would become, the prominent leaders of California, respected him.

John Sutter was impressed. In a letter to the U.S. Consul, Thomas O. Larkin, he wrote, "P. Lassen is building a water saw and griss mill. He have already a good horse mill. He will be rich in a few years. He is a very industrious man."[47]

Bosquejo was the northern most settlement in California, and was ready to play a part in California's future.

J. Goldsborough Bruff, *Indian Lodge at Lassen's Rancheria.*
This item is reproduced by permission of The Huntington Library,
San Marino, California.

LEGENDARY TRUTHS

1846
Fremont's Trip to Klamath
from Rancho Bosquejo

(Northernmost Outpost on the California Oregon Trappers Trail)

Once the pursuit of truth begins to haunt the mind, it
becomes an ideal never wholly attained.

—Agnes E. Meyer

In the spring of 1846, the future of settlers in the Mexican province of Northern California was tenuous. The carefree pastoral life and the easy-come easy-go attitude of the settlers was giving way to rumors that were spreading about Governor Jose Castro's intent to drive them out and burn their houses and crops.

The Mexican officials had been suspicious of strangers before, but the defeat of Governor Micheltorena and Sutter in the Battle of Cahuenga, near Los Angeles on February 20, 1845, which had resulted in their capture and later release, set the scene for unrest. It divided California between Governor Pio Pico in the south and Governor Castro in Monterey to the north. California became more distanced than ever from Mexico, and both Britain and America were watching.[1]

In addition to this unsettled question of rule in California, the mission Indians were becoming unruly. Governor José Figueroa had secularized them in 1834, and without the patronage of the priests, they were now exercising their newly acquired independence from mission rule. The skills and knowledge of horsemanship and the use of firearms that they had learned from the priests, were now used to increase their raids on the settlers. They had become known as the "Horse-thief" Indians.

Captain Fremont had entered the state by coming over the mountains in winter conditions, and subsequently had a run-in with Governor Castro, who sent him two letters that were blunt and to the point, ordering him to exit California immediately.

Showing disdain for Castro and a disregard for the orders to leave, Fremont built a rough log fortification on Gavilan Peak near Pueblo de San Juan and the mission of San Juan Bautista, and raised the American flag over it. This greatly incensed Castro, who gathered troops and marched toward the fortification; however, no battle was fought, and Fremont removed his men and traveled northward, crossing the Feather River.

On March 27, they stopped at the rancho of Samuel Neal, a blacksmith, who had formerly been one of Fremont's men. Then three days later, on March 30, they arrived at Deer Creek and Lassen's rancho. Fremont wrote in his memoirs:

> In the afternoon, about half a mile above its mouth, we camped on Deer Creek, another of those beautiful tributaries of the Sacramento...Mr. Lassen, a native of Germany, has established a rancho here, which he has stocked, and is gradually bringing into cultivation. Wheat, as generally throughout the country, gives large returns; cotton, planted in the way of experiment, was not injured by frost, and succeeded well; and he has lately planted a vineyard, for which the Sacramento Valley is considered to be singularly well adapted... [2]

Fremont was greatly impressed with Lassen, and with what he had accomplished at *Bosquejo*. They became good friends, and Fremont was invited to stay at the rancho as long as he wanted. Lassen was so impressed with Fremont that he decided to name the settlement he was planning to build after Fremont's father-in-law, Senator Thomas Hart Benton. The settlement was to be called Benton City.

While staying at Lassen's, Fremont sent Alexis Godey, Tom Martin, and four of his Delaware Indians southward to purchase horses. While they were gone, Fremont crisscrossed the Sacramento Valley exploring and looking over the country.

On April 5, he went up the Sacramento and camped near the present site of Anderson. There he crossed the river and followed up Cow Creek, which he said was named for cattle that escaped from a party going to Oregon. Fremont's party encountered stormy weather and was turned back by a hailstorm near Mount Shasta. They returned to *Bosquejo* on April 11 to await better weather.

In mid-April, Martin and Godey returned with the newly purchased horses. Word came down from the north that a war party of 1000 warriors had arrived there. It had killed Reading's majordomo, burned out Reading's Rancho, and was preparing to make an attack on other settlers.[3]

Thomas Martin reported that, "Settlers asked for help but Fremont refused because he didn't have government authority."[4] He did allow Kit Carson to take some men to fight the Indians, and on the way, according to Martin:

> ...they saw from *"4,000 to 5,000" Indians![5] The sun was setting when the enemy was sighted at Reading's Ranch, rigged out in their war time regalia of black paint and white feathers. They were engaged in a dance to work themselves into the proper state of frenzy to perpetrate the intended massacre...The redmen were taken completely by surprise, but held their ground until driven into the woods and river.*

Twenty-four were killed in the initial rifle attack, and then sabers were used to cut a red path of death. When the battle was finished three hours later, over 175 Indians had been slain.[5] Kit Carson, in his account of the fight, said it was a "complete butchery." Samuel Hensley later testified, "There is an island called Bloody Island, named by myself in consequence of a battle with the Indians in which I personally engaged. It is opposite the mouth of Cottonwood Creek, which island still retains the name, and same island is called by the Mexicans 'Isle de Sangre'."[7]

After they returned to Lassen's, the men wanted to celebrate their victory, and Thomas Martin wrote:

> *While we were at Deer Creek, there was encamped on another creek about 12 miles S. from us a large number of immigrants bound for Oregon. Having received permission from Fremont to have a barbecue, we enlisted a large quantity of Bear, Elk, & Deer Meat. Then we took a number of our horses and went down for the emigrants among those who came were about 15 ladies. A place had been cleared away. As we began dancing which we kept up for 2 days. Then the third day the emigrants returned to their camp.*[8]

Fremont left Lassen's again on April 24, but his presence in California and later exploits would prove to greatly affect and influence Lassen's future travels and trail experience. So we will follow Fremont's ventures throughout the year of 1846 to better understand the circumstances that led to Lassen's visiting the Klamath area and the reaches of the Pit River (then known as the upper Sacramento River), and also the experiences and impressions he would gain in traveling east to Missouri in the following year.

After leaving *Bosquejo*, Fremont traveled north along the Oregon trappers trail on the east side of the Sacramento River. The trail had been well established and used for years by the Hudson's Bay trappers coming from Fort Vancouver into the Sacramento and San Joaquin Valleys to trap beaver. It had also been used for stock drives and by emigrants traveling between California and Oregon.

> *Chief Trader Alexander Roderick McLeod had opened the way down the Pit River and over Burney mountain to Cow Creek on his first journey to California in 1829....*

> *Chief Trader John Work and his Snake Country Expedition had taken a lower route in 1832. Traveling south, Work left the Pit River at the big bend and crossed overland to Hat Creek, then up Hat Creek. He then had crossed the foothills southeast of Burney Mountain to Cow Creek.*[9]

Kit Carson, Fremont's guide and scout, had been over the route as far as the Pit River when he had entered California with Ewing Young's trapping party in 1830. They had met Peter Skeen Ogden and traveled with him as far north as the Pit River.

Charles Preuss was Fremont's cartographer, and his map showed that Fremont's expedition to Klamath Lake turned east into the mountains soon after crossing Battle Creek, a few miles north of Lassen's *Rancho Bosquejo*. The expedition then crossed the headwaters of the "Poisett River" (Hat Creek) and the Sacramento River (Pit River) near the falls.[10]

Fremont reached the confluence of the Fall River and the Pit River on May 29, and camped beside the upper Sacramento (Pit) River above Fall River. Traveling up the river, he came to and named Round Valley (now Big Valley), then turned north toward Klamath.

On May 1, he camped on the south side of Rhett Lake, which he named in honor of an old friend. The lake has later come to be known as Tule Lake. Continuing on, he then camped on McCrady River (now Lost River), and finally reached upper Klamath Lake on May 6.

He had wanted to get to a Klamath Indian village on Williamson River inlet of the lake, to find the friendly Klamath Indian who guided him in 1843 when he had come south from Fort Vancouver. The Klamath Indian had guided him from his camp in Klamath Marsh to Winter Ridge, and Fremont was trying to connect the areas of his explorations for his map of the West, but arising conditions later prevented that from happening.

Fremont wrote in his memoirs:

> *My plans when I started on my journey into this region were to connect my present survey of the intervening country with my camp on the savannah, where I had met the Tlamaths in that December; and I wished to penetrate among the mountains of the Cascade ranges. As I have said, except for the few trappers who had searched the streams leading to the ocean, for beaver, I felt sure that these mountains were absolutely unknown. No one had penetrated their recesses to know what they contained, and no one had climbed to their summits; and there remained the great attraction of mystery in going into unknown places—the unknown lands of which I had dreamed when I began this life of frontier travel.[11]*

Meanwhile back at Lassen's rancho on May 1, Lieutenant Archibald

Gillespie arrived in search of Fremont. He was a United States Marine Corps officer with military orders for Fremont but, to avoid arousing Mexican suspicion, he disguised himself as an American merchant traveling for his health. He claimed to be a friend of Fremont and claimed he had family letters for him, which he was anxious to deliver.

Lassen warned him of the dangers of the territory and the hostile Indians, but Gillespie insisted on going after Fremont.

Lassen and three others—Sam Neal, Levi Sigler, and Bill Stepp—agreed to guide Gillespie and his Negro slave, Benjamin Harrison, to Fremont. On May 2, the six men started north, traveling up Cow Creek, and crossing just north of Lassen Peak, following the established Indian and trappers' trading route to the Pit River Crossing near Fall River. They then proceeded on to Klamath Lake, where they caught up to Fremont on May 9, a distance of about 200 miles in seven days of hard and dangerous riding.

Swartzlow wrote, "Whether Lassen was guide on this route, or whether, on the contrary, the trip provided him with an opportunity to add to his own geographical knowledge, is not apparent."[12]

While it may not be clear as to whether Lassen acted as the guide, and whether they were following Fremont's tracks, or the well-beaten route of the Indians and trappers, what is apparent and obvious, is that he saw the route. He traveled over it both directions, and the way was established well enough that his party was able to follow it directly in pursuit of Fremont.

Considering Lassen's interest in exploring and his desire to build Benton City on his rancho, he undoubtedly was beginning to think about bringing emigrants from the East. Lassen would now have ample time to discuss with Fremont and his men their earlier expedition in the Klamath area and the lay of the land to the east.

On the evening of May 8, Fremont and his men were warming themselves by the campfires when they heard the sound of approaching horses. They quickly moved from the firelight into the shadows for safety, when Neal and Sigler, who had been sent ahead, rode into their camp, which was perhaps near Klamath Marsh.[13] Neal said that shortly after they had picked up Fremont's trail, Indians had tried to cut them off and that, thanks to his superior horses, they had enough speed and strength to outrun their pursuers. He also told Fremont that an officer was on his trail with dispatches from the government, and if he did not receive help at once, the Indians would kill him.

LEGENDARY TRUTHS

As soon as they could see the trail at daybreak, Fremont started back with the two messengers and a small party of his Indians and trappers. They rode forty or fifty miles that day and stopped near the west shore of Klamath Lake. Just at sundown, Lassen, Stepp, Gillespie, and Harrison reached their camp.

Fremont was excited about the messages and as he contemplated the future he let his men rest, but for some reason he failed to post a watch. Hearing something that seemed to be moving among the horses, he went to check. "Drawing a revolver I went down among them. A mule is a good sentinel, and when he quits eating and stands with his ears stuck straight out taking notice, it is best to see what is the matter."[14]

Seeing nothing, he returned to camp. Later, as he was just dozing off, Carson's voice awakened him. Kit had heard the sound of an axe striking the head of Basil Lajeunesse. He gave the alarm to the rest of the camp, but the half-breed, Denny, and Wetowka Crane were killed in the attack. By this time the rest of the men, including Lassen, were firing. They shot down the Klamath chief who was leading the attack.

> *Three of our men had been killed: Basil, Crane, and the halfbreed, Denny, and another Deleware had been wounded; one fourth of our number. The chief who had been killed was recognized to be the same Indian who had given Lieutenant Gillespie a salmon at the outlet of the Lake. Hung to his wrist was an English half-axe. Carson seized this and knocked his head to pieces with it, and one of the Delewares, Sagundai, scalped him. He was left where he fell. In his quiver were forty arrows... all headed with a lancet-like piece of iron or steel—probably obtained from the Hudson Bay Company's traders on the Umpqua—and were poisoned for about six inches. They could be driven that depth into a pine tree.*[15]

If Gillespie had not found Fremont that night, the Indians, without doubt, would have killed him and his party. In addition, Fremont would have gone farther into Oregon, and the history of the United States might have been changed had he not received the orders to return to California.

Reports vary as to where Fremont's main camp was, where Gillespie had camped before meeting Fremont, and where Gillespie met Fremont, or where Fremont met Gillespie, and the battle took place.

Some accounts say Fremont's main camp was at Klamath Marsh, and it would have been a forty to fifty mile ride back to a place on the western shore of Klamath Lake, where a small stream flows between Aspen Lake and Klamath Lake. Fremont supposedly camped there on the shore of Klamath Lake, where a thicket of trees behind their camp provided some protection.

The small creek nearby was named Lajeunesse Creek by Fremont in honor of one of the dead, but it is now called Denny Creek in honor of the half-breed who was killed. Highway 140 passes close by, and a small stone marker beside the road marks the site. It was also said that the Indian chief who was killed had offered Gillespie a salmon when they crossed the river. The distance to Denny Creek, from the river, would probably have taken Lassen and Gillespie the rest of the day on horseback to get there.

A different account said Fremont rode into Gillespie's camp on Klamath River after darkness had overtaken them.[16] This would also have been a forty to fifty mile ride for Fremont if his main camp had been on the northwest bay of Klamath Lake. If this were true, perhaps

Marker at Denny Creek. Site of Indian attack on Fremont's camp near Klamath Lake in 1846. *Photo by Ken Johnston*

the marker at Denny Creek denotes the place where Fremont buried the bodies of the dead after packing them on horseback part of the day following the attack, and then having to abandon them when many Indians were observed approaching the lakeshore in canoes.

Eagan wrote, "…the delay in burying their comrades saved Fremont and his men another battle on the trail." But he also claimed, "John Charles and his weary men rode into the main camp" by afternoon.[17] This contradicts his report that Fremont left the main camp at daybreak and arrived at Gillespie's after dark. He had to travel the same distance, and taking time to pack, then to bury the bodies (hiding them so the Indians wouldn't find and mutilate them), wouldn't have allowed him to arrive in the afternoon.

Another discrepancy appeared in Bancroft's *History of Oregon*, where it was reported that three months later the Applegate Party discovered a different site south of Lower Klamath Lake, west of the Stone Bridge on Lost River. "Keeping down the shore of the lake they encamped on Hot Creek, at the identical spot where Fremont's party had been a couple of months previous, and where the Hot Creek Modocs murdered his three faithful Delawares."[18]

Wherever the site of attack was, the record clearly indicated that in order to appease the remaining Delaware Indians, as well as his men and his own anger, Fremont continued around the lake punishing any and all Indians he encountered. They sacked a major village where the Williamson River enters the lake, and killed many Indians. Lieutenant Gillespie admired the men who fought with Fremont and commented on their fitness. He said, "By heaven, this is rough work. I'll take care to let them know in Washington about it."[19]

Fremont then made it clear to Gillespie no mention of the day's events were to be reported in Washington, and indicated that he didn't think heaven had any role in it. Lassen remained with Fremont as he led his men around the east and south sides of the lake, attacking any Indians he could find to avenge the deaths of his men.

Charles Preuss' map showed only one track from Klamath Lake to the Sacramento Valley, passing overland from east of Rhett Lake on its way to the Pit River near Rose Creek—then down the Pit River to Hat Creek.[20] They crossed the Cascades just north of Lassen Peak and followed a different route (according to Swartzlow and Scott).[21]

This different route came over the northeastern flanks of Lassen Peak, where it crossed close to or over what would later become known as Nobles Trail. Later reports would say Lassen claimed to know of this route before Nobles did. Fremont's party then followed down Battle Creek, a more direct route to Lassen's rancho than the Cow Creek route he followed in going to Klamath.

By May 24 Lassen, Fremont, and his men were back at *Bosquejo*, where they learned that on April 17 Castro had issued a proclamation ordering all noncitizens out of California, and denying entrance to any future American emigrants.

News had not reached California of the outbreak of the Mexican American War, which was now being fought in Texas and Mexico. However, conditions were such that the conflict would extend into California, where Fremont would play a leading role. Some sources claimed that Lassen enlisted under Captain Fremont and took an active part against the Mexican forces.[22]

It isn't clear what part Lassen played, if any, in the following events that led to California's political takeover. But what is important to our narrative about Lassen's life is how his association with Fremont— including Fremont's role in the war—affected Lassen's opportunity to return to Missouri with Stockton's party in 1847, and the influence that would have on Lassen's later return to California and the development of his trail.

Fremont and his men left Lassen's on May 25, riding south to Sam Neal's Rancho, where they heard rumors that Castro had been inciting Indians to burn crops and wheat fields, barns and houses, and kill Americans whenever the chance prevailed.

Fremont then moved south to Bear Valley to avoid being caught in a trap. There he learned from "Stuttering" Ezekiel (Zeke) Merritt, a rugged, fearless old Rocky Mountain trapper, that the rumored devastation hadn't actually taken place yet. So, he returned to the Sacramento Valley and set up headquarters near Sutter's Buttes, about sixty miles north of Sutter's Fort.

On June 14, 1846, while Fremont remained at the Buttes, William Ide, with Long Bob Semple, and Zeke Merritt and his men, captured General Vallejo of the Californios at Sonoma, in a bloodless coup that was to become known as the Bear Flag Revolt.

Fremont then joined the cause of the Osos (the participants of the Bear Flag Revolt) at Sonoma. He promised to protect the Americans against General Castro, but was vague about getting involved in the political takeover of California.

LEGENDARY TRUTHS

On July 2, Commodore Sloat sailed into Monterey Bay aboard the Savanna. With solid information about the start of war between Mexico and the United States; knowledge that Sonoma had fallen; and the report Fremont had joined the Bear Flaggers, Sloat raised the American flag over the Customs House in Monterey. On July 9, forces under his command occupied San Francisco and Sonoma, and claimed California for the United States. Commodore Sloat sent a letter to Fremont ordering him to bring his men to Monterey.

After Sloat talked to Fremont and learned there were no specific orders from Washington to take action against the Mexicans, Sloat resigned his position, claiming illness and age, and prepared to sail back to Washington. His resignation put Commodore Robert Stockton into the position of command.

Stockton's personality and style of leadership were complimentary to Fremont's; both were men of action. Subsequent events would segue into a return journey across country to Missouri, which would include Peter Lassen and provide Lassen with experience and knowledge of the known and proposed routes to California.

On July 23, 1846, Stockton promoted Fremont to major and put him in command of the California Battalion. Fremont and his men were transported by ship to San Diego, which they occupied, as well as Los Angeles.

Fremont was to command the military forces in California and to increase their numbers through enlistments. Stockton then withdrew his naval forces from California in order to protect merchant vessels in the Pacific Ocean. The commodore then stated that if Fremont managed to have things well in hand by October, he would appoint him governor of California.

Kit Carson was then sent back East with government reports and letters from Fremont and Stockton. One letter from the commodore was a report to President Polk of the political status in California. In traveling east, Carson met Brigadier General Stephen Watts Kearny and the Army of the West. They had just captured Santa Fe, and were now headed to California. Carson reported that California had fallen into the hands of the Americans and things were peaceful there, so Kearny sent some of his men back to Santa Fe, and ordered Carson to guide him on to California. Carson's letters were then sent on to Washington by another courier.

By the time Kearny, with his troops and Carson, reached California, the peaceful conditions had deteriorated into all-out war. Stockton had to recapture San Diego, and Fremont was moving his troops south to help quell the uprising. When Stockton received a letter from Kearny with information of his arrival, Stockton immediately sent Captain Gillespie with a detachment of volunteers to warn Kearny of the nearness of Andrés Pico and his lancers.

Both Kearny and Gillespie were wounded in a battle that followed with Pico, but they finally made it to San Diego. While Kearny's forces were recapturing Los Angeles, Fremont captured Santa Barbara, and through diplomacy and acting as commandant of the California Battalion of the United States, he negotiated the surrender of the Mexican forces, and issued a proclamation of peace to the Californios and to Andrés Pico.

He wrote up seven Articles of Capitulation on January 13, 1847, and instigated terms that would end the war without rancor or bitterness from the Californios—terms that were diplomatic and appreciated by the Californios, but that would later be questioned by jealous and glory seeking superiors.[23]

Both Brigadier General Kearny and Commodore Stockton were unhappy with the terms Fremont had negotiated, and thought the conditions stipulated were too easy on the Mexicans. "Kearny would not receive the treaty as he claimed he [Fremont] was not the officer in charge."[24] However, Stockton indicated that he intended to appoint Fremont to the office of military governor of California. Kearny, although upset with the treaty, indicated that he, too, wished to make Fremont governor of California.

Later, jealousies and questions of superiority of rank and authority intensified between Commodore Stockton and General Kearny. Although Stockton had been in charge, Kearny claimed command. Stockton had pointed out to Kearny that he, Kearny, and his men would have perished in battle on Mule Hill if they hadn't been rescued by a unit of sailors and marines.

In addition, Stockton had offered Kearny the opportunity to command the forces that captured Los Angeles, but he had not accepted. Stockton therefore claimed credit for the victory.[25] He also pointed out that California had been conquered and a new government had been established. News of these proceedings had been sent to President Polk long before Kearny had arrived in California, even though Kearny possessed letters dated June 3 and 18, 1846, signed by the Secretary of War and approved by President Polk, assigning him the duty of establishing the new government.[26]

Conditions were developing in which Fremont would be caught in this rivalry. Stockton informed Kearny that he was going to ask President Polk to recall him, and that Kearny should consider himself "suspended from the command of the U.S. Forces in this place."[27] He then issued a letter "To all whom it may concern…" appointing J.C. Fremont governor and commander-in-chief of California.[28]

Instead of acknowledging this, Kearny issued a letter to Fremont telling him to maintain his command of the California Battalion. It stated, "The general directs that no change will be made in the organization of your battalion of volunteers or officers appointed to it without his sanction or approval being first obtained."[29]

When confronting this dilemma, Fremont logically—but with military naiveté, considering he was an Army officer—chose to follow Stockton's leadership.

1846
Trail Development and the Donner Tragedy

...never take no cutofs and hury along as fast as you can.—Virginia Reed, thirteen-year-old surviving member of the Donner Party, written in a letter to her cousin.

While California was undergoing the throes of political change in 1846, other events were taking place in the East and on the California Trail that would affect future emigration and would influence, also, the development of alternate routes both to California and to Oregon. News of the Donner tragedy would exacerbate fears of dangers and hardships presented by the older, more established route and would stimulate hopes for a new and easier route (a hope the Lassen Trail would later fulfill).

The year 1846 was one of high hopes for the annual migration westward because word had reached the East that wagons, under the command of Elisha Stephens, had actually crossed the mountains and entered California in 1844. Earlier emigrants, although successful in getting through to California, had to abandon their wagons on the way. Guidebooks and maps for emigrants headed to both Oregon and California were available—though fraught with vagaries and inaccuracies. Perhaps more important were letters sent home by people who had experienced the trails, which were being improved each year. Hometown newspapers in the East published many of these letters, providing news of their native sons' adventures, giving trail information, and piquing interest of those wanting to see for themselves.

Five years earlier, in 1841, the first emigrant party to attempt taking wagons to California was the Bidwell/Bartleson Train. Although interest was high and talk was "cheap," some five hundred people from Missouri had signed up for the Western Emigrant Society, and many others had shown interest in leaving that spring and traveling to California.

However, when John Bidwell arrived at the starting point in Sapling Grove he found only one wagon waiting. Slowly people began to arrive, and when the party numbered about fifty, including about thirty-five men, five women, and ten children, they felt the party was large enough to proceed. Later they joined a party of three Jesuit priests, including Father Pierre Jean De Smet, going to Fort Hall with Thomas "Broken Hand" Fitzpatrick as guide.[1]

From Fitzpatrick they learned skills for the trail and stayed with him until they reached Soda Springs in Idaho, southeast of Fort Hall. Some of the party continued with Fitzpatrick, but a group of thirty-three was determined to proceed on to California, although they had no guide, and there was no established route. They had to abandon their wagons in Nevada, put packs on their animals, and proceed on foot, but they were successful in crossing the Sierra Nevada and became the first emigrant party to enter California overland across the Great Basin.

One party member, Nancy Kelsey, wife of Benjamin Kelsey, carried their one-year-old daughter, Ann. Walking barefooted part of the way, Nancy proved women and children could make the trip. Of the hardships she later said, "Where my husband goes, I go. I can better endure the hardships of the journey, than the anxieties for an absent husband."[2]

In 1842, no wagons started for California. No wagons would make it overland to California until the Stephens Party of 1844 succeeded in getting their wagons to the Sacramento Valley. However, in 1842, wagons broke the trail all the way to Oregon by following the ruts of the Bidwell/Bartleson Party to Soda Springs, then following the tracks of the group who had left the Bartleson Party for Fort Hall, nearly getting their wagons through. Wagon trains using the trail to get to Oregon for the next couple of years account for the more common usage of the name Oregon Trail being applied to the route from Missouri to Fort Hall. However, California emigrants used it more heavily in later years.

Also in 1842 a group of thirteen men, including Joseph Chiles, left Sutter's Fort in April to return to the States with news of the success of reaching California overland, and firsthand information about the opportunities to be had there. They crossed the mountains via Tejon Pass, then went north to Mary's River and followed it to Fort Hall. From Fort Hall they went over trappers' routes south to Santa Fe, and then followed the Santa Fe Trail back to Missouri, traveling a total distance of approximately four thousand miles over nearly every type of terrain in the West.

Having gained a great amount of experience, both as a member of the Bidwell/Bartleson Party of 1841 and from the return trip overland in 1842, Chiles was well qualified for his job as wagonmaster in 1843. He left Missouri in May with eight wagons and about thirty people, again bound for California. His party met John C. Fremont at Elm Grove, and Fremont noted the meeting in his journals, commenting that the wagons were freighting various goods, furniture, farming implements, and machinery for a mill. The two parties traveled together for a few days. Chiles and one of his men hunted wild turkeys and deer for both parties, but ended the arrangement in disgust, due to Fremont allegedly appropriating the hindquarters of the deer for his men, leaving only the forequarters for Chiles' people.[3]

Although they would not meet again on the journey, their trails would again cross near Lake Abert, in eastern Oregon, where they would both learn the lay of the land that would provide a northern access to California without having to surmount the rocky steeps of the Sierra Nevada.

Earlier, when Chiles was west of Fort William (later to be renamed Fort Laramie), he met Joe Walker, an experienced mountain man who had led an expedition to California in 1834, and who had discovered Walker Pass, named after him, at the southern end of the Sierras. Walker agreed to act as guide for a fee of $300, and according to George Stewart:

> No one living was better qualified to act as a guide on the trail to California. Besides knowing something about the route, he would be useful as a hunter and for his knowledge

LEGENDARY TRUTHS

of Indians. But Walker had traveled as a mountain-man, on horseback. He knew little of the problems of handling a wagon train.*

The Chiles/Walker train traveled on to Fort Hall, and due both to the shortage of provisions for the train and the lack of availability of provisions from the fort, they decided to divide the party. Walker was to take the wagons and emigrants down the Humboldt River to California, while Chiles would lead a group of twelve men, traveling fast on horseback, to enter California by a northern route, to buy supplies, which they would then pack over the mountains to aid the wagon train.

It was a good plan, and the horseback party reached the Hudson's Bay post of Fort Boise on October 3. The fort's commander gave them information about the route and a hand drawn map. The Hudson's Bay trappers had traveled the route under the leadership of Peter Skene Ogden, and Indians had used much of the route through the Malheur country for centuries. The only problem was that they underestimated the distance, the difficulties with Indians, and the dearth of game for food.

Among the party, though, were several capable men, who would later play prominent roles in the political change coming to California and/or in the development of the California Trail. Along with Joseph B. Chiles were Pierson B. Reading, Samuel J. Hensley, John Gantt, John J. Myers, and Milton McGee. Of them, George Stewart would write, "In fact, this little horseback party might be said to have served as a school for guides and explorers."†

As it turned out, Chiles was late getting into the Sacramento Valley, and was unable to aid the Walker contingent, who had to abandon their wagons in the Owens Valley of California, and continue on foot with

---

*   Stewart makes allowances for Walker not having used wagons on the route he had previously traveled, but later Stewart will not make the same allowances for Peter Lassen when he leads a wagon train on a route with which he had previous knowledge, but had not taken wagons over!

†   Later, when writing about Myers and McGee applying this knowledge of the land in leading wagons over the Lassen Trail, it is interesting that Stewart seems to have forgotten this. He then wrote that McGee, like Hudspeth and Myers "had only the very slightest idea of what he was doing."

pack animals around the southern end of the Sierras.

The Chiles/Walker train of 1843 did succeed, however, in getting the people through to the Sacramento Valley, and they proved that the valley could be accessed from both the south and the north.

In 1844, a train of forty wagons with a party of about forty-six men, women, and children bound for California met at Council Bluffs, Iowa. This train was destined to be the first to get wagons all the way into the Sacramento Valley, and to establish the route later followed by thousands of emigrants. The group included Martin Murphy and his family; Doctor John Townsend, his wife and brother-in-law, Moses Schallenberger; Isaac Hitchcock; and Elisha Stephens (or Stevens). Stephens would be elected the captain, and henceforth the train would be called the Stephens Party. They hired Old Caleb Greenwood, a mountain man of much renown who claimed to be in his 81st year, accompanied by his two half-Indian sons, as their guide.

They followed the established route to Fort Hall, and then eleven of the wagons followed Walker's wagon tracks down the Humboldt. Near the Humboldt Sink, they encountered a Paiute Indian chief named Truckee, who talked to Old Greenwood through sign language. He allegedly drew a map in the sand and told of a way over the mountains, by following a river that would later be named the Truckee in his honor.[*]

Crossing the desert and following the river was difficult, but they managed to get their wagons up the river canyon to a point where it turned south. Thinking it prudent to continue taking the wagons west up the canyon of a broader tributary stream, they decided to split up, sending an exploring party of six men on horseback, south. The horseback party then passed by Lake Tahoe and went west over the mountains to alert Sutter of the need for help.

The wagon contingent then built a cabin and left Joseph Foster, Allen Montgomery, and Moses Schallenberger, all of whom volunteered to guard six wagons and their heavy contents from the Indians. Thus, allowed to travel faster, the rest of the party then managed to get five wagons beyond what was later to become known as Donner Lake, and over the pass. However, they were not able to get far enough down the western slope before winter set in, and four feet of snow

---

[*]   Fremont had named this river the Salmon/Trout River in 1843, but it is now called the Truckee, named by the Stephen's Party.

prevented further progress with the wagons. Remaining a few days with the wagons, they butchered cattle for food, and left the women and a couple of men with the wagons. The rest of the men then went on, floundering through snowdrifts to Sutter's Fort, where they again met the horseback group who had gone via the Tahoe route.

Expecting to form a relief party to return for the women, the men were surprised to find California and Sutter in the throes of a revolution against General Castro. The men were either forced or cajoled, or at least enticed, into joining forces with Sutter and marching with him on January 1, 1845. The women would have to survive on their own, and besides, the snows would probably prevent relief parties from returning anyway, or so they rationalized.

Meanwhile in the mountains, the three young men made snowshoes and left the wagons they had stayed behind to guard. They realized with the increasing depth of snow that there was no danger of Indians taking their belongings, hunting would be nearly impossible, and escape was the best measure. Schallenberger, though, was not strong enough to make it over the pass. He returned to the cabin, where he survived the winter by trapping foxes, as he found the other available game of coyotes and ravens unpalatable.

When spring arrived, the people, including Schallenberger, were rescued and the wagons were taken on into the Sacramento Valley, thus opening the trail all the way to Sutter's Fort. In spite of the winter ordeal, no lives were lost; in fact, two births increased the party's size.

As soon as the snows melted and the return route was open, Greenwood with his two sons rode eastward with the news of the opening of the trail. He was on his way to Fort Hall, as an emissary for Sutter, and was to divert emigrants going to Oregon, enticing them instead to go west to Sutter's Fort. Greenwood also hoped to hire himself out as a guide to the wagons that would go to California.

The success of the Stephens Party in getting wagons through to the Sacramento Valley was a turning point in western migration, with travel to California increasing. Of the five thousand emigrants going to Oregon in 1845, Greenwood was successful in convincing about 250 people with fifty wagons to change their destination to California. Then by charging $2.50 per wagon for guiding them, he earned an additional $125.00. He was also successful in getting them through to Sutter's Fort, with the exception of one man, named Pierce, who was killed by Indians—the first fatality of a California emigrant on the trail.[4]

Also in 1845, John Charles Fremont returned to California by horseback. In coming west, he rode along the southern shores of Great Salt Lake, and crossed the Salt Lake Desert to the west. He passed by and named Pilot Peak. The Bidwell/Bartleson Party had stopped there four years earlier at the springs, now named Donner Springs, located near its base. Fremont then followed the Mary's River—renaming it the Humboldt River—and entered California following the Truckee River and the traces of the Stephens Party over the pass, following down the American River into the Sacramento Valley.

Although Fremont was not experienced with wagon travel, he reported that the route he had followed was "decidedly better" for wagon travel, "shorter," and "less mountainous, with good pasturage and well watered."[5]

Lansford Hasting's party of ten riders was the last to enter California in 1845, arriving at Sutter's Fort on Christmas Day. He had followed the established road to Fort Hall, down the Humboldt, and over the pass that Stephens had opened. He had previously entered California in 1842 from Oregon by following the Siskiyou Trail, and returned to the States by ship in 1844.

Early in 1845, Hastings published *The Emigrants' Guide to Oregon and California*, offering descriptions of both Oregon and California. He vaguely described routes and wrote, "Wagons can be as readily taken from Fort Hall to San Francisco, as they can, from the states to Fort Hall." He also recommended leaving the established trail south of Fort Hall and heading in a more direct route to California; however, when he wrote these words, he didn't have information about the success of the Stephens Party or of wagons actually having made the journey through to California. It was a prediction on his part, but he presented it as fact, for he had grandiose plans of leading emigrants from the States, creating a force that would liberate California from Mexican rule, and he readily voiced his aspirations to those about him.

Lansford Hastings and John C. Fremont would strongly influence future travel on the California Trail. Fremont's descriptions of his route through the desert bolstered Hastings' claims and stimulated his aspirations. He planned to retrace Fremont's route, evaluate it for wagon travel, meet emigrants heading west, convince them of the advantages of this new route, and guide them to California. So early in 1846 Hastings left the Sacramento Valley with a company of nineteen men, three women, and three children to seek his destiny. In so doing,

LEGENDARY TRUTHS

he would set the scene for the Donner tragedy and the realization that safer routes to California were needed.

At about the same time in Oregon, a party headed by Jesse Applegate, Lindsay Applegate, and Captain Levi Scott left the Willamette Valley in search of a safer southern route into Oregon. Both Lindsay and Jesse had lost sons in the rapids of the Columbia River section of the Oregon Trail near Wallula when they came west with their families in 1843. They followed the Hudson's Bay Trappers Trail south to the Rogue River area, then turned east to Klamath Lake, following a route disclosed to them by Jesse's friend, Peter Skene Ogden, who had trapped throughout the area in 1829 and made a map of the area, which Jesse possessed.[6]

As they passed around the southern end of Klamath Lake, they apparently crossed the tracks of Fremont, who had been there three months before. As reported by Bancroft, "Keeping down the shore of the lake they encamped on Hot Creek, at the identical spot where Fremont's party had been a couple of months previous, and where the Hot Creek Modocs murdered his three faithful Delawares."[7] They had to have crossed the path of Fremont, but it is doubtful that this description of the massacre site is accurate.[*]

Continuing east to Goose Lake, the Scott/Applegate party then followed the same route traveled by Fremont in 1843 on a well-traveled, but ancient Indian trail through High Rock Canyon to the Black Rock Desert. From here, they left the route pioneered by Fremont and, traveling to the southeast, discovered Rabbit Hole Springs and Antelope Springs, before reaching the Humboldt River, which they then followed on their way to Fort Hall.

Applegate estimated the new "southern route" to be about two hundred miles shorter than the established Oregon Trail, and stated that it had the distinct advantage of avoiding the rapids of the Columbia, where his son and nephew had drowned when they entered Oregon by the original trail.[†] At Fort Hall, he promoted the route to emigrants headed up the Oregon Trail, and to those headed to California,

---

[*] See description of massacre site in chapter 1846 Trail Development and Donner Tragedy.

[†] This labeling of the trail as a "Short Cut" may have carried over to the later Lassen Trail that followed the same route from the Humboldt. There is no record that Lassen ever promoted it as a shortcut.

convincing them of the advantages of traveling his route.

Jesse Quinn Thornton was one of the emigrants he convinced. Thornton later wrote disparagingly of the Applegates and their trail after he had experienced the hardships of the Black Rock Desert, and later the rainy weather and rugged route through Canyon Creek Canyon.

In spite of Thornton's negativity and the hardships the route presented, it became an alternate road to Oregon and opened up the eastern part of what was later to become the northern route into California—The Applegate/Lassen Trail.

In 1846 Hastings explored Fremont's desert route south of Salt Lake, and continued east as far as the Sweetwater River, where he promoted his new "Cutoff to California" to arriving emigrants, inviting them to meet him at Fort Bridger. Some men with experience, including James Clyman, argued against the new route, and most of the early arrivals stayed with the proven route. However, later arrivals, concerned about time, were swayed by the professed shorter route, and listened to Hastings, who was to wait for them at Fort Bridger to lead them across the new route.

On July 20, Hastings started from Fort Bridger with about forty wagons and two hundred people, heading westward to Bear River and beyond, where no wagons had previously gone. Another twenty wagons followed later. They ran into steep barriers and a nearly impassable canyon following the Weber River through the Wasatch Mountains. Hastings was finally able to get about sixty wagons through with the loss of only one wagon and its team of oxen. But the route was so difficult that he sent word back to the following wagons, instructing them to camp, send a messenger for him, and he would return and guide them through, too.[8]

The next wagon train of about twenty-three wagons and eighty-seven people was under the leadership of George Donner. They camped as directed and sent James Reed ahead to get Hastings. When Reed met with Hastings, he refused to return to lead the rest. Reed returned with this news and a report of the dangers and difficulties of the canyon ahead. A decision was made to cross the mountains rather than risk the Weber Canyon.[9]

The route was very difficult, and they were without sufficient manpower. They had to cut trees and build a road, which took much time and effort, tiring the party and weakening the oxen. Then they encountered the next ordeal of crossing the Salt Lake Desert—eighty-three waterless miles of wheel-trapping mud, salt, and sand.

Hastings' first group had crossed this stretch of desert with difficulty, but there was no loss of life or wagons; however, there was a toll on the oxen. The Donner Party fared less well. Their oxen, having been stressed with the mountain ordeal, required ten days just to cross this section. They lost precious time, and they lost oxen and had to abandon wagons and their contents.

Far behind the other trains now, they continued slowly across the "Cutoff," down the Humboldt, and across the Forty Mile Desert. When they finally started up the Truckee River route and over the mountains, they were arriving so late in the season that they became entrapped by snowstorms. Some made it as far as the lake that would later be named Donner, and the Breens made use of the cabin where Moses Schallenberger had spent the winter two years earlier. Farther back down the trail, the Donners and others built cabins or erected shelters of branches and canvas or hides.

Trapped, without supplies and weakened from their arduous journey, they began an epic saga of winter hardship, starvation, and survival, ending with the *dénouement* of death, cannibalism, and heroism that would give rise to legendary tales of macabre events for years to come.[*]

Of the party, forty died and forty-seven survived. The year of 1846 became known as the "Year of the Donner Tragedy." Fears of suffering the same fate largely affected the choices of routes to be followed by future emigrants.

1846 was also a year of many wagon trains successfully arriving in California, and it was a year of several improvements to the routes, so that land travel to California in 1846 (1,500 emigrants) eclipsed that to Oregon (1,200 emigrants).

The Donners had opened a new way into the Salt Lake area that would benefit later emigrants, especially the Mormons, who came into the area the following year.

Also in 1846, the opening of the Applegate Trail connected the California Trail, on the Humboldt River, to the Siskiyou Trail. It was used by the Hudson Bay's trappers to travel from Oregon to California, providing a logical northern route into the Sacramento Valley, thereby avoiding the rugged steeps of the Sierra Nevada over Donner Pass.

---

[*] See *Winter of Entrapment* by Joseph A. King, *Ordeal by Hunger* by George R. Stewart, or many other books detailing the Donner Tragedy.

In a letter written in Oregon City by Robert Cadden Keyes, brother of Margaret (Keyes) Reed, dated December 10, 1846, he confirmed that the connection of these routes was commonly known long before Peter Lassen "pioneered" the route leading wagons over it in 1848. The letter was addressed to James and Margaret Reed of the Donner Party. Keyes knew they were coming to California in 1846, but he didn't know their party was trapped, at the time, in the snows of the Sierra Range. He wrote:

> *Dear Brother & Sister,*
> *I again take my pen in hand to wright you that I am well at this time and hope that this letter may fine you all in good health. I am in Oregon I reach this place the 16 of Ju last after a trip of 40 Days and a Vary plesant trip (word illegible) with the exception of me loosing one Horse and pack crossing Sacrimento Mountin I lost everything I had but the Shirt and pantaloons that I had on me. That was the 4 day from Mr Lasons the Mountain is vary thick with brush and like the Old Horse got out of the trace and I couldnt find him, the things that I lost cost me $100 but I got hear in good health with milling work (apparently the name of his mare) & one Maule & two others Horsis milling work is aflected at this time with a sore leag and is very poore but I think that she will be well so as to come to California in the spring as I intend to come to sea you befor I go home. This is a good timbered and soiled Country this of wich I wright is the valie of willamet it is to much shut in from Ship navigation I want to go across the Columbia River to (?) in (?) May to look at pugts Sound and the Country around iot this valie don't please me you can youse your pleasur to come and see it or not I would recommend you take leave of your family thare if you don't like that Country till you looke at this for if you can git land thare I think thare will be large Company thar next Somer from hiar with packs and Wagons for they can go on to Applegats Road within one Hundred Mils of P Lasons and that Houndred mils is a valie vary (? easy ?), so I am told, the folks are in the Mountains yet on Applegates Road that is what is arrive of them...*[10]

LEGENDARY TRUTHS

Keyes had come to California in 1845 with the same party as William B. Ide and had gone to Oregon in April 1846, passing Lassen's rancho and traveling up the old trappers trail (east branch of Siskiyou Trail) to the Willamette Valley. Whether he met Lassen is unknown, but his trip was only a few weeks earlier than when Fremont came to *Bosquejo*, and subsequently when Lassen followed the same route to Klamath in pursuit of Fremont. Note that in his letter he wrote, "packs and Wagons… can go on to Applegats Road within one Hundred Mils of P Lasons and that Houndred mils is a valie vary (? easy ?)."

/

1847
Donner Fallout and Lassen's Trip East

We came to the Donner Camp whear the most of them perished the winter before. They had trimmed the pines of their limbs for fuel...Their camp was in a thick forrest of pines, not far from doner lake. The snow was verry deep. We found bones and sculls scattered about it was a most horrible sight-they had mashed the bones to get marrow...I stood guard in the latter part of the night. And thoudt of all the ghosts and hobgoblins I could think of or ever herd of. Besides the sculls bones and the dark forest it was a most dismal place. Day come and drove all the specter away. * [1]

—Abner Blackburn, 1847

There is little remaining record of the part Peter Lassen played in either the Bear Flag Revolt or the capitulation of California from

---

*   Unedited quote from actual journal.

LEGENDARY TRUTHS

Mexican to American rule, but some sources claim that Lassen enlisted under Captain Fremont and took an active part against the Mexican forces.[2] Franklin Scott wrote, "Neither Lassen nor the other recent Mexican grantees played any part—directly, at least—in these events, for they honored their Mexican oaths of fealty."[*][3] If he participated, and when he returned to his rancho isn't known for sure. However, early the following year, he traveled from his rancho downriver, perhaps to meet with, or to support, Fremont.[†][4] For his involvement in the power struggle between Commodore Stockton and the General, Fremont was now under the command of General Kearny. Fremont would be escorted back to Washington D.C. to face a court martial. Or, perhaps, Lassen just learned on this trip of Stockton's upcoming return to Washington.

On February 13, 1847, as he was traveling south, Lassen was given the following letter, written by George McKinstry to deliver to the *California Star* newspaper.[5]

> *Mr. E.P.Jones*
> *Dear Sir.—*
> *An opportunity offering to send to your town by Mr. [Peter] Lassen on his way down in a canoe, I write to inform you of the latest news from the mountains—Capt. E.M. Kern, commander of this district returned from Johnson's Settlement on the 11th inst. After an absence of some 10 days; he traveled on horseback and found the road very good both going and returning. On his arrival at that settlement he found five women and two men that had succeeded in getting in from the unfortunate company now in the mountains, in much better health than could have been expect[e]d; in fact they were suffering merely from their feet being slightly injured by the frost....*
>
> *(One of the men [William Eddy] returned with the party...)*
> *All the horrid reports that they have received, part of which*

---

*   Bancroft in *History of California*, said that Lassen was probably one of the Bears in 1846.

†   Some sources say that one reason Peter Lassen returned to the East later in the spring with Stockton's Party was to support Fremont in his court martial.

I wrote you in my last were corroborated by those who were so fortunate as to get in.

Earlier on January 16, the *California Star* published this headline, "Emigrants in the Mountains" and broke the news to the people of California about a party of "about sixty persons, men, women, and children," who were trapped in the mountains "in a most distressing situation," and it said, "They were almost entirely out of provisions."

If Lassen hadn't previously known of the Donner incident, he was now obviously aware of the news. This awareness—about the hardships the established route presented, over what would from now on be called Donner Pass, and the dangers of winter entrapment that loomed for those arriving late in the season—would later influence his opinions and those of his contemporaries.

News of the tragedy appeared in six issues of the *California Star* in the spring of 1847. The paper reported the ongoing struggles against the snow in the mountains and grim tales of the famished emigrants, who had resorted to cannibalism in order to survive. Elder Sam Brannan, a Mormon and owner of the *California Star*, took sixteen copies of the paper to Salt Lake City and gave them to Brigham Young. On his journey over the mountains, Brannan met William Fallon, one of the rescuers, as he was bringing Keseberg out of the mountains. This was the first news of the tragedy to reach the East, but it engendered fear among future emigrants, and was probably responsible for turning most of the 1847 emigrants north to Oregon.[6]

As spring in the mountains progressed, rescuers brought out the survivors and lurid descriptions of their ordeal. The site of the "Donner Tragedy" was abandoned until travelers would later encounter the remains. General Kearny's party was reportedly the first to pass by. Kearny's party left Johnson's Ranch on the Bear River on June 17 with Fremont in tow. However, Kearny would wait until he reached Fort Leavenworth to formally place him under arrest and charge him for a court martial. In spite of the fact that Fremont had traveled over the route to be followed, and had extensive experience, Kearny snubbed him by hiring William O. *(Le Gross)* Fallon to guide them over the mountains.

On June 22, they arrived at the cabins by the lake where members of the Donner Party had been trapped for the winter. Kearny ordered

LEGENDARY TRUTHS

Major Swords and his men to bury the "gruesome remains." Edmund Bryant wrote:

> *When the return party of Gen. Kearny (which I accompanied) reached the scene of these horrible and tragical occurances, on the 22nd of June, 1847, a halt was ordered, for the purpose of collecting and interring the remains. Near the principal cabins, I saw two bodies, entire with the exception that the abdomens had been cut open and the entrails extracted. Their flesh had been wasted by famine or evaporated by exposure to the dry atmosphere, and they presented the appearance of mummies. Strewn around the cabins were dislocated and broken bones— skulls, (in some instances sawed asunder with care for the purpose of extracting the brains)—human skeletons, in short, in every variety of mutilation. A more revolting and appalling spectacle I never witnessed. The remains were, by order of Gen. Kearny, collected and buried under the superintendence of Major Swords. They were interred in a pit which had been dug in the centre of one of the cabins, by the order of Major Swords, were fired, and with every thing surrounding them connected with this horrid and melancholy tragedy, were consumed.* [7]

Other members of the party also recorded their observations and experiences:

> *Reached the 'Cabins,' where 25 or 30 of a party of emigrants, in attempting to pass the winter, had perished from starvation. Their bodies & bones were strewn about, presenting a revolting & distressing spectacle. The Gen'l directed Maj. Swords to collect these remains & inter them.* (Turner, 1847) [8]
>
> *We came down to the lake to some cabins that had been built by some emigrants last fall. They were overtaken in the snow. There were eighty of them in number, and only thirty of them that lived. The rest of them starved to death. The General called a halt and detailed five men to bury the deserted bodies that were lying on the ground. Those that lived the longest lived on the dead bodies of the others.*

One man lived four months on human flesh. He sawed their heads open, ate their brains and mangled their bodies in a horrible manner. This place now goes by the name of Cannibal Camp.... After we buried the bones of the dead, which were sawed and broken to pieces for the marrow, we set fire to the cabin. (Jones, 1847)[9]

About a month later, Commodore Stockton and his party left Johnson's Ranch on July 20, 1847. But before he started east, he had the *Californian* publish in its July 17, 1847 issue a long article stating "he had been commander-in-chief of all military operations in the conquest of California, and that General Kearny had been second in command."[10] Stockton had apparently submitted the article earlier, but the publisher delayed publishing it because Kearny had threatened to hold him accountable. The rivalry of command continued, and it would later be argued in Fremont's court martial in Washington.

With Stockton was a mixed party of about forty-five men, including Peter Lassen, Joseph B. Chiles, Archibald Gillespie, J. J. Myers, Milton McGee, and Samuel J. Hensley.[11] Hensley, along with Lassen and Chiles, would return to California the following year leading parties of their own. McGee and Myers would lead wagon trains to California in 1849.

The guides for the Stockton Party were Joseph B. Chiles, working as head guide for $2 per day, James Beckwith, Garrett Long, and Francis Drake Brown acting as secondary guides.

Being a few weeks later than the Kearny Party when they arrived at the Donner site, considerably more snow had melted, exposing additional examples of the "grisly remains," and they, also, stopped to bury them.

Having experienced firsthand the steep, rugged terrain and seen the results of a winter entrapment on the established road to California, Stockton, Lassen, and the others were convinced that the route should be avoided. They advised the emigrants they met on their way to take a northern route, which was also known as the "southern route" to Oregon. Although this new route hadn't been traveled by wagons going to California, the general idea of the route had been known by putting together its parts.*

---

* See Trail Development & the Donner Tragedy chapter, letter from James Keyes and corresponding footnote.

LEGENDARY TRUTHS

The Applegates had led wagons from the meadows (later to be known as Lassen's Meadows) north across Black Rock Desert to Goose Lake and beyond to Oregon. Fremont had been through High Rock Canyon in 1843. Chiles, with Hensley, McGee, and Myers had ridden from Goose Lake down the Pit River to Hat Creek and entered the Sacramento Valley via the old trappers' trail (known as the eastern route of the Siskiyou Trail) in 1843. Lassen, himself, had ridden up that trail to Klamath Lake in pursuit of Fremont in 1846, and seen the lay of the land from the Pit River (also known, then, as the Upper Sacramento River) south to his rancho.

Lassen had spent a lot of time talking with Fremont and Carson, and was now traveling east with Chiles and other notable guides, including Myers and McGee. Undoubtedly, they discussed the Donner tragedy and considered the attributes and difficulties of another route as compared to the traditional route. It is known that they advised westbound emigrants to avoid the Truckee Route and take the northern route instead. A letter, apparently written by Jesse Applegate, published in the *Oregon City Spectator* on November 25, 1847 stated:

> *A company of 16 wagons, under the direction of Mr. Gordon left the forks of the road on the 27th day of August, bound for California. They met the party of Com. Stockton, who advised them to keep the southern route to Oregon, until they arrived at the Sacramento River, and by descending it they would avoid the Sierra Nevada.... They followed his advice, but after laying by one week at this river (i.e. Lost River) examining the Country, they concluded it would be safer to follow the road to Oregon.* [*] [12]

Some sources referred to this train as the Gordon/Wiggins Train or alternately the Wiggins Train. Stewart wrote:

> *This year instead of Hastings, it was William Wiggins. A New Yorker of no great ability or distinction, he had lived in California since '40. He had been to Sutter's Fort for a while, but there is no likelihood that he knew anything more*

---

[*]   The Sacramento River mentioned here refers to Lost River near Klamath Lake. Fremont in 1843 had misidentified the Sycan River as the headwaters of the Sacramento and Preuss drew it into his map, later causing this confusion.

*about the mountainous northern area than he might have
picked up in gossip with the few people who had traveled
there.*[13]

Yes, much information passed by "gossip" or word of mouth,
including the advice and directions he undoubtedly received from
Stockton and the members of his party. Fremont's report and map, as
well as the Applegate's Waybill, were available to Wiggins and other
emigrants on the trail that summer.

Wiggins had traveled the Oregon Trail with Lassen in '39, and
they had wintered in the Willamette Valley, where they received
information about the old trappers trail that went south to California.
They had wanted to enter California from Oregon via the mountain
route, but conditions at the time prevented them from organizing a
large enough party, thereby causing them to enter California by ship.
Therefore, Wiggins did have some previous knowledge of the route,
or at least parts of it.

Stewart continued:

> *He went east on horseback in '46, and in the next spring
> started back to California. With this experience behind
> him, he became either the captain of a company or its
> paid guide. Somewhere along the Humboldt, as Wiggins
> himself later told it, he and his men met 'a company from
> California' who gave them a 'waybill' from there to a river
> called Sacramento. Most likely this document was what has
> been preserved in another copy as Applegate's Waybill, an
> itinerary of the Applegate Route to Oregon, including the
> name, 'Sacramento River.'*
>
> *Wiggins and his men need not have been merely naïve in
> accepting this 'information.' Doubtless they had a copy of
> Fremont's report with them, and they would have found that
> it apparently checked with the waybill....*
>
> *Putting all the 'information' together, Wiggins decided
> to avoid the Forty-mile Desert and the other difficulties of
> the California end by following the Applegate Route until
> he came to the 'Sacramento.' So far, we can commend him
> for basing himself on the best authorities. But his next idea
> was a bad one—that, having come to the Sacramento River,*

LEGENDARY TRUTHS

he would simply follow down along it to the Sacramento Valley. By so doing, indeed, he could be sure that he would not have to cross a high mountain divide. But anyone should have known, as the difficulties along the Truckee and Weber had shown amply, that trying to follow a river could get you into trouble. Nevertheless, Wiggins and his party so decided. They turned off the main trail—eighteen wagons, about twenty-five men, and twice that number of those hostages of fortune, women and children. Through the hard desert country they followed the trail of the emigrants who had headed that way for Oregon the year before. They must have been well equipped and efficient, for they took their wagons in good–enough time across three hundred miles of hard going. Eventually they came to the 'Sacramento,' which did, indeed, flow southward at that point.

Scouting a few miles downstream, however, they found that the river flowed into a lake. To the south of the lake were lava beds and high country, and no indication of an outlet. In addition, the lake water may have been brackish to the taste, and doubtless the evidence of different water levels indicated a lake without an overflow. Wiggins at once became convinced that the waybill was 'entirely erroneous,' and that the river was not the Sacramento.[14]

Was this the truth? Or was he on the Pit and blocked by a canyon, as Helfrich seemed to suggest? Did Lassen later blunder into the same trap following his tracks? Is this the same canyon where Gray[*][15] later had to turn around? Is this the Pit River canyon near the Thompson's Ranch in Bieber, California? Here is where "legendary truths" become contradictory in an interesting way and lead to speculation that then engenders more "legendary truths." Helfrich wrote, "The Wm. Wiggins train of about 17 wagons, California bound, seem to

---

[*]   On September 13, 1849, when he was camped in Big Valley, he wrote: "In the afternoon started on a road which led over a high hill & thinking we were on the wrong road, turned back & took up our route through a canon & after driving awhile found our road completely block'd up, as it was only a 'turn off' so we had to return & take the road we took first…".

have been the first train, by a week, to turn into the Applegate Trail...
Sidetracked somewhere in the Goose Lake - Pitt River country, they
became the last train to enter Oregon in 1847." [16]

Stewart concluded the Wiggins episode:

> *He then acted with excellent judgment. He did not waste*
> *precious time in trying to force his way southward,*
> *pigheadedly, through almost unknown mountains. Instead,*
> *he brought the wagons back to the Applegate Trail, and*
> *followed it westward to the Oregon settlements, arriving*
> *there about November 1.* [17]

Stewart later added:

> *The disappearance of this party raised much to-do in*
> *California. People feared, with good reason, that another*
> *Donner disaster was occurring somewhere in the tangled*
> *northern mountains. Two expeditions pushed northward*
> *in attempts to find the vanished emigrants. On account of*
> *the snow neither expedition was able to get far, and their*
> *failures only renewed the strength of the rumors. As if in*
> *repetition of the Donner story, some men were said to have*
> *come in from the company and reported that the people*
> *were trapped in a canyon. The mystery was at last resolved*
> *in April, when Wiggins himself arrived in San Francisco by*
> *sea.* [18]

This last statement by Stewart is interesting in that it agrees with
Helfrich's rendition of the Wiggins' train getting stuck in a canyon
and having to retrace its steps, but earlier, Stewart places them at the
location where Lost River enters Tule Lake. There is no canyon that
could have trapped them there. Did some of his men separate from the
group and get through to California?

Helfrich continued:

> *...Their intention was to follow the Applegate Trail to the*
> *headwaters of the Sacramento (Pitt) River, then turning*
> *southwest, follow down that stream to the Sacramento*
> *Valley. This they seem to have partially done, turning from*
> *the Applegate Trail probably at Goose Lake. How far they*

traveled is unknown, but they were forced to turn back and eventually fell in behind the main Oregon bound migration. When the Wiggins Party failed to arrive in California, their friends feared another Donnor tragedy, or an Indian massacre. It was not known until the next April, when Wiggins arrived in San Francisco by boat that the party had made their way in safety to Oregon.[19]

Calhoun's version of the Wiggins story generally agreed but had the date wrong and said Wiggins rode from Oregon to California over the "Shasta Trail" (old trappers trail):

A wagon train, in 1846 (date wrong), turned off to follow the Applegate trail at the Humboldt Meadows, (later called Lassen Meadows). When they arrived at Goose Lake, snow was already beginning to fall. They gave up California, and made a dash for the Rogue River Vally. They found the country so lush that all but Wiggins, the train captain, decided to settle there. Meanwhile, news got through to California that the Wiggins train was on the way. When it did not arrive at Johnson's Ranch on the Bear River, word spread that it must have suffered the fate of the Donner Party. Only this time the entire company had either starved, or had been frozen by the bitter cold of the desert or foothills east of the mountains.

Not until late in the spring of 1847, did the news spread that Wiggins, alone, had ridden down the 'Shasta Trail', to the real head of the Sacramento River, and on down to Lassen's Ranch at Vina in the Sacramento Valley.[20]

In Davis's version, he speculated:

It may have been Augustus Mitchell's 1846 map that led the Wiggins-Gordon wagon train[21] *to attempt to break a way down the Sacramento River to California in 1847. The Wiggins-Gordon wagon train followed the South Road to the Rio Sacramento. They planned to follow the Sacramento*

---

* Bagley explained that these were two separate trains.

River to the Sacramento Valley. The Wiggins train wasted a week trying to locate the fictitious Rio Sacramento south of Tule Lake, then gave up. They continued down South Road with the Oregon emigration and ended up in the Willamette Valley separated from their friends who were worrying about their safety in California. Some of the party caught a ship and went to California the next spring. [22]

The Wiggins train has led to some "legendary" speculation about the route he actually took, and whether the Sacramento River he followed, was the Pit or the Lost River. Where did Stewart hear, "some men were said to have come in from the company and reported that the people were trapped in a canyon"? Unanswered questions provide food for the myth. But, in *Wiggin's Recollections*, he didn't mention people leaving his group, and he described the place of his decision to go to Oregon as being where Lost River flows into Tule Lake.* [23]

These speculations make interesting lore. But the important point, here, is that in 1847 the opinion of many qualified trail leaders, like McGee, Myers, Chiles, and Lassen—all members of the Stockton Party—considered the "southern route" to Oregon, better for going to California than the Truckee Route. It should also be noted that when Lassen led the first wagons into California over this route that he was not "an incompetent Dane"[24] exploring an unknown route, as suggested by Lavender and others, who seem to think the idea of entering California by this route originated with Lassen.

Meanwhile, the Stockton Party continued east, and near the present-day town of Reno, they had a battle with a "combined force of 1,500 Piute and Pit River Indians," as estimated by Brown, one of the guides. After the battle, "they had more Indian trouble along the way, and during one battle, Stockton received an arrow wound through both thighs."[25] They crossed the Great Basin following the Humboldt River, and then proceeded to Fort Hall and east to South Pass.

---

* Tule Lake was earlier named Rhett's Lake by Fremont, but usage at the time suggests that it may also have been known as "Goose Lake" giving rise to confusion as to Wiggins' location when he "supposedly got lost." Burnett, in his recollections seems to refer to Tule Lake as "Goose Lake," where he turned south off the Applegate trail in 1849. Thomas McKay, who also had previously been to both "Goose Lakes," was guiding Burnett. Did he call Tule Lake "Goose Lake," and did he refer to Goose Lake as "Pitt Lake" as Ogden had originally named it?

LEGENDARY TRUTHS

Before they arrived at Fort Hall, they met the party of Abner Blackburn, who continued on west over the Truckee Route and noted in his journal:

> *At Goose Creek [we] met Comodore Stockton and suite, Captain Gelespie, Peterson, and J. Parker Norris with fifty two marenes with them to keep them from harm. They were ordered to Washington to settle the quarrel between Kearny, Freemont, and Stockton. They said the Trucky [Truckee] Indians attacked them at night killing some of their horses and wounding some of their men. Stockton was wounded in his [k]nee with an arrow. They cautioned us to be on our guard all the time. Our pilot said he knew dem ingen and he could slip us true.* [26]

"Legendary truths" relate another interesting story claiming Peter Lassen got lost from the Stockton Party somewhere along the Platte River. If this story is true, it may confirm the reputation of Lassen "always getting lost." Or does it? Was he really lost, or did he just leave the Stockton Party for some reason? At any rate, he arrived in Missouri as soon as, or even earlier than Stockton, as reported by Missouri newspapers.

The arrival of the Stockton Party was noted in the St. Louis, Missouri paper of November 4, 1847:

> *The steamboat Meteor, which arrived here this morning from Weston, on the Missouri River, conveyed to this place Commodore Stockton and suite, who are now on their return from California. The party which traveled with Com. Stockton left the Valley of the Sacramento, near Fort Sutter, on the 19th of July, and numbered 46 persons...The party, while crossing the mountains, encountered large bodies of snow, but found the streams in the valleys low— the effects of a drought...* [27]

The November 4, 1847 issue of the *Brunswicker* printed: "The meteor, last Sunday, brought down our old county man Peter Lawson, who has been absent to California since the spring of 1842. He comes in the train of Commodore Stockton on the 19th July...He brings in a young Indian chief with him to show the sights and will take him back next spring."[*]

The *Brunswicker's* mention of Lassen being accompanied by an Indian from California is the only record we have of this, but it does lead to some speculation that on the return trip the Indian could have helped Lassen navigate his new route by contributing his knowledge of the area, especially as they neared Lassen's rancho.[28] Not documented by the newspapers of the time is the claim of David Dutton, who traveled to Oregon and California with Lassen in 1839-40, that he accompanied Lassen and Stockton on the trip to Missouri in 1847, and that he returned with Lassen in 1848. Dutton claimed that he went east "by special invitation from Lassen," to be his traveling companion and "body guard." He said Lassen went east "to encourage emigrants to come to California and bring back a Masonic charter concealed in Lassen's boot."[29]

Lassen probably spent the winter in Missouri with friends, visiting and perhaps recruiting people to return to California with him, but there is no evidence he went on to Washington to attend Fremont's court-martial.[†] [30] Probably the main motive for Lassen's trip back to Missouri was to visit the area where he had owned property and to drop in on friends, some of whom would return to California with him the next spring, when he departed leading a train of twelve wagons.

On May 10, 1848, Lassen, along with Sashel (alternately spelled Sarchel, Saschel, Satchel) Woods and Lucien E. Stewart, received a charter from the Masons of the state of Missouri to establish the Western Star Lodge No. 98 at Benton City. Lassen was the Junior Warden. Stewart was the Senior Warden, and Woods was the Master. Lassen had previously been a member of the Chariton chapter, and it was his desire to take the charter back to California to establish a chapter at his proposed Benton City, but there is no confirming documentation to Dutton's claim that Lassen "brought the Masonic charter back hidden in his boot."[31]

It is interesting to note discrepancies in the date of Lassen's departure for California. The May 4, 1848 issue of the *Brunswicker* reported Lassen had left for California, but May 10 was the date the

---

[*]   The *Brunswicker* was the newspaper of Brunswick, the county seat of Clariton County at the time. Keytesville is the present County seat.

[†]   Bruff suggested Lassen went east to attend the court-martial.

LEGENDARY TRUTHS

Masonic charter was issued. Possibly the paper announced his future departure, and he waited until he received the charter before leaving; however, according to journal entries, Lassen's train was one or two days ahead of Chiles' train, which had left Independence some time before Richard May arrived there on May 12.

1848
Lassen's Return and News of Gold

They tell me there is more real pleasure in one year in the mountains than in a whole Lifetime in a disease Settled Country.—Richard May[1]

The westward migration from Missouri that year, led by Peter Lassen, Joseph Chiles, James Clyman, Samuel Hensley, and others would open new routes and secure the usage of some established ones. However, the most significant event in 1848 to influence the further development of the California Trail and emigrants using it was the discovery of gold at Sutter's mill and the resultant rush of '49. Word of the discovery, although slow to get out, caused some immigration of gold-seekers, especially from Oregon to California in the summer, as news of the strike seemed to reach there first. Oregon's proximity to the Sacramento Valley by following the Applegate and old trappers' trails resulted in increased travel from there, but it would be another year before the rush would start from the East.

Following the Mexican-American War, concern in the East over postwar conditions in California seemed to direct the emigrants toward Oregon, so that only four hundred to five hundred started to California, and usage of the California Trail that year would be fairly light in comparison to future years.

Among the parties heading east from California that year was a Mormon party of forty-five men, one woman, seventeen wagons, and about 150 horses organized on July 18 to return to Salt Lake City. They were under the command of Samuel Thompson. Henry Bigler kept a diary of the journey and parties they met on the way. Having heard "horrendous stories about the difficulties of the Truckee Canyon with its many river crossings—'very deep and rapid,'"[2] they were determined to avoid that route and pioneer a safer road over the mountains farther to the south, coming out on the West Fork of the Carson River. This new Mormon road also crossed the high mountains, with steep ascents and many difficulties, but it possibly provided a safer alternative to the Truckee Route, and would later be chosen by thousands of emigrants as the preferred route going to California. Oddly enough, though, it would be called "The Carson Route" because it followed the Carson River rather than honoring the Mormons who discovered it; however, some modern historians prefer to call it the "Mormon-Carson Route."

Many authors have written that Lassen went East in 1848 (Note! he was already in Missouri!) to meet emigrants somewhere along the Humboldt or at Fort Hall and lure them to his proposed city at *Bosquejo* primarily for the reasons of enriching himself with the sales of land, livestock, and "exorbitantly priced provisions." In doing so, they contributed to the "legendary truths," shadowing the legacy of Peter Lassen, or perhaps we should refer to them as "legendary fantasies." Among those writers were: David Lavender in *The Great West*, Thomas Howard in *Sierra Crossing*, F. D. Calhoun in *The Lassen Trail*, George Stewart in *The California Trail*, and even Fariss and Smith in *History of Plumas County*.

Fariss and Smith wrote:

> *Lassen, accompanied by Paul Richeson, went to Fort Hall in the summer of 1848, and induced a train of emigrants to submit themselves to his guidance, and try the new route to California...There were twelve wagons in the train that decided to attempt the new road, and Lassen led them along safely, though they encountered some extremely rugged and*

*difficult mountains, until they reached Mountain Meadows
or Big Meadows, where their provisions and animals both
became exhausted, and they stopped to recruit the one and
supply the other. Here they were overtaken by a company
from Oregon with twenty wagons, on their way to the
gold fields of California—news of the great discovery not
having reached Oregon till the last of August. This was
about the first of November. With the aid of the Oregon
party they made their way safely to Lassen's ranch, where
the train disbanded.*[3]

At least Fariss and Smith wrote, "Lassen led them along safely"
even though they encountered difficulties (as nearly all trains did), and
remarkably, there was no mention of "being lost," as others claimed.
Lavender wrote:

*Early in '48, quite unaware of Marshall's discovery, Lassen
rode east to the Humboldt River to lure farmers close to
his property so that its value would increase. Ten wagons
heeded him. He led the party along the Applegate Trail
until they were far north of where they should have gone.
Totally lost. Lassen then floundered toward the Pit River, a
tributary to the Sacramento.*[4]

Thomas Howard wrote, equally as erroneously:

*In 1848 Peter Lassen, a Dane who had arrived in
California by sea in 1840 and acquired a land grant in
the northern Sacramento Valley, took a notion to bring in
emigrants to his land and set himself up in the baronial
style of John Sutter. Lassen was somewhat familiar with
northeastern California, and his idea was to follow the
Applegate Trail from the Humboldt through Fandango Pass
in the Warner Range, and then leave it to angle back to the
southwest. In the summer of 1848 he journeyed east to a
point on the Humboldt, apparently after crossing the Sierra
via the Truckee route rather than by giving his own route
a trial run in reverse (which might have saved him a lot
of trouble later), and intercepted some emigrants whom he
persuaded to take his 'shortcut' to the Central Valley.*[5]

74

LEGENDARY TRUTHS

F. D. Calhoun wrote:

"In 1846, Lassen made the first of several trips to St. Louis. There he obtained a 'Charter' for a Masonic Lodge.'" * Calhoun went on to say:

> *In 1847, and in 1848, he crossed the mountains early. Then rode on east to meet the expected wagon trains bound for California, or for Oregon, at Ft. Hall. He sold his services as an experienced guide, over the most dangerous part of the road west, to the highest bidder...In 1848, however, he was not interested in the guiding fee alone. The news of Marshall's discovery of gold reached Vina. He raced ahead to tell the travelers the wonderful news. He had no trouble turning wagons south from Ft. Hall, and then on to the Humboldt River. Then he convinced ten or twelve wagon owners to follow him over a new and quicker route to the gold fields. [6]*

Even George Stewart, in his chapter on the development of the California Trail in 1848 wrote legendarily:

> *As usual, people also started eastward from California.... In the spring of '48, like another Hastings, he rode eastward, presumably having some others in his party. To have explored the new route as he went along would have been the wise course, but the evidence suggests that he took the regular trail, probably going as far as Fort Hall. [7]*

Leaving this realm of "legendary truths," we will now return to Peter Lassen in Missouri, and to where the 1848 migration was forming. Hafen and Young wrote in *Fort Laramie* that about four thousand Mormons took the trail to Salt Lake City, seventeen hundred emigrants made their way to Oregon, and only about 150 went to California. Historian Hubert H. Bancroft estimated lower numbers. However, Helfrich, in *The Schreek of Wagons*, used Henry Bigler's journal recordings of meeting about one hundred wagons and Hensley's twelve-member

---

*   Lassen received the Masonic charter on May 10, 1848.

75

pack train[*][8] to estimate the number going to California at about 450.

These emigrants would first meet the party of Isaac Pettijohn and be recorded in his journal. Pettijohn had left Oregon by way of the Applegate Trail and was traveling east with a party of about twenty on pack mules and horses. The emigrants going west would later meet Bigler on the reaches of the Humboldt River, and be recorded by him.

The May 4, 1848 issue of the *Brunswicker* reported Lassen's westbound departure.[†][9] Also, "a letter dated 'Pacific Springs 16 July 1848' and signed 'Peter Lassen' is reproduced in the 'Brunswicker' of 9 Sep. 1848. 'Clearly Lassen went all the way to Missouri in 1847.'"[10]

Will Bagley reported that, "Among the members of Lassen's train were a Master Mason, Rev. Saschal Woods, who carried a Masonic charter issued by the Grand Lodge of Missouri on 10 May 1848 for Western Star Lodge No. 98 that listed L.E. Stewart as senior warden and Peter Lassen as junior warden."[11]

No diaries, journals, or other documentation from members of the Lassen Party detailing the trip have survived, or at least turned up to date. Therefore, we have to extrapolate their journey from the topography covered and from the writings of others on the trail at the time. Fortunately, several encounters with eastbound travelers that summer were recorded in their diaries.

A vanguard of wagons under the leadership of the old mountain man, James Clyman left before and stayed ahead of Lassen's train of eleven or twelve wagons.[‡][12] As noted above, Lassen departed on May 4, and was somewhere in the middle of that year's migration. He was followed by Joseph Chiles' train, which consisted of forty-seven wagons. The last to leave was Hensley's pack train.

Richard M. May arrived by boat in Independence after the last of the wagons departed and after Hensley had left for the year. He was told that no more wagons would leave until the following year, so he sent a dispatch ahead to Chiles announcing his desire to catch up, asking Chiles to wait for him.

Richard May left Independence on May 12 and caught up with

---

[*] Later on, he lists Hensley's number at ten.

[†] Fairfield lists several publications that document Lassen's presence in Missouri in 1848.

[‡] Rene Lassen states there were twelve wagons.

LEGENDARY TRUTHS

Chiles on the 21st, during a thunderstorm. May was one of the few to keep a westbound diary for 1848, and his descriptions of the journey give us the closest depiction of general events, road conditions, weather, eastbound parties on the trail, and the eastward spread of the "word" about the discovery of gold in California.[13]

Lassen was to maintain his lead ahead of Chiles for the entire distance to the Humboldt Meadows (later to be called Lassen's Meadows). But apparently, he was not far ahead, because Pettijohn's packing group recorded meeting them only one day ahead of Chiles' Train when they crossed the North Platte.

Traveling across the prairies, they encountered rain, sometimes in torrents, and high winds that blew down their tents. However, the face of the land was beautiful, with spring flowers blooming and a luxuriant growth of grass for the oxen. Averaging eight to ten miles a day and sometimes making twelve or more, they found the road easy across the flat, undulating landscape, but they often had to cross steep ravines, and occasionally double-team the oxen to ford a shallow, sandy-bottomed river.

May wrote:

> The dull Monotony of a Prarie Journey is quite Tiresome it being So very uniform that the variety which we Seek is no where to be found The Crack of the whip the clanking of Chains and the Still more disagreeable Schreek of Wagons is all that the Sense of hearing Conveys to the mind. Now and then the Lark and linnet will give you of their best, and Sweetest notes to emulate you while Journeying in these endless prarie.[14]

Francis Parkman also mentioned the monotony in his *Oregon Trail*, but he added, "Here and there a crow, or a raven, or a turkey-buzzard, relieved the uniformity." Occasionally the emigrants saw antelope (pronghorns), buffalo, turkeys, or an elk to rally the would-be hunters of the group. Also, many journals of the time mention the nearly endless "towns" of the prairie dogs.

An eastward bound party came from the mountains with twenty-two wagons laden with buffalo robes and tongues, passing the emigrants on the way to markets in the States, and attesting to the wanton slaughter that was going on at the time.

Then in early June, Lassen's Train passed "La Grand Isle," which was wooded and afforded firewood in a land otherwise destitute of wood. For much of the journey the emigrants burned *bois de vache* (wood of the cow)[15] or cow and buffalo chips.

A few miles upriver from Grand Island, May wrote that they saw the tents, wagons and four companies of the Oregon Battalion who were busily engaged in building Fort Child. In December it would be designated Fort Kearny after the general we met in preceding chapters.

On the plains, as they neared the towering landmark of Chimney Rock, mosquitoes became a problem, and buffalo gnats ("black galinippers" as called by one emigrant, George Holliday) were at times so pestilential that some emigrants reportedly contrived to make cheesecloth veils to protect themselves from the onslaught.

The prairie began to give way to a stark, uplifted and eroded landscape, and "we have found the grass Verry Short Since we reached buffaloe range The whole Country appears to be grased down by the red Mans Cattle Our present encampment the grass is verry good."[16]

Now the monotony of the prairies was broken by spectacular rock formations: Jail House Rock, Court House Rock, Chimney Rock, "Buttresses and barbican, bastion, demilune and guardhouse, tower, turret and donjon-keep"[17] of Scotts Bluff. Lassen had seen them all in 1839 and again on his trip East in '47. Other wagon train leaders had passed them in various years.

May described the landscape as:

> *The country through which we passed for the Last 3 days; Has the Most Romantic appearance of any my eyes ever beheld; The Wagoners Language fails to describe the Magnificent Grandeur of the rocks & Sand hills on the Nebraska [Platte]; I have Taxed my imagination to See if I could add another Variety to the different Shapes & figures presented to view in particular on the North fork But Such is the Sublime & picturesque Scenery that I would as Soon undertake to add an othe[r] tinge to the Rainbow...*[18]

At Fort Laramie, trade with the Indians was brisk; there were about one hundred fifty lodges nearby. Emigrant trains found a welcomed haven to rest and recruit. Wagons were repaired, the services of a blacksmith shop were available, lame animals were disposed of, and trade items were available. Mr. Bordeaux, the proprietor, provided entertainment and several young ladies and gentlemen of the Chiles Party danced and partook of his generosity. It is assumed that other trains, including Lassen's, received the same welcome.

On June 28, a party of ten "mostly disillusioned" men on their way back to the States from Oregon passed them. They reported the grass ahead was all dried up due to 1848 being one of the driest seasons ever known. Of the many going west with high hopes, many would return dispirited, and writers would describe them variously as in the "slough of despair," or "wonderfully sick of their romantic journey." That year, as in years to come, there was an ebb and flow of emigrants leaving and returning to the states of their origin. One returning group affixed a sign to their wagon stating, "Pennsylvanians Going East; And don't you forget it."[19]

A couple of days behind this party was the pack train of Pettijohn, who met the Lassen train and wrote, "July the first Crossed North Platte today with the assistance of the brethren Met 11 wagons." Then on July 2 he wrote, "met 47 wagon to day mostly for California." This was Chiles' train. May also recorded in his diary on that date, "We met Some twenty on pack mules & horses returning from Oregon. I had a few minutes conversation with them but nothing worthy of Note in the way of news." Obviously, news of the gold strike in California hadn't reached Oregon when they left.

Traveling up the Sweetwater River, the emigrants found the water pure and limpid as the name suggests, but May mentioned the dust that was notorious in the area. From the Sweetwater, they gently climbed to the Continental Divide at South Pass,* where they came to the headwaters of the eastern flowing waters. He also noted that the grass was good and not as the disgruntled Oregonians had reported.

We know from the letter Lassen sent to the *Brunswicker* that his party reached Pacific Springs on July 16. The following year, on August 2, Bruff gave a description of the area and mentioned camping in a moist bottom near Pacific Springs on South Pass. He said the grass was tolerable, that there were plenty of grouse of several varieties, that fine white dust in annoying clouds affected the men and the animals.

---

* At South Pass the trail actually crosses the Continental Divide twice (elevations are 7,412 ft. and 7,550 ft.).

He also mentioned the putrescence from dead oxen along the way. Probably conditions had changed some from the previous year, due to the increase of trail usage during the year.[20]

Chiles' train reached Pacific Springs on July 18, 1848, so he was still only a day or so behind Lassen. A few days later, May met Joseph Walker, the renowned mountain man, and was so impressed as to write:

> *Mr. Walker appears to be about 45 years of age and Steps off with the alearity [alacrity] of a youth. But this much may be Said of any one that has Lived in these mountains a few years. To See the Life the buoyancy of a mountaineer Compared to one of Missouri's Sons would astonish the most of men There is quite a number of men from the States throughout this Mountain Wilderness; They tell me there is more real pleasure in one year in the mountains than in a whole Lifetime in a disease Settled Country There is no political Strife no Religious Contention no domestic Broils no agricultural persuits to tire and weary the Limbs. Though Last not Least no Law nor Lawyers to Pettifog among them to mar their Peace and Sow discord among them Their duties are confined to the horse and gun and when they become Tired of one place they remove to another Their squaws performing all the labor.* [21]

Interestingly, May didn't address the effects of this mountain life on the "…squaws performing all the labor."

From South Pass, most the migration of '48 traveled west and north from the headwaters of the Green River, following the Bear River to Soda Springs, then northwest to Fort Hall. Most of the emigrants arrived there early in the month of August. At the fort, some provisions could be purchased and livestock replaced, reportedly for lower prices than at any other place on the road.

Which route Lassen followed from South Pass isn't documented other than an August 26, 1848 mention in Samuel Hollister Rogers' *Trail Journal* stating that Lassen "came by way of Salt Lake." Will Bagley, in *So Rugged and Mountainous*, noted, "Roger's intriguing entry raises the possibility that it was Lassen and his wagons, not Samuel Hensley, who opened the Salt Lake Cutoff." Bagley added, "Rogers was probably mistaken about Lassen's route."[22]

LEGENDARY TRUTHS

From Fort Hall, the road followed southwest down the Snake River crossing the Portneuf River and continuing to where the Raft River flowed from the southwest toward its confluence with the Snake. Here was where the two trails diverged—the Oregon Trail going down the Snake toward Oregon, but the California Trail turning southwest, generally following the Raft River through "Scenery bold and rich peak after peak Rising to great heights on both sides of our road," until the City of Rocks was reached near the Nevada/Idaho border. "Here all the language that I command Will not describe the Scenery around our encampment it is rich beyond anything I have ever beheld Single and isolated rocks Standing in the plain from 50 to 200 feet high encircled by a chain just giving admission & dismission from the bason."[23]

From the City of Rocks, it was about a day's drive to Goose Creek. On August 17, Hensley's pack train caught up with the Chiles' train again. Hensley had lost time by trying to go west through the desert south of Salt Lake, but due to bad weather and muddy conditions he had to return and rejoin the California Trail near the City of Rocks, and he now traveled with the Chiles Party for a few days. The trail then entered the Nevada territory to the south, passing by Thousand Springs, coming to the Humboldt River.*

In Franklin Langworthy's 1850 journal, he wrote, "The Humboldt is a singular stream; I think the longest river in the world of so diminutive a size. Its length is three or four hundred miles, and general width about fifty feet. From here, back to where we first saw it, the quality of water seems about the same. It rather diminishes in size as it proceeds." [24]

On August 23, Hensley's pack train started on ahead of the Chiles' train, expecting to arrive in California earlier and possibly sending provisions back to help the wagon train if help was needed. From this time until they reached the lower Humboldt, Hensley would maintain a position about a day ahead of Chiles and about a day behind the Lassen train, but he hadn't caught up to Lassen by the time the Mormon train from California met them on the lower Humboldt, just

---

* The Humboldt River had previously been called Ogden's River for Peter Skene Ogden, who followed it with his Hudson's Bay fur brigade in 1828. Ogden's men variously referred to it as "Unknown River," Swampy River," and "Paul's River," for one of their party who was buried on its banks. Later it became commonly known as "Mary's River," allegedly after Ogden's Indian wife. In 1845 Fremont renamed it the Humboldt River.

east of Lassen's Meadows.

Along the Humboldt, the road was generally good but monotonous, and marshy places had to be avoided. Mosquitoes could be troublesome, and grass and firewood could be scarce in places. The biggest complaint, though, was the horrendous clouds of dust that bothered both the people and the oxen; however, a dusty road had the benefit of providing softer walking for the oxen's trail-worn hooves.

This was also the area of the Paiute (or Digger) Indians who had wounded Stockton the previous year. They were a continual threat that had to be guarded against, as they would surreptitiously launch arrows at the livestock. When wounded, the stock would have to be butchered or abandoned to the Indians' profit and great hardship to the emigrants, who could be stranded without animals to pull their wagons.

By the middle of August, the first of the westward bound emigrants arrived at the Humboldt Sink, where the Humboldt terminated by sinking into the desert. The Mormons coming east from California had completed their new road and were also arriving at the Sink.

On August 15, the Mormons met a westward bound train of eighteen wagons, probably led by James Clyman. The next day they met another party of twenty-five wagons, and in the vanguard of wagons was Hazen Kimball, an apostatized* Mormon, who had taken wagons north from Salt Lake City, following along the east side of Salt Lake then going north to Fort Hall, where he had then joined the movement to California. In doing so, he had pioneered a new route that would later be followed and improved.

Another eastbound Mormon group, in a pack train, was a couple of days ahead of Thompson and Bigler's wagon train. As Lassen's party was nearing the Big Bend of the Humboldt, and just before he arrived at the meadows that would later bear his name (the same place where the Applegate Road turned north toward Oregon), they met this pack train coming east from California. It carried surprising news. A couple of days later, meeting the same party, Richard May would write:

> *Friday 25th Aug...We met a train of packs from California 23 in Number Several of them had specimens of the Gold Lately discovered in that Country about 70 Miles above Sutter's establishment (They represented the Mines as being Verry*

---

* Apostatize is to renounce a religion previously professed.

LEGENDARY TRUTHS

Rich yealding on an average of two oz) of gold to the days Labor and that one particular Man had made 700 dollars in one day. The train giving us this information were Mormons bound for Salt Lake Valley. [25]

It is unlikely that any of the westbound emigrants had any knowledge of the discovery of gold in California until news was carried east by the Mormons. Ackerman and Helfrich wrote of May's journal entry:

Probably the only contemporary writing in existence of the breaking of the gold discovery to any train anywhere, anytime. I lack the words with which to describe this probable bombshell to an unsuspecting group of emigrants, alone and hundreds of miles from any habitation, worn out from travel, and running short of provisions. It can well be surmised that the members of this pack train each had samples of gold which they themselves had actually mined and that each displayed these samples. Also it can well be imagined the stirring tales that each had to recount and it is only too true that these tales lost nothing in the telling. Therefore imagine excitement that would be set afoot in the emigrant train. The speculations, the dreams and the cravings that were started among members of the slowly plodding wagon train. [26]

Shortly after passing the Mormon pack train and coming closer to where he would turn off toward Oregon, Lassen met the next party of Mormons with wagons. They got more news of the gold discovery and, undoubtedly, first hand reports about the newly opened Mormon alternative to the Truckee Route. However, this new road would be too far to the south of Lassen's destination to appeal to him. Bigler recorded this meeting in his journal on August 26, saying they met ten wagons having passed the Big Bend.

On the next day, Bigler recorded meeting Captain Hensley's pack train. Hensley reported to them the route he had followed around the north side of Salt Lake, that he thought it would save them about eight days of travel by not having to go as far north as Fort Hall and then turning south to Salt Lake Valley.

Interestingly, earlier in the season he had taken his pack train to Salt Lake City and tried to cross the Salt Lake Desert, following the

Hastings' Cutoff, but heavy rains so softened the desert that his mules bogged down. He had to return to Salt Lake City to re-supply. He then went north following Kimball's tracks as far north as Bear River, which he crossed, then veered north and west to intercept the California Trail without having to go all the way north to Fort Hall. He then met up with Chiles' train near Goose Creek, as noted by Richard May.

Two days after meeting Hastings, the Mormons and Bigler met the Chiles' train of forty-eight wagons. Stewart wrote that Chiles "reacted vigorously to the news of a freshly discovered pass."[27] Considering his experience the previous year at the Donner site with the Stockton Party and the general misgivings and trepidation associated with the route, he was undoubtedly happy to learn of an allegedly safer route, and one that crossed the mountains in a more direct line toward his destination, which was considerably south of Lassen's destination at *Bosquejo*.

What was not disclosed nor discussed was which route he would have taken had he not received this news. It is highly likely, though only speculative, that he, too, would have gone over the Applegate Route.* Chiles was still upriver from the Big Bend. Therefore, he hadn't reached the place where he might have contemplated following the southern Oregon route.

Considering the opinions held and advice given by the Stockton group, of which he was a member and guide, along with Lassen, McGee, Myers and others, he probably would have turned north at Lassen's Meadows, as did Lassen who was just ahead of him on the trail, in 1848. The following year, 1849, Milton McGee and J. J. Myers (who had been with Chiles in 1843 and with Chiles and the Stockton Group in 1847) would choose the northern route at Lassen's Meadows.

If Chiles had not heard of the Mormon (Carson) Route, and had instead followed Lassen over the route into the northern Sacramento Valley, which he had partially ridden over in 1843, it is interesting to speculate the effect his usage of the new route would have later had on the opinions people held about it. For instance, he was only a couple of days behind Lassen. The addition of the manpower from Chiles' large group would have made the roadwork needed to open the way, much easier for the small party Lassen led, thereby precluding the need

---

* Some historians contend "that Chiles wouldn't have gambled on the Applegate-Lassen trails had there been no option of a Carson route...Chiles previous experience in Northern Calif. had been near a disaster, so why would he want to chance it again?"

for Burnett's help and the later assumption that the Lassen Party was destitute and "lost."

Chiles, upon hearing of Hensley's advice to the Mormons of a cutoff to Salt Lake Valley, gave them a waybill of an even shorter route, which he allegedly had followed in 1841 with the Bidwell/Bartleson Party. The Mormons then went east following Hensley's shortcut, but gave up on finding the route Chiles suggested, because they didn't find the trail. Stewart implied that they might have thought Chiles had just come that way, rather than in 1841 when he was with the Bidwell/Bartleson Party. Failing to find Chiles' tracks the Mormons felt there was a mistake.[28]

How the news of the discovery of gold in California affected Lassen and his train isn't known. But considering his adventuresome spirit and the enthusiasm he later exhibited in prospecting, it is most likely that he and his people were as excited as May noted that the Chiles' train was "...the glowing stories of the Mormons of the gold mines nearly ran us all mad."[29]

How long Lassen remained at the Meadows isn't known, or what precautions he took—like cutting grass and hauling water—before starting over the desert on the Applegate Trail. But there is no doubt he turned off with the same deep conviction that the southern route to Oregon was the best route—a conviction held by his contemporaries, who had promoted it to parties the previous year and would choose it the following year, in 1849.

The rest of the California bound emigrants continued down the Humboldt, and most took the new Carson Route over the mountains. On September 12, as the Chiles' train was near the Humboldt Sink, May recorded an interesting event:

> We Traveled 35 miles during the day & night and made our 21st and last camp on this Stream It was 4 oclock' in the morning We were forced into this drive for want of grass We had a delightful time driving the teams during the night The moon fulled at an early hour and Shone with great Clearness. But all at once She appeared to be covered with clouds. It grew quite dark I Looked and behold the shadow of the Earth had fallen on her. The Eclipse was total and of course Lasted Some time The Indian fires were plainly to be

seen on the right and Left; it is their habit when Strangers get into their neighborhood to do this in order to give warning to their friends of the fact.[30]

Lassen's train was probably somewhere near Surprise Valley when the eclipse occurred. In that desert area, chances are the sky was clear, and he and his party, also, marveled as the moon disappeared, then reappeared, but then again clouds may have obscured it. Anyway, no other known journals for 1848 recorded the event.

LEGENDARY TRUTHS

Trail Beginnings:
Lassen's Meadows to Rancho Bosquejo

*So Lassen led his wagons southward. There was no
trail. Thus began a journey which must have seemed to
the emigrants to have about it a nightmare quality of
uncertainty, vagueness, and terror.*

　　　　　　　—George R. Stewart (a "legendary truth")[1]

Lassen arrived at what would be named Lassen's Meadows on
the Humboldt River sometime around the first of September 1848.
According to Bigler's journal, there were ten wagons with him. What
happened to the other two wagons can only be surmised—they could
have been abandoned or perhaps, as often happened in other trains,
they separated from Lassen's train and joined another.

Stewart wrote that, "There were women and children, and ten ox-
drawn wagons. So we may consider that it was a typical emigrant
party."[2] Yes, a typical emigrant party, but it differed from the other
"typical" parties in that Lassen, the guide, was leading a group that

Author with Lassen's Meadows (Rye Patch Reservoir) pictured in the background, before bicycle trip over the Lassen Trail.

included personal friends and acquaintances from Missouri. And it was unusual, also, that he was taking them to his home in California, not just guiding them to "California."

Among them were William Myers and Colonel Peter Davis, who were friends from Lassen's Missouri years. Myers later built a comfortable home at *Bosquejo*,[3] and Davis leased the house Daniel Sill had built on the first piece of land Lassen had earlier sold.[4] The Indian who had accompanied Lassen east[*] was surely with him, as were his Masonic brothers—Master Mason Rev. Sashel Woods and Senior Warden L.E. Stewart—who were carrying the Masonic charter for the lodge Lassen wanted to establish at Benton City, on his rancho.

Leaving the Meadows, Lassen followed the road the Applegates had established in 1846. With wagons and pack trains using it for the two previous years, the route was easy to follow. Earlier in the summer, as stated before, the Isaac Pettijohn packing group from the Willamette Valley had left Oregon via this route, and following up the Humboldt

---

[*] November 4, 1847 issue of the *Brunswicker* said, "He brings in a young Indian chief with him to show the sights and will take him back next spring."

LEGENDARY TRUTHS

River, had later met Lassen at the North Platte crossing.[5] Pettijohn's party surely encountered the same difficulties inherent in crossing any of the deserts those before, and those following later, were required to cross in reaching California—no matter what route they chose.

From the Meadows, the Humboldt River flowed toward the south, and the trail Lassen followed turned off toward the west. It crossed an expanse of sage and greasewood, and gradually gained elevation to Antelope Springs, where one emigrant, a year later, wrote, "...we found several weak springs and a little grass, on the mountainside."[6] The road then continued over Antelope Summit, turning northwestward, where it crossed a high open plain to Kamma Pass, and then dropped through the colorful hills of Painted Canyon to Rabbit Hole Springs. Rabbit Hole Springs have now been bulldozed to form a large watering hole, but when the Applegates found them in 1846, they filled a small "rabbit hole." In Lindsey Applegate's reminiscences, he wrote:

> *Digging down in this clay we made a basin large enough to hold several gallons and by dark we had quite a supply of good pure water. We then began issuing it to our horses, a little at a time, and by morning men and horses were considerably refreshed. Great numbers of rabbits came around us and we killed all we wanted of them. This is the place always since known as the Rabbit Hole Springs.*[7]

By 1849 they had become "...springs or rather Wells dug out by the emigrants some four or 5 feet deep with plenty of water. ...I saw three oxen in as many wells of water about 4 feet square & 6 feet deep into which they had plunged head first in the eagerness to [slake] their thirst."[8] From the springs, the trail dropped in elevation across a stony alluvial peneplain to the white expanses of the alkali playas of the Black Rock Desert. It was about twenty-three miles from Rabbit Hole to the hot springs at the foot of the Black Rock. The terrain in itself wasn't difficult. However, the drag of the soft playa soils on the wagon wheels—in addition to the long drive without water and grass, and the burning summer heat—often proved to be the *coup de grace* for oxen and mules. These creatures had been weakened by the arduous distance from the States, the three hundred miles of poor water, and dubious grass along the Humboldt River.

Peter Lassen & His Gold Rush Trail In Fact & Fable

How Lassen's Train fared here isn't recorded first hand, but *Fairfield's Pioneer History of Lassen County* stated:

> *Lassen followed the Applegate road until he reached the lower end of Goose lake, and here the Lassen Trail really begins...Lassen kept down on the north side of the river and crossed it near the mouth of the canyon below what is now called Canby. He then went over into Stone Coal valley and down that to the river, and again followed down the river, being obliged to cross it frequently and sometimes to go along the sides of the hills above it. About ten miles above where Lookout now stands he crossed it for the last time,[*] going over to the east side of it, and then went down through Big valley, then called Round valley, keeping close to the river and passing through the present site of Bieber.[9]*

Note that Lassen turned south at Goose Lake to follow the Pit River, which was at that time also called the Upper Sacramento River, as it was the main tributary to the Sacramento. Here, Lassen displayed his knowledge of the land and the route to follow, whereas, Wiggins, the previous year, with the same destination in mind but not having had the previous experience Lassen had, continued on to Lost River and Tule Lake before trying to turn south. As noted before, in 1846 Lassen had been in the Pit River area and on to Klamath Lake and returned to his rancho with Fremont and Carson, who had undoubtedly discussed their travel experiences and the lay of the land with him. Lassen had also associated closely with Chiles, who had ridden from Goose Lake down the Pit River and followed the trappers trail into Northern California in 1843.

Several writers have contended that Lassen became lost shortly after leaving Goose Lake, but considering the obvious route of following the Pit River as far as Big Valley (Round Valley in Fremont's description), where the river enters a steep and rugged canyon, it is virtually impossible to get lost in this area.

When they reached the Pit River Canyon, Lassen turned south where

---

[*]   In this statement, Fairfield was inaccurate. Lassen's Train also crossed the Pit River south of Bieber near where Thompson Ranch is located and again west of Muck Valley. In 1849, he would return as guide to the Warner/Williamson government survey party, and again in 1850 in search of the legendary Gold Lake with Bruff.

LEGENDARY TRUTHS

Mount Shasta from near Bieber Summit, California
Photo by Ken Johnston.

the Hudson Bay trapper, John Work had crossed in 1832, and where Lassen, with Fremont, probably crossed when returning to *Bosquejo* by a different route than they had taken in getting to Klamath Lake. Will Bagley, in *The Lassen Thread* summarized this legend as, "When Lassen turned south at Goose Lake and left the Oregon road, it quickly became apparent that there was no trail and the trailblazer was lost."[10]

Fairfield commented on the legend:

> *It looks as though Lassen didn't know where he was going. They used to say that when he got to Goose Lake, he saw Mt. Shasta one day and Lassen's Butte the next. He didn't know the difference, and traveled one day toward one of them and the next day toward the other.*

However, he added this disclaimer: "...The writer will not vouch for the truthfulness of either story, but he has heard both of them told a good many times."[11]

The order of the above is correct. From the Goose Lake area and along the Pit River, just west of where Alturas is located, Mount Shasta looms to the west and becomes the dominant landmark toward which

91

Mount Lassen from near Bieber Summit, California.
Photo by Ken Johnston.

to guide. Farther west, near Big Valley, Lassen Butte (Lassen Peak) becomes visible to the southwest, far to the left of Mount Shasta as one is facing downriver. The peaks, although both snow covered, have easily distinguishable profiles from this area,* and it is highly unlikely that Lassen, the members of his party, and especially the Indian traveling with him, would confuse the two. Gold rush emigrants in 1849 easily recognized, differentiated, and recorded seeing the two mountains.

Stewart also wrote:

So Lassen led his wagons southward. There was no trail. Thus began a journey, which must have seemed to the emigrants to have about it a nightmare quality of uncertainty, vagueness, and terror. (The historian, [Stewart] too, feels about it this uncertain quality. The only detailed record is a reminiscence written years later—vague about time and place, as such reminiscences are. All that can be done is

---

* Both of the author's daughters at ages ten and twelve could easily distinguish between the two peaks.

92

to compare this account with the actual topography. When the two fail to agree, as sometimes happens, one can only attempt to reconstruct a somewhat reasonable story.) * [12]

But was Stewart being "reasonable"? Or was he the one who was "vague" and writing with an "uncertain quality"? Let's visit the facts and not the "legendary truths"!

Stewart later stated:

Then after three or four days' journeying (though the record is too vague and uncertain to be trusted for exact time) the inevitable happened! The river flowed into a canyon too 'tight' for wagons. Soon everyone must have come to the realization that Lassen did not have much idea of where he was going. As a contemporary summed him up: "This route he had not previously explored. He only had a correct idea of the courses, and some general knowledge of the country through which they must pass." [13]

Although Stewart's *California Trail* is a classic history of the development of the various routes and the men who developed them, his penchant for aggrandizing extremes and unknowns was addressed by Joseph King, who said:

When he wrote history Stewart employed many of the techniques of the novelist. He knew how to tell a good story, full of suspense, with heroes, villains, and the in-between.... This being said, one has to remember that historians write with a bias, bringing their own backgrounds in time and place to their work. [14]

"So came the first suggestion of nightmare." [15] Nightmare? This is a good example of Stewart's "aggrandizing" as King stated. In the Pit River area, where the grass was lush and the water plentiful, the emigrants were most likely thankful for a respite from the monotony of the plains, the boredom of the Humboldt, and the hardships of the desert. In addition, with the prospects of arriving at their destination not far in the distance, not to mention the added enthusiasm the other

---

*   The reminiscence or "only detailed record" isn't referenced.

emigrants expressed at the Mormon's news of the gold discovery, their minds were more likely preoccupied with future possibilities than being troubled with "nightmares," hardships of the trail notwithstanding.

Lassen's troubles probably started in the thickly forested area still to be encountered south of Big Valley, where their wagons would have to be maneuvered around and between giant trees and other obstacles. A wagon with two yoke of oxen would be approximately equal in length to an automobile with a camper trailer—about thirty feet long. A wagon with three yoke of oxen would be comparable to maneuvering a semi-truck (forty feet long) through the obstacles. And, with the oxen weakened from the long journey and only a small workforce of trail-worn men, it is no wonder that some decided to cut down the wagons and make carts that were more maneuverable. Other emigrants had done this on other trails.

Lassen was probably never "lost," as in "not knowing where he was or where he needed to go." But, it is highly likely, as supported by evidence and testimony of Peter Burnett and Peter Lovejoy, that he made some judgmental errors in choosing which way to take wagons, and scouting of practical ways would have been necessary. Most of us in trying to reach a destination, perhaps even within sight, have experienced not being able to get through because of obstacles or enforced detours. This wouldn't have meant we were "lost" or deserving of being called some epithet such as a "bungling or incompetent Dane."[16]

In *Peter Lassen, Northern California's Trail Blazer,* Swartzlow wrote:

> *Students and woodsmen can only assume that Lassen really did not know where he was going. Legend says that after Lassen had left Goose Lake he used Mount Shasta as a landmark one day and Lassen Peak (then called Joseph's Mountain) the next.*[17] [Obviously! as explained above]. ... *He did not know the difference and traveled one day toward one and then the next day toward the other.* [Again, this is pure "legend."]

> *The story is told that in the Country near Poison Lake, around Pine Creek Valley, Lassen got lost and the men in his party threatened to hang him. Lassen said if they would allow him to climb to the top of the mountain nearby*

LEGENDARY TRUTHS

[supposedly Lassen Peak] *he could find his way and would show them the lush Sacramento Valley. At the point of their guns he is supposed to have climbed the mountain which now bears his name. Fortunately it was a clear day and he could show them the Sacramento Valley. His would be killers then allowed him to continue to guide their train to Benton City.*[18]

This, too, is food for "legend." Lassen may very well have climbed some hill, or perhaps to the tops of several hills, to scout the route ahead, but to lead a party up Lassen Peak would have been so time consuming and distant from where he allegedly became "lost," that it is highly unlikely. If he could see the mountain, he would have, as well, known where his rancho was, as if he had been on top of the mountain looking into the Sacramento Valley.

Fairfield, too, supported this idea in writing:

It is also told that out in the Pine Creek country he got lost, and the men in his train threatened to hang him. He told them that if they would let him go to the top of a mountain near by, he could find the way. They let him go, and from the mountain he was able to get on the right course again.[19]

The source of this was, undoubtedly, what Peter Burnett wrote in his reminiscences after overtaking the Lassen Party on his way to the gold fields of California.

Another factor contributing to the disintegration of Lassen's wagon train, as noted by Burnett, was low provisions. This would have contributed to the party's low morale. Several in Lassen's party were his fellow members of the Masonic Brotherhood and would have stood by his side even in hard times and not allowed such an extreme measure, even though there may have been murmurings of "hanging" among the discontented. His Masonic brothers were the ones who were still with Lassen after the mutinous members had left and foolishly descended into the canyons, disregarding his advice.

While Lassen's wagon train was struggling southward, word of the gold strike in California had already reached the Oregon settlements, and Burnett (who would become the first elected governor of the State of California) was organizing a group of Oregonian gold-seekers to go to California. Before leaving the Willamette Valley, he had asked John

McLoughlin about taking wagons to California, and:

> *Without hesitation he replied that he thought we could succeed, and recommended Thomas McKay for pilot. No wagons had ever passed between Oregon and California. Thomas McKay had made the trip several times with pack trains, and knew the general nature of the country, and the courses and distances; but he knew no practicable wagon route, as he had only traveled with pack animals.*[20]

Asa Lawrence Lovejoy, who was also a member of the group, later recalled, "General Palmer was along in that trip. We had an old gentleman by the name of McKay, who undertook to pilot us. He had been through that country, but it was a great many years before, and he did not seem to know much about it."[21]

The party Burnett organized consisted of 150 "stout, robust, energetic, sober men," and fifty wagons, well stocked with provisions so they could survive the winter if they became entrapped by snows as the Donner Party had in '46. They left on September 10 following the Applegate Road south and east to Klamath Lake, where they left the road turning south to what was then called "Goose Lake." It was actually Tule Lake that McKay led them past. He had traveled this route with Peter Ogden and gone up the Pit River to Goose Lake, which Ogden had called "Pit Lake." (Remember, Wiggins had also thought Tule Lake was "Goose Lake.")

Separated from the rest of the party and scouting ahead, Burnett was hungry and recalled killing a badger:

> *This was all the meat we had. We dressed and cooked it well; and, to our keen and famished appetites, it was splendid food. The foot of the badger, the tail of the beaver, the ear of the hog, and the foot of the elephant are superior eating. I have myself eaten of all but the last, and can speak from personal knowledge; and, as to the foot of the elephant, I can give Sir Samuel Baker as my authority, in his 'Explorations,' etc.*[22]

Traveling south, as they neared the Pit River, they saw wagon tracks.

> *Who made this road we could not at first imagine. A considerable number of those coming to California with*

pack animals decided to follow our trail, rather than come by the usual pack route. These packers had overtaken us the previous evening, and were with us when we discovered this new wagon road. It so happened that one of them had been in California, and knew Peter Lassen. This man was a sensible fellow, and at once gave it as his opinion that this road had been made by a small party of immigrants whom Lassen had persuaded to come to California by a new route that would enter the great valley of the Sacramento at or near Lassen's rancho. This conjectural explanation proved to be the true one.[23]

Burnett's party continued following the Lassen Road down the river until the river entered a canyon. After crossing the river, they followed the road south about ten miles:

...when we came to a beautiful grassy valley, covered with scattering pine timber. This valley was about two miles wide where the road struck it, and ran west, the very direction we wished to go. It seemed a defile at right angles through the Sierra Nevada Mountains, as if designed for a level road into the Sacramento Valley. [24]

The Lassen Party probably thought the same thing when they arrived here, and were equally "as pleased at the prospect" as Burnett wrote in his recollections:

We were much pleased at the prospect, and followed this splendid road rapidly about eight miles, when, to our great mortification, we came to the termination of this lovely valley in front of a tall, steep mountain, which could not be ascended except by some creature that had either wings or claws. Upon examination, we found that old Peter Lassen and his party had marched west along this narrow valley to its abrupt termination, and then had turned about and marched back to near the point where they entered it, thus wasting some ten or fifteen miles of travel. The two portions of the road going into and coming out of this pretty valley were not more than half a mile apart; but this fact was unknown to us until after we had brought up against that impassable mountain.[25]

Burnett then went on to say, "We spent the greater part of one day in exploring a new route, but found it impracticable. In our explorations, we found a lava-bed some two miles wide."

In doing this, Burnett, under the guidance of Thomas McKay, had done exactly what Lassen had done in searching for the Trappers Route, but Burnett concluded that, "...old Peter Lassen was lost, except as to courses, and was wholly unacquainted with the particular route he was going. Our own pilot knew about as little as Lassen, if not less."

Thus determined to follow Lassen, he later wrote, "We found the road an excellent one, going in the right direction; and we soon found ourselves upon the summit of the Sierra Nevada Mountains."[26]

Lassen's mistake of turning up the promising valley and Burnett's later account of it, probably gave credence to the later "legends" that Lassen was lost. The location of the valley described is not known for certain, but it was most likely in the vicinity south of Harvey Valley, maybe west of Blacks Mountain, and perhaps as far south as Willow Springs.

The eastern branch of the old trappers trail, which was part of the Siskiyou Trail network (see map), crossed over the mountains into the Sacramento Valley between Magee Peak and Burney Peak just to the west. Lassen, McGee, and Myers undoubtedly knew this, because the following year, in 1849 during the Gold Rush, McGee and Myers (both of whom, in 1847, had been with Lassen in the Stockton Party returning East to Missouri) would follow Lassen's route to this location, and then search for a route west to the Sacramento Valley. Myers and McGee had both been with the Chiles/Reading Party in 1843, when they entered the Sacramento Valley after following the Pit River.

Myers was also with Fremont and Lassen in 1846, when they returned from Klamath Lake by a route passing near here. No one has dared suggest that either Myers or McGee, both noted mountain men, were "lost," when they turned west as Lassen did. They all knew of the route crossing the mountains north of Lassen's Peak. It was just that a practicable route for wagons eluded them.

George Kirov wrote:

> At Pine Creek Lassen became lost and the tired men of his party showered him with abuses, but, taking his sights from a nearby mountain regained the trail, turned south, passed Feather Lake, crossed the Susan River just west of

LEGENDARY TRUTHS

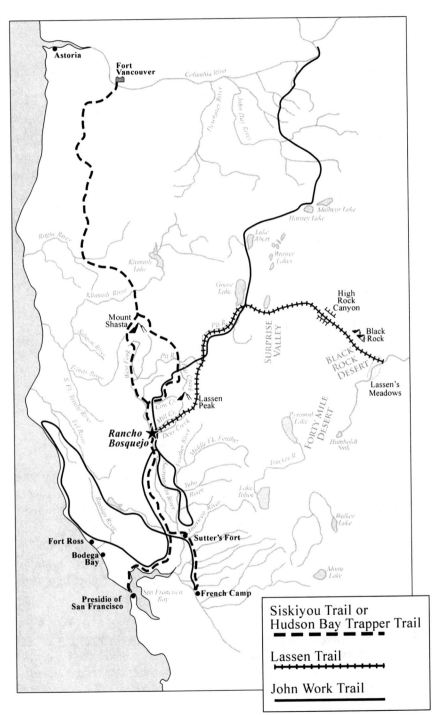

Siskiyou Trail or
Hudson Bay Trapper Trail

Lassen Trail

John Work Trail

Norvall Flat and went around Duck Lake and Clear Lake
to the place where the town of Westwood is now located.
At Big Meadows the provisions and the animals gave out.
Since it was the first of November and snow storms were
momentarily expected, the party was forced to stop for
hunting and to allow their stock to get food and rest.[27]

The answer to the question of when—and if—Lassen's knowledge of the area and his leadership failed, falls back to legend and speculation. But after many months and miles of wearying travel and the depletion of supplies, it is easy to speculate that impatience and discontent could have contributed to mistakes in judgment—not only on Lassen's part but also on the part of the others, who mutinied and went ahead on their own. Lovejoy recalled:

We struck that trail and followed it; but it led to a very bad
place. We found some wagons, away down there, that had
got in and could not get out. * *They were out of provisions.*
It was a terrible place. It had no name. Nobody was ever in
there before, I think. The women were riding on the cattle.
We gave them flour. We were very well provided and gave
them what they needed. They got mad at this Lassen, and
would not follow him any farther, and struck off and made
terrible work of it. They got into a ravine. When we found we
were getting out of track by following them, we found their
wagon beds and everything in a terrible state.[28]

Lovejoy also alluded to the truth of the speculation rather than the legend by recalling, "This man, Lassen, who was their pilot, had been across three or four times, but the emigrants got very much fatigued and tired, and they thought they could get there quicker, so they would not follow him any farther."[29] Had they remained with Lassen, though, they would not have got into the "very bad place" where Lovejoy found them. They had to abandon their wagons and belongings, and pack out with whatever they could carry.

---

* The "very bad place" was in the ravines Lassen warned Burnett not to go down into but rather to stay on the ridges, which led more easily to his rancho. These emigrants were some days later arriving at Lassen's, because of not staying with him or following his advice.

LEGENDARY TRUTHS

Burnett's party, with Lovejoy, had caught up with the struggling Lassen Party of five cut-down carts about forty miles above the Sacramento Valley and somewhere south of Mount Lassen, most likely at Deer Creek Meadows. Burnett and his men, who had now pioneered the California-Oregon Road for wagons, joined with Lassen, and together completed clearing the route to Lassen's rancho. "It took only ten or fifteen of Burnett's men to clear the obstructions and 'cut out the road in one day as far as the timber extended—say fifteen miles—and did it as fast as the wagons could follow.'"[30]

"Old Peter Lassen insisted that our wagons should keep on the top of the ridges, and not go down to the water."[31] He obviously knew this part of the country and knew which ridge led directly to his rancho, thereby avoiding the difficulties encountered by the mutinous packers, who had set out on their own following the ravines. In addition, according to Lovejoy's narrative "this man Lassen…had been across three of four times." The packers didn't arrive at the rancho until several days later.

Burnett recalled:

> We left the first camp in the valley the next morning, and, after traveling a distance of eight miles, arrived at the rancho of old Peter Lassen. The old pilot was in the best of spirits, and killed for us a fat beef; and we remained at his place two or three days, feasting and resting.[32]

The packers, having descended into the impassable canyons, had to retrace their steps, leading to the credence of the speculation that it was the mutineers who were lost, rather than their guide.

With the Burnett Party, which joined the Lassen Party, was another train of twenty wagons and twenty-five men from the Puget Sound country of Washington, who had taken full advantage of the new routes. The worst part of the trip from Oregon was not in California but in the notorious canyon in the Umpqua Mountains, which had brought so much grief to the 1846 emigrants following the Applegates.

According to Swartzlow, a group of Lassen's followers met at "Bentonville" on October 31. They wrote a tribute to the Lassen route they had just followed, which was printed in the *New York Herald* on February 12, 1849:

> We found the ascent and descent to and from the mountains, very gradual and easy; and upon the whole, your committee

consider the pass discovered by Captain Lawson, one of the finest in the world, through mountains so extensive as the one through which it passes. In the opinion of your committee, a most practicable road can be made, with very little labor, through this pass; and that this route will prove of lasting benefit to parties traveling to and from Oregon and California, and from the United States, as it has proved to us. Your committee think Captain Lawson entitled to the thanks of this meeting, for the energy and decision displayed by him in surveying the route....[33]

Adobe home of Peter Lassen.
Photo Courtesy of Shasta County Historical Society, Redding, California.

LEGENDARY TRUTHS

PART 2

GOLD RUSH 1849

Easterners Respond to
News of Gold Discovery

*It's not a matter of what is true that counts but a matter of
what is perceived to be true.*—Henry Kissinger

No one could have anticipated the great surge in numbers of emigrants
that would be following the trails to California in 1849. No one could
have anticipated the needs of the people or the routes they would choose
on their way to the anticipated gold fields. Likewise, no one should be
blamed or held accountable for the choices made by the 49ers.

Whether the report published in the *New York Herald* had any
influence on the choice of routes the following summer, is doubtful.
Over half of the gold-seekers had passed by on the established route to
California before mention of the Lassen route appeared in the journals
of the 49ers. And that was after reports of the shortage of grass from
grazing by previous trains had trickled back up the Humboldt. At
any rate, it was more the lateness of the later trains, rather than the
route they chose that, as in earlier years, caused the winter hardships

encountered by many who, for whatever reason, were arriving later in the season.

The summer of 1849 was known variously as the "Year of Madness," the "Year of the Greenhorn," and the "Year of the Gold Rush." It was a year of madness, because men from all walks of life mortgaged farms and businesses and left family behind for the opportunity to strike it rich. It was the year of the greenhorn, because, unlike previous years, many of the people were truly "greenhorns," inexperienced in handling teams and not possessing the farm and country skills required for wagon travel. It was, also, a year when many diarists and journal keepers recorded their daily impressions and experiences.

Estimates of the numbers of emigrants who traveled the trails range as high as 50,000; however, Stewart thought this was an exaggeration and estimated that about 6,200 wagons with 21,000 persons and another 1,000 packers were on the trail. But Mattes in *The Great Platte River Road* wrote, "Available data gleaned from emigrant journals, newspaper accounts, and reports of the official Fort Kearney [sic] and Fort Laramie registers, indicate something like 30,000 Argonauts for 1849."[1]

Although most emigrants were greenhorns, the trails to California were by then open and easily followed. Books and trail guides had been published and were available if, however, not very detailed or accurate. From information printed in these, Stewart credited some interesting differences in the appearances of the emigrants and travel that year. He said the differences were due to the Mexican War and influences it had on the citizen soldiers, who had brought their experiences back to the States. Information from those who had "seen the elephant" and letters from those who had already traveled the routes, were also available to those, like Joseph Goldsborough Bruff, who wanted to research and plan the route before traveling it.

Mule teams were more common, and many of the companies were organized as military units, reflecting the war experience.[2] Some emigrants used an odometer, variously called a roadometer or a viameter, attached to the wheel of a wagon to measure rotations and, therefore, distance and functioned similarly to modern odometers.[3] Bruff had a precision odometer made in St. Louis and was thus able to record somewhat accurate distances.[4] Guitars rivaled banjos and violins in popularity around the campfire, where people might enjoy a "fandango" rather than a dance. Pinole, precooked cornmeal with seasoning, became a favored food item, and big sombreros became popular hats.

California gold was the news in the shops, streets, and newspapers, and various items were advertised:

> *To Companies going to California.—Slakin's celebrated six-barrelled Revolvers"; "California Goods...which are particularly recommended to gentlemen about starting for California: Colt's and Allen's Revolving Pistols Allen's Self-cocking do...Bowie Knives, assorted qualities and prices. ...Belt Hatchets and Axes...Jenk's Patent Carbines and Rifles"; Money Belts, made exclusively for gold"; "superior Wax Taper Matches, in round wooden boxes perfectly safe and portable"; "California Maps..."*[5]

However, perhaps the greatest difference this year was reflected in the greater numbers of emigrants on the road. Fortunately, it was a wet year in the Midwest,* and the grass held out more or less until they neared the end of the Humboldt, where rumors of scarcity and hardship would, later in the season, become influential in the choice of a route to follow. Crowding at river crossings and other bottlenecks on the trail helped to spread out the migration so that in places it looked like a solid line of wagons. Some reported continuous lines of up to five hundred wagons stretching out toward the horizon.

According to Mattes:

> *It was all very well to get a head start and beat the crowd, but if animals weakened from malnutrition an outfit would find itself stalled while the 'tidal wave' swept by. Dalliance in getting an outfit together permitted the crest of the wave to roll ahead; the nice green grass would be eaten off and the waterholes fouled. Everyone laid bets on the magic date, and when it was suddenly revealed by rumor, or 'prairie telegraph,' everybody tried to take off at once. Average 15 miles per day–2,000 miles in 4 months or 120 days.*[6]

---

*   In the far West, 1849 was an average rainfall year. 1850 was a wet year (floods in Sacramento). In 1849, diary accounts show emigrants keeping close to the Humboldt River, but in 1850, they had to stay higher up, away from the river bottom.

LEGENDARY TRUTHS

It was recommended that each emigrant start with $500 as a minimum and five hundred pounds of food. The bread-bacon-coffee formula was the usual emigrant diet, but additional items included: salted pork or beef, rice, tea, dried beans, dried fruit, baking soda (saleratus), vinegar, cheese, cream of tartar, pickles, ginger, and mustard. As an alternative, some took cornmeal, also known as Indian meal or pinole, as well as wheat products such as pilot bread, hardtack, hard bread, sea biscuits, and preserved fruits.[7]

Fresh eggs and milk were available to those who took along chickens and milk cows—traveling dairies. Extra animals were sometimes taken along to butcher, and as the draft animals—horses, oxen, and mules—failed along the way, they were often butchered and eaten in emergencies.

Game such as buffalo, elk, and pronghorns were hunted by some to supplement the larder, but these became more wary or scarce as more emigrants traveled the trail. Some journals mentioned sage hen, rabbit, badger, and rattlesnakes, which were known as "bush trout."

Whiskey was commonly carried in casks for "medicinal purposes"— to cure snakebite, to treat cholera and colds, as a trade item, or to be used for celebrations on special occasions, like the Fourth of July, a birthday, or the arrival at a milestone on the trail. One emigrant mentioned mixing it with "bad water" under the notion that in some mysterious way it would become healthy and purified. Mixed with molasses, as an extender, it was known as "skull varnish," and was one of the last items to be discarded after other valuables to lighten a load.

Berries, such as gooseberries, chokecherries, and serviceberries abounded on the prairies in season, and were mentioned in some journals. Mattes wrote of a Mrs. Parker, who was ahead of her day, when she "gathered fresh greens for our delectation as well as to prevent scurvy."

Over the years, the trails to California had been developing and techniques for making travel more efficient had been passed on to this year's travelers. The people on the trail were always open to new suggestions and to news of new trail developments.

The road (as it should be called by this time, as it was too heavily used to be called a trail) from Missouri, up the Platte, as far as Fort Laramie was easy going for experienced teamsters, but proved arduous for those who were more accustomed to city life. In his *Overland Guide,* Haun wrote, "...the route designed by nature for the great thoroughfare to the Pacific. This was the road selected by nature's civil engineers, the buffalo and the elk, for their Western travel. The Indians followed them in the same trail; then the traders; next the settlers came."* [8]

After Fort Laramie, though, the emigrants had choices to make. There were mountains to cross, desert stretches to encounter or avoid, and areas where the Indians were more troublesome. Newer, easier, and sometimes shorter routes were being developed as guides experimented with different possibilities. Over the previous years, several "cut-offs" or "shortcuts" had been added to the choices, and in 1849, Myers and Hudspeth added the "Hudspeth Cutoff." Some of the emigrants, like Bruff, left home with researched knowledge of the choices, and some were just content to follow the flow. But, all were anxious to hear of new developments and conditions along the trails.

Communication along the way was achieved by several ingenious means. Messages could be sent ahead by couriers moving faster than the emigrant trains, or they could be sent back on the trail with people returning to the States. The "roadside telegraph" or "prairie telegraph" included signs and messages posted along the trail, and proved an important factor in influencing emigrants' decisions. "Bone Express" messages were posted by writing on sun-bleached bones and skulls that were left in prominent places beside the trail. [9]

J. Goldsborough Bruff commented, "Some of the travelers, among other rascalities, are in the habit of putting up erroneous notices to mislead and distress others. I had the pleasure of correcting some of these statements, and thereby prevented misfortune." [10]

Perhaps the most famous and controversial example of the "Roadside Telegraph" was the "Post Office," where information and advice was left pertaining to what would later be known as the Lassen Cutoff (Lassen Trail). J. Goldsborough Bruff described it on September 19, 1849 when he wrote in his journal:

A broad and perfectly semi-circular area, very dusty, sweeps around the bend—and the two trails or roads, are broad as well as any traveled thoroughfare can be. On the right, about a hundred yards from the Bend, the Desert route

---

* Haun, also known as Major Horn was married to Catherine Haun who also kept a diary in 1849. He traveled the trail in 1849 and Bruff noted Haun passing by his camp on October 30, 1849.

branches off, and in the forks of the road, I observed a red painted barrel standing. - I rode up, to examine it. - It was a nice barrel, about the size of a whiskey-barrel, iron hoops, and a square hole cut in the head; and neatly painted in black block letters, upon it, 'Post Office.' On looking in, I found it half full of letters, notes, notices, &c. - Near this was a stick and bill-board, also filled with notices. - These were chiefly directed to emigrants in the rear, hurrying them along, giving information about the route, telling who had taken this or the southern route, &c. By these I ascertained that few had taken the Southern road. I inscribed a card and left, here, for the benefit of all whom it might concern, as follows:

The Washington City Company.
Capt Bruff, pass'd - on the right-hand trail,
Septr 19th. 2 p.m. 1849.

Other than increased numbers depending on grass supplies and water sources, crowding at favored camping places, and congestion at river crossings, travel, experiences, and hardships were similar to previous years on the trail. However, due to increased numbers, later arrivals found less grass. This was especially true as the emigrants approached the desert areas farther west, and by September, rumors were rampant about shortage of grass ahead on the Truckee and Carson Routes. As early as September 1, Bruff noted this and the loss of animals in his journal as he approached the Humboldt River and followed down it:

September 1: "Passed 8 dead oxen, 2 do mules,
  & 2 do horses."
September 2: "Passed to-day, 10 dead oxen,
  6 dead mules, and 2 do horses."
September 3: "Passed 4 dead oxen, 1 do mule,
  1 do horse, and 1 discarded ox—exhausted."
September 4: "Passed, this forenoon, 6 dead oxen,
  6 do mules, and 2 dying oxen." * [11]

In September, as they came down the Humboldt River, the rear guard of the migration was facing these shortages, as well as the imminent

---

*   Bruff used the word "do" to mean "ditto," in this place meaning "also dead."

approach of winter. The known difficulty of crossing the Forty Mile Desert was looming ahead. Closely following that hardship was the Donner/Truckee route over the Sierra, or the equally depleted and difficult Carson Route. Also, their position at the rear of the migration made the grim rumors and reputation associated with crossing the Sierra more threatening.

The conditions made the opportunity of a new route sound more promising. It was no wonder Joseph Middleton wrote in his journal, that by following the "Oregon Road" to the Feather River, they "… will cross the Sierra Nevada," and "by doing so they will avoid the tremendous mountains so difficult to pass, on the route by Salmon River, and Mary River Sink."[12]

In *Longing for Frontiers*, Flemming Fischer wrote:

> *What could have been relatively easy crossing for a small, efficient party was becoming a nightmare on a trail where 25,000 people had to fight for water and grass for 40,000 animals, and for decent campsites for themselves.*"[13] *Stewart added confirmation that,* A special rumor was circulating that the grass on the lower Humboldt had been exhausted.[14]

After 12,000 or more emigrants and their livestock had passed there, this "rumor" was undoubtedly true. It was, therefore, a godsend that Lassen had opened his alternate route a year before.

LEGENDARY TRUTHS

Beginning Use of the Lassen Route

Truth is simply a collective name for verification processes.

— William James

Legend tells that Peter Lassen sent messengers to the Humboldt River to entice emigrants, with lies and misinformation, to follow the "new route" to his rancho. However, there is no mention of Lassen's name in any of the early journals of people on the trail at that time. So the question looms as to why a large percentage of the last third of the 1849 migration turned north to follow the route he had taken the previous year—a route pioneered by Jesse Applegate and Levi Scott in 1846. Who influenced this change? And where was Lassen at this time? Also, what was he doing? Perhaps facts recorded in history and journals can set the "legendary truths" aright.*

---

* According to Dr. Jack Fletcher: "It was Bancroft who outright wrote that Lassen only went as far as Fort Hall, with the express intent of luring unwary travelers. Masonic records recorded that Peter Lassen took the Applegate from Goose Lake to Fort Hall and then to Missouri in 1847 (probably with Stockton and Chiles) to procure

As previously stated, reports were circulating back up the trail that grass on the lower Humboldt had been exhausted, and what had merely been a rather difficult journey in earlier years was becoming a nightmare, due to the increased numbers of people and animals competing for water, grass, and campsites. Vincent Geiger, in his journal, noted, "Already the grass is so scarce that we will not be enabled to get through, if at all, by merely the skin of our teeth, & what the seven thousand teams behind us are to do—God Almighty only knows."[1]

It was therefore fortuitous that Lassen had opened an alternate route considering the overused condition of the traditional trails and the difficulty of crossing the steep passes. The emigrants now had a choice when they arrived at Lassen's Meadows. At the time, Israel Hale recorded in his journal that a man who had scouted ahead, had advised them, "that by doing so we would cross the mountain at a lower gap and would find better grass than we would by the sink route and furthermore we could get to the Sacramento in nine days travel."[2]

New routes were commonly called "cutoffs" or "shortcuts." Jesse Applegate had estimated his trail, which turned off at Lassen's Meadows and followed the same route to Goose Lake, to be two hundred miles shorter than the old route to Oregon. This may have carried over to the reputation of "shortcut" for the Lassen route, too. Those who didn't have maps or waybills, and hadn't really researched the trail information, were easily influenced by rumors.

Because the Pit River was the main tributary of the Sacramento River, it was sometimes referred to as being the Upper Sacramento River. In addition, S. Agustus Mitchell's 1846 map[3] showed the "Rio Sacramento" originating near Goose Lake. This may have misled people into thinking that it was at the head of the Sacramento River Valley. Too, the Lassen Route crossed the headwaters of the Feather River near Mount Lassen, and although the Feather River Mining Area was considerably downriver, this information contributed, also, to the idea of a cutoff or shortcut. Even so, some were not unaware of the extra distance the new route presented.

---

a Masonic charter, the first in California. Lassen returned in 1848, took the road again at Fort Hall to the Applegate as far as Goose Lake and turned south on his unfinished road. Peter Burnett, leading Oregonians south to the new gold fields, with his men helped Lassen finish the road."

LEGENDARY TRUTHS

Kimball Webster wrote on September 14:

> *The other, or right hand road is called the Cherokee Cutoff,* *and the distance is said to be but 180 miles to the Feather River gold mines.*
>
> *The question arose, which of the two roads we pursue— follow the old road—the advantages and disadvantages of which we are pretty well informed; or shall we risk the new one of which we know nothing, except from unreliable reports...The question was submitted to a vote of the company, and it was in favor of trying the "Cutoff" as it is called, with scarcely a dissenting vote.[4]*

Webster also added, "Haynes and Fitfield, who left the company at Raft River, left a posted notice here, which showed them to be several days in advance of us. They chose the old trail, and cautioned us against taking the new one, as it was their opinion that it was a longer and a poorer road."[5]

David DeWolf was another who knew that the so called "Cutoff" was farther, as he wrote on September 24, 1849:

> *...we came to a forks of the road, the right hand road being what is termed the Oregon road. A large amount of the emigration has taken this road to avoid the mountains; the distance by this road is nearly 200 miles further than the left hand road. We took the left hand; at the forks of the roads was a post office consisting of a large water cask; it had a large amount of communication in it.* [6]

Pardon Dexter Tiffany arrived at the meadows and wrote:

> *...came to where the new road branches off to the right & found here a general Post office that is a great many letters & notices the trains who had passed struck in split sticks written on slips of paper, cards, & boards...I advised the leader not to go but he urged us...*[7]

---

* Rumors of a Cherokee coming from California, who had found this new trail and created a waybill were recorded in some 1849 Journals (Tiffany and Israel Lord). Bruff copied several of these in his journal, but they probably originated with Jesse Applegate.

His train voted to follow the Lassen Route, and in spite of his misgivings, he went with them.

Edwin Booth wrote that his company believed the rumors that the distance of the new route was only 160 miles to the gold mines, and were in favor of following it. But he claimed:

> *I showed them by Frémont's map that the distance, even in an air line, was much greater and the story therefore was entitled to little credit...without saying anything or taking a vote, one old fellow took up his whip and drove on, another followed and another. So we all kept on the old route, and well we did so.*[8]

Abram Minges wrote:

> *August 13th Left Camp at Six came on down the river eight mile to where we came to a nother rout it is cald Appelgates rout to oragon a few years a gow where Some[?] got lost in the mountains [not true, he is referring to the Truckee Route and the Donner Party] good many died some ware in the mountains most all winter we take this rout on account of Scarsity of feed on the old ro[a]d this rode is a bout too hundred miles far[t]her we Struck this rode a bout ten oclock came on over a barren of twelve mile to a Spring where we camped grass & wattr rathr Scarce we drove our animals a bout a half mile up a revene to grass maid out to get enough wattr to wattr our Stock & coock Cap Mc Gees train took this rode yesterday morning the first wagons that travld hit[it] this Summer, this is the first spring wattr that we have had in too weeks it tastes mighty good...* [9]

From these journal entries, it is obvious that information pertaining to trail distances was available to emigrants trying to decide on the route to travel even before they left Lassen's Meadows. Some chose not to follow the "new" route because of the distance, and some chose it in spite of the extra distance, knowing that it avoided the steep mountains of the other routes. Others apparently followed blindly along without getting the necessary information to make their own decision. These were the ones who would later complain that they were tricked or deceived.

LEGENDARY TRUTHS

On August 11, Milton McGee changed the course of the migration by turning his train of eleven wagons off the Humboldt onto the route previously followed by the Applegates in 1846 and Lassen in 1848. Stewart said, "No three men that season (1849) had greater reputations for knowing what they were doing than had Mcgee, Myers, and Hudspeth."[10]

Stewart then wrote a contradiction in stating that McGee, "had only the very slightest idea of what he was doing."[11] This was a surprising opinion considering that McGee had been with Chiles, Reading, Hensley, and Myers in 1843, when they had ridden into northern California by following down the Pit River. (The Pit River was named after the pits the local Achumawi Indians dug to entrap animals.)

Reading noted in his journal that the country there was very rough and barren as they traveled past Fall River. He also noted in his journal of the trip that one of the men, a:

> ...*Mr. McGhee* [McGee], *who was walking ahead a short distance very suddenly disappeared. In a few minutes we saw the top of his head rising in the path, he having met with the misfortune of stepping into one of these traps. The accident was attended with no further injury than a few slight bruises.*[12]

In addition to having traveled the route in 1843, McGee had accompanied Chiles, Myers, and Lassen with the Stockton Party going east in 1847, and was privy to their discussions and advice to others to avoid the Donner Route. He had doubtlessly heard the reports of the exhausted supplies of food and other hardships that emigrants were expecting and experiencing on the other trails.

Stewart then wrote:

> *To give him his due, he did not attempt to get others to follow him. He was only trying to get his own party through, and was doubtless disgusted at first, then horrified, to discover that he was being followed by hundreds of wagons and thousands of people.*[13]

Stewart's alleged sentiment contradicts advice McGee, Myers, and others in the Stockton Party of 1847 had continued to give out to emigrants, after their travel east over the Donner Route in 1847, when they observed firsthand the difficulties and dangers of that route.

How, one may ask, did McGee "discover" that he was being followed by hundreds of wagons and thousands of people? He did travel slower than many emigrant trains and many passed him, so they may have brought news of others behind. But how would he divine that they would be worse off than they would have been had they chosen the route that had proved disastrous for the Donners? In his mind, he had chosen the best route, considering the conditions, for his own train and would probably have advised the followers that this was the better of the choices.

Next in significance to take the trail was John Jacob Myers, who arrived at the meadows after McGee. Myers was guiding the Hudspeth train,* which had earlier experienced success opening the Hudspeth Cutoff. This success had gained him some credibility among the trains that would follow. Myers, too, had been with Chiles, Reading, and McGee in 1843 when they came down the Pit River. He was a veteran of Fremont's California Battalion and was also with the Stockton Party going east in 1847.

Earlier in 1849, Myers wrote to Brigadier General Roger Jones from Jackson County, Missouri, offering his services as a guide to any army expeditions heading for California. "It is a well known fact that whare the Waggon Road crosses the California Mountain it is both Difficult and Dangerous," Myers noted. He claimed he had spent five years in the country trapping beaver, and had:

> ...examined every stream South of the San Joaquin to the head of the Sacramento" and had "crossed the Mountain in Several places and whare the waggon road now cross it and from what I have seen the Head of the Sacramento is by far the best Rout through the Mountain and can be passed at any Season. † 14

Myers had seen Truckee Pass when he returned to the States with Commodore Stockton in 1847, and though he had probably not actually

---

* J.J. Myers and Hudspeth had been with Fremont in 1846 when he went to Klamath Lake and returned with Lassen to *Bosquejo*. Reportedly, Myers had also married Hudspeth's niece in Independence in 1848.

† Myers to General Jones letter, 13 February, 1849

crossed the pass Applegate and Lassen had used, he suggested "leaving Marys River about one hundred miles above its sink whare the Suthern road to Oregon now leaves it."

Myers was confident that "with very little work a good waggon road can be maid Down the Sacramento" with "but one small mountain to cross not exceeding ten miles over it which can be passed any time during the Winter."

He boldly speculated that "if this Route is examined it will be found as I have stated and in a few years will be the only Rout traveled by land from that Country."[15]

Van Dorn, after hearing reports of six hundred dead cattle along the southern (Applegate) route, was camped in the meadows, considering taking the new route. He wrote in his journal, "Some speculation exists as to the practicability of a new shute-to avoid the desert across the sink."

Van Dorn added, "We learn today that Jack Myers, in charge of Headspeth's train, decide by a vote today whether they take the new route. Myers has been over it twice with packs, but it has never been travelled with wagons."[16]

This information tends to collaborate with Myers' claims about his knowledge of the route, but one wonders if these two trips with packs were in addition to his trip with Chiles in 1843.*

A large percentage of the emigrants on the trail following the greatly respected guides—McGee, Myers, and Hudspeth—who had turned onto the northern route, recorded in their journals that they were duly influenced to follow. William Hoffman explained why his company chose the new route, "One of the companies registered there (at the junction post office) had, we knew, very competent leaders, and that decided us to take this way."[17]

In his book, *The Plains Across*, John Unruh commented:

> *A host of forty-niners similarly reported that they were much influenced in their decisions to follow the Lassen trail when they learned that such respected leaders as Benoni Hudspeth and John J. Myers had taken the cutoff. Since the Lassen Cutoff proved to be one of the biggest 'humbugs' of*

---

* According to Tom Hunt, Myers hadn't been over it twice before with packs, so one wonders where Van Dorn came up with his information.

1849, this was one instance when it would have been just as well had the overlanders really been traveling in the isolation of popular legend.[18]

Opinions vary today—as they did in 1849. However, castigations, such as Unruh's saying it was "one of the biggest 'humbugs' of 1849," failed to consider the consequences of some 8,000 more trail-worn emigrants. These emigrants with their hordes of tired, emaciated livestock having to cross an equally long and forbidding desert, a desert with all grass long overgrazed, then having to ascend a much steeper and difficult range of mountains, which had proven its potential for tragedy and disaster to the Donners in 1846.

A similar ordeal on the Donner and Carson Routes in 1849 would have far exceeded the toll taken on the Donners in 1846 or on those who chose the Lassen Route in 1849. This consideration was clearly stated at the end of the '49 emigration by Major Rucker, who was in charge of a government relief party sent to all the incoming trails. He reported to General Persifor Smith (Dec. 20, 1849):

Although the distance [via the Lassen Trail] *is much greater than by the old routes, and some of the emigrants were much longer in getting in, I cannot but think it a fortunate circumstance they did so, for the loss of property would have been greater on the old trail, as the grass would have been eaten off long before they could have arrived.*[19]

LEGENDARY TRUTHS

Misconceptions of the Trail

Sometimes legends make reality, and become more useful than the facts.—Salman Rushdie

By the middle of August, about two thirds of the migration had passed down the Humboldt. The impact from the numbers of animals grazing on the recruiting areas of the trail and the stress on the animals from the distance already traveled, was becoming evident even on the upper stretches of the river. Rumors, concerns, and fears were being passed back up the trail, and the emigrants, who were all too well aware of the Donner tragedy, were eager to try a new route—especially if it promised to provide better grazing and "was shorter," to boot.

In the words of Will Bagley, the route Lassen had taken the previous year soon took on "...a wishful mythology all its own as thousands of weary sojourners pinned their hopes on the new shortcut."[1] Undoubtedly there was more grass on the new route that had not seen the numbers of emigrants and livestock pass by; however, there was still a grueling desert to be crossed by already weakened animals and emigrants who were arriving dangerously late in the season. The distance, although avoiding the rugged mountains of the south, proved to be farther than the older routes.

It was, therefore, an unfortunate twist of circumstances and fate that the adjectives of "shortcut" and "cutoff" became associated with the new route, as it definitely was not shorter. Undeservedly, Lassen became the brunt of accusations that he promulgated a deceit on the people, when actually a geographic misunderstanding can be traced back to John Charles Fremont's 1843 expedition and the resulting map, drawn by Charles Preuss. On this journey, Fremont had wanted to find Klamath Lake, which he thought was the headwaters of the Sacramento. He was also looking for Mary's Lake, which was reported to be the headwaters of the legendary Buenaventura River. Traveling east from Klamath Marsh, they crossed what is believed to have been the Sycan River near Long Creek. An Indian's drawing on the ground, and knowledge of the Sacramento in California, led him to conclude that he was on the headwaters of the Rio Sacramento.[*2] In his journal Fremont wrote, "...we became immediately satisfied that this water formed the principal stream of the Sacramento River."[3]

In his 1846 map, S. Augustus Mitchell made the same erroneous connections. Most 1846 emigrants over the Applegate Trail, and a few in 1847 referred to Lost River as the Sacramento. The Wiggins Train of 1847 may have used this map. "The Wiggins Train wasted a week" at Lost River, thinking it was the headwaters of the Sacramento. Preuss, after having revisited the area in 1846, no longer connected these rivers on his maps.[4]

Adding to this geographical confusion was the fact that the Pit River was the main tributary to the Sacramento River. Its headwaters were just south of where the Applegate Trail passed around Goose Lake. This river was often referred to as the upper Sacramento River, and distances to this point were considerably shorter than to the actual Sacramento Valley. Farther on, the Lassen Trail also crossed the headwaters of the Feather River near Lassen Peak. The Feather River was known for gold discoveries, and people mistook the distance to its headwaters and the distance to "the mines."

---

[*]   Preuss was a member of Fremont's Party and was the mapmaker.

LEGENDARY TRUTHS

The Cherokee Cutoff

*You can bend it and twist it...You can misuse and abuse
it...But even God cannot change the Truth.*

—Michael Levy

Another confusing but provocative story surfaced at this time about
a "Cherokee Cutoff" and was recorded by Israel Lord in his journal on
September 9, 1849:

> *Lay over...We are laying in for a long drive without grass...
> Report here says that there are four routes, the old one,
> across the desert; another, striking Truckey River twelve
> miles north lower down; a third north of Pyramid Lake, by
> Mud Lake, crossing over to Feather River; and a fourth,
> still farther north, called the Government Road. The last
> two leave the road about sixty miles below, at the next great
> bend of the river. The first of these two is called the Cherokee
> route, and promises so much that, if I mistake not, it will be
> found a humbug. A Cherokee who resides in California has
> been through to this point, and started back with the great*

Cherokee train, as it is now called, of one hundred wagons. The real Cherokee train was reduced to a dozen wagons, I should think, before this manoeuvre. This man reports a good route across the desert, and water and grass at some points.

If there was not a northern route besides this into California, I certainly should not venture. If it should fail, the Government route is sure, though certainly far round. I shall consider it. All the men, I find, are determined to go that way; and probably any attempt to take the old route would lead to a division of the train. There are one hundred and fifty wagons in sight, preparing for hard times, and others rolling in hourly....[1]

This is "provocative," but it also raises some questions. The "Government Road"* he referred to was apparently the Applegate/Lassen route farther north. Lord already knew that it "is sure, though certainly far round," indicating an awareness of the Lassen Route and its distance. Did he think the Cherokee Cutoff was a shorter route, perhaps foreshadowing the later discovery of the Nobles Road?

But, the Cherokee route went "north of Pyramid Lake, by Mud Lake, crossing over to Feather River." This described the Applegate/Lassen Trail, which passed Mud Lake north of Black Rock Desert just before entering High Rock Canyon.

If the Cherokee route followed a more direct path north of Pyramid Lake, it would probably have gone more directly west across the Smoke Creek Desert on the route later to be opened by Nobles. Again, there is some confusion here, because in many of the journals and on modern maps, the area near High Rock Canyon is referred to as Mud Lake, which the Applegate/Lassen Trail clearly went by. However, Fremont and others referred to the playas of the Black Rock and Smoke Creek Deserts farther south, near the present town of Gerlach, also as Mud Lake.†

---

*   The term "Government Road" may have derived from the fact that Lieutenant Hawkins had led a government supply train from Oregon to Fort Hall over the Applegate/Lassen Route and met westbound emigrants with news about the road.

†   In a personal conversation with Dr. Jack and Patricia Fletcher in January 2009, they speculated that Dick Owens might have led his Cherokee pack train over this route. Owens had been with Fremont in 1843 in the Mud Lake area. Fremont named

LEGENDARY TRUTHS

At Lassen's Meadows, Tiffany wrote:

...learned that a Cherokee had come through from California to guide a train of Cherokees and had given the distance on an entirely new route which shortened the road very much avoided the desert at the sink of Mary's River and went through a pass in the mountains without any steep hills to go over, with fine grass and water all the way.[2]

Also at the meadows, Kimball Webster wrote:

The other, or right hand road, is called the Cherokee Cutoff, and the distance is said to be but 180 miles to the Feather River gold mines...The question arose, which of the two roads shall we pursue—follow the old road—or shall we risk the new one...The question was submitted to a vote of the company, and it was in favor of trying the 'Cutoff,' as it is called, with scarcely a dissenting vote.[3]

Where the name "Cherokee Cutoff" came from for the Applegate/Lassen Route is subject to speculation, but it was obviously recorded as such in the journals of later emigrants in 1849.

According to legend, and to John Henry Brown, who claimed in his *Early Days of San Francisco*, that earlier, in 1843, a company of Cherokee fur traders under the command of Captain Dan Coody traveled to California via the Humboldt and Truckee route. [*4] They wintered on the site that later became Johnson Rancho, and when they were returning to the Cherokee Nation in 1844, they met the Stephens-Townsend-Murphy Party and gave them information about California.[5] Again, legend suggests some of this knowledge or experience (however, as inaccurate as that may be) may have later come to play in 1849, as it is well documented that a large contingent of Cherokees traveled from Oklahoma to California in 1849. Various factions traveled by wagon trains, and one by pack train. They entered

---

Owens Valley in his honor.

* John Henry Brown accompanied the Cherokees to California in 1849, and his records were published in *Early Days of San Francisco California*.

California by different routes.*

As the Cherokees traveled north across Colorado into southern Wyoming, they followed an old trappers' trail along the Front Range of the Rockies leaving their name on what is known today as the Cherokee Trail. Later, when some of them turned off on the Applegate/ Lassen Route, it too picked up their name as the Cherokee Cutoff.

While in Pueblo, Colorado, part of Evans' party of Cherokees hired Dick Owens to guide them to California by the Truckee Route. This group then left the Evans' wagon train and became an independent pack train. Captain Evans later took some of his followers over the Truckee Route.[†6] On November 20, Jos. A. Sturdivant wrote a letter home saying:

> *I am now in camp with Wm Shores and Capt Evans, who arrived here about three weeks ago with about half the Arkansas teams. The balance of the train took the northern route on Humboldt River, and my team with them. Learn from Lieut. Rucker who has been with supplies to relieve the emigrants that they had been caught in a snow storm, and have lost all the stock that belonged to the train.[7]*

Read and Gaines wrote, "It is perhaps not idle to speculate on the routes followed by some of the other Cherokee."[8] It is speculated that Dick Owens, who had been over the area with Fremont in 1843 and in 1845-1846, led his Cherokee and white packers over the northern route, as they were obviously part of "the balance" of Evans' train, as mentioned by Sturdivant.

The Fletchers and Whiteley, in *Cherokee Trail Diaries*, wrote that Owens met the party of Amos Josselyn on August 8 and 9 on the Humboldt. They may well have convinced the Owens Party to take the northern route, as they turned on to it on August 13, "...making

---

* Tom Hunt has pointed out that Brown's account is highly questionable, since the Truckee Route wasn't opened until 1844. Further research has shown that there are many errors in Brown's recollections of geography and the sequences of events he claimed. For instance, he claimed Caleb Greenwood guided them to "Hooter's Damm" and directed them to go on past Steep Hollow. "Hooter's Damm" is a term that was applied to the Sturgeon Bend section of the San Juaquin River near San Juaquin City and Steep Hollow was on the west side of the Sierra—conflicting sequences.

† Some of Evans' wagon train went over the Carson Route.

no mention of letters, notices, or other inducements to take the route, which were noted by later emigrants."* [9]

They also wrote:

> *It is probable that Owens took his Cherokee and white pack company over a route similar to Fremont's that followed the present Applegate Trail—to Rabbithole Springs, then to Mud and Pyramid lakes, and west into California's golden valleys—a route mentioned by Israel Lord.* [10]

Again, which Mud Lake would be significant? But, going then to Pyramid Lake, as Fremont did, would have led them too far south.

Owens was familiar with the Sierra, as he had been over the mountains with Fremont in 1843, when they had come south through High Rock Canyon, across the Black Rock Desert by the hot springs near present day Gerlach, to Pyramid Lake, and the "Truckey" River.

Owens was also a good friend of Kit Carson, and both had accompanied Fremont to California in 1845. Fremont subsequently named a river, a lake, and Owens Valley in California in his honor. In 1846, he fought in Fremont's Battalion of Mounted Riflemen and was captain of Company A. Then in 1847, he accompanied Fremont to Washington D.C., prepared to testify in defense of Fremont at his court martial.

As guide to the Cherokee pack train in 1849, Owens was probably as knowledgeable of the route to California as any of the guides on the trail that year.

J. Goldsborough Bruff copied some versions of what he called the "Cherokee Guide" into his journal, listing distances to Mud Lake and High Rock Canyon, but these were essentially based on the Applegate waybill. Bruff also noted in his journal on several occasions, seeing the Cherokees on the trail, even dining with them near Fremont's Castle, and on the trail between Lassen's Meadows and Lassen's rancho.

Read and Gaines wrote, "The Cherokee were renowned as pathfinders, sharing honors with the Delawares as guides...One might not go far wrong in surmising that Cherokee were among the first converts to take the north trail at the bend of the Humboldt... "[11]

---

* Josselyn wrote in his journal on August 9, "Owens was their guide."

Apparently, a Cherokee named Senora Hicks came over the trail with an earlier train in 1849, and he was employed by Major Rucker as a guide for the government relief party. He later was an advance courier for the major, carrying a circular to the emigrants advising them to proceed as fast as possible. It stated, "The bearer of this, Mr. Hicks, has passed over the whole of the route to Lassen's in the valley of the Sacramento, and will give any information to the emigrants that is necessary for the preservation of their stock or their speedy progress."* [12]

---

*   Hicks was first cousin to Flora Coody, Major Daniel Rucker's first wife, who died at Fort Gibson in 1845.

LEGENDARY TRUTHS

Responsibility For Trail Choice

When in doubt, tell the truth.—Mark Twain

Although legend accused Lassen of having sent out messengers to influence emigrants to take his trail,* it was the choices of both Myers and McGee to follow the Lassen Route that turned the tide. Lassen, at the time, was employed as a guide for the government exploring party under the command of Captain William H. Warner. There is no written evidence that he ever sent out messengers to Lassen's Meadows or westbound emigrants; however, both Bruff and Delano recorded meeting the government supply train, under the command of Lieutenant George W. Hawkins, headed east from Oregon to Cantonment Loring, near Fort Hall. Lieutenant Hawkins reported good road conditions.

Delano wrote on August 23, 1849:

---

* The government party under the command of Lieutenant Hawkins gave favorable information about the new route, and he probably was mistakenly thought to have been an emissary of Lassen.

...it was with much satisfaction that we learned that there was a good and feasible wagon road, leading from Goose Lake, beyond the Sierra Nevada, to California, which was opened last season; that the passage of the mountains was not difficult, and now there was grass and water all the way....[1]

Patricia and Dr. Jack Fletcher correctly noted:

...it was the members of the Fort Hall-bound supply train from Oregon, and not Lassen, who gave poor advice and incorrect mileages to many along the Applegate route, and along the Humboldt River. So far as is known, the only circular sent out over the Lassen Trail was the one from Major Rucker, who noted the bearer, Senora Hicks, had been over "the whole route to Lassen's."[2]

Wherever the credit or blame lies, what Stewart wrote about the California Trail in general, also applied to the Lassen Train in particular:

The most remarkable feature of the whole movement was its success against all reasonable expectation. A trail which had been developed for the use of a few hundred people was suddenly required to accommodate many thousands. And, in general, these people were not well qualified by experience or training to survive such a test. This success may be attributed to many factors. The heavy rains of the preceding winter and spring had produced grass along the trail such as had never been known before. The equipment and techniques of travel which had been developed in the years from '41 to '48 were sound, and proved workable under the greatly changed conditions.[3]

Add Lassen's alternate route and John Peoples' aid to the stragglers when snows threatened them, and we get a tale that ranks as one of the heroic stories of the West.[*][4]

---

[*]   John Peoples was in charge of government relief sent by General Persifor Smith to stragglers on the Lassen Trail.

LEGENDARY TRUTHS

PART 3

Lassen's Gold Rush Trail and Alternate Routes

LEGENDARY TRUTHS

Lassen's Meadows to Black Rock

Having made their decision at the Meadows, the emigrants were now committed to a new chapter in their journey. "The new road takes immediately to the desert of fifty-five miles extent with two weak springs on the route." (Virgil Pringle, 1846) It began with a long, gradual ascent west toward Willow and Antelope Springs, their first water after leaving the Humboldt River. Traveling westerly about fifteen miles, it crossed an upland valley floor "...through greasewood and a sprinkle of sage, a little of it heavy," as described by Israel Lord in 1849. Surrounded by high mountains and expansive vistas, the area was both scenic and daunting.

Looking to the north, Israel Hale wrote in 1849, "From the road is seen a round mound that appears to be in or near the center of the valley and is eight or ten miles...from the Humboldt River. By that mound, the bend in the river, the cut-off may be known."[1]

It was a new chapter, begun after a long journey, by trail-jaded emigrants with draft animals already pushed to, or nearly to, their

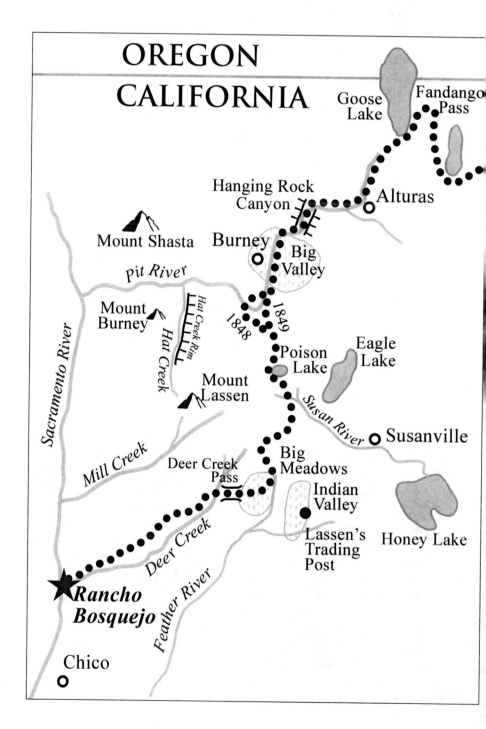

OREGON

CALIFORNIA

Goose Lake

Fandango Pass

Hanging Rock Canyon

Alturas

Mount Shasta

Burney

Big Valley

Pit River

Mount Burney

Hat Creek Rim

1849

1848

Hat Creek

Poison Lake

Eagle Lake

Mount Lassen

Susan River

Susanville

Sacramento River

Mill Creek

Deer Creek Pass

Big Meadows

Indian Valley

Honey Lake

Deer Creek

Lassen's Trading Post

Rancho Bosquejo

Feather River

Chico

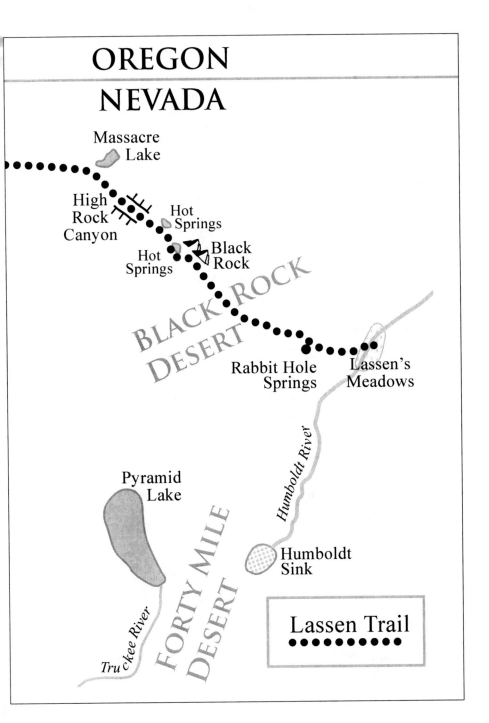

limits. J. Goldsborough Bruff, who had been recording dead draft animals in his journal since September 1 as he was approaching the Humboldt, recorded here, "Passed, on road, since we left the river, 22 dead oxen, and 2 dead horses, any countless wheels, hubs, tires, and other fragments of wagons; ox-yokes, bows, chains, andc."[2] Much of the reported difficulty of the "new road" had already begun, and thus any route undertaken would inherit it.

As we follow the trail and its travails, we should keep a couple of things in mind for perspective. Earlier trains fared better because the grass and water along the way hadn't been as depleted, so timing and numbers of trail users were significant factors for difficulties encountered, and some—who had planned better, were better prepared, or were more experienced—seemed to do better.

> *It should also be noted that those 49ers who traveled the Lassen Trail at the beginning of the diversion recorded no excess suffering; it was the tail-end portion of the emigration—slow moving and containing a much larger proportion of families—that suffered.*[3]

Another factor in 1849 making the trail experience more difficult or distasteful, was caused by the undisciplined lack of consideration by some emigrants for following trains, including damaging or polluting waterholes and burning off the grass.

> *We came 10 miles to a patch of bushes on the right, where we found a little bad water in a Rabbit hole. Two or three miles further on and one mile on the left of the road, we found several weak springs and a little grass, on the mountain side. The water was tolerably passable until the stock got to it. They made a thin mud of it all.*[4]

The first spring came to be known as Willow Spring, and the second as Antelope Spring. Later arrivals dug out the springs to increase the flow.

J. Goldsborough Bruff described the springs as:

> *These were mere drippings—percolating from small clay cliffs in the shallow slope of a mountain. Travelers had dug out hollow reservoirs below each spring, which filling*

enabled the animals to drink...The selfish proprietors had permitted their animals to crowd in and muddy up the water.

However, Bruff reported that higher up the mountainside (Antelope Springs), "in a gulch, were other, small springs, of good clear water..."[5]

From the springs, the trail ascended to Antelope Summit, where it crossed the Majuba Mountains, and the pull was taking its toll on both people and animals. Joseph Middleton wrote:

People are driving their poor exhausted cattle behind or sometimes before their wagons-and when they lie down from exhaustion, they will sometimes wait awhile for them to rest, at other times they will beat them, or split the skin of the tails, or set a dog on them (if they have one) or go through all three operations in succession; and if the poor creature can bear all these operations without moving then they are abandoned. This has been for some time back, and still continues to be a daily occurrence. The cruelty exercised on oxen by some is revolting to all the better parts of the human heart.[6]

At Antelope Summit, the country opened out, and looked down onto a wide sage-covered upland with daunting vistas of the vast landscape ahead and mountains surrounding in the distance.

Crossing this upland plain the trail then dropped into the Rabbit Hole Watershed, and soon began to climb over Kamma Pass, following through a narrow constriction in the Kamma Hills, where the first glimpse of the white desert playa could be seen in the distance ahead. At this place, Royal Tyler Sprague commented:

...and a more perfect scene of barren desolation I never witnessed for a barren plain of 40 miles lay between us...the plain was white and seemed entirely destitute of vegetation or water. Many members of our train were alarmed at the prospect before us...[7]

The trail then continued down through Painted Canyon, where the emigrants were impressed with the mineral hues, and where Alonzo Delano wrote, "Descending a couple of miles through a defile, we passed the most beautiful hills of colored earth I ever saw, with the shades of pink, white, yellow and green brightly blended."[8]

Israel Lord added more colors to his description, "There are red, chocolate, purple, peach, blue, yellow, pink, green, etc."[9]

A couple of miles farther, the trail came to Rabbit Hole Springs, where most of the emigrants watered their stock and rested overnight. But some waited until night to travel on to the desert, thus avoiding the heat while crossing the next stretch of it, then the playa.

When the Applegates, by following rabbit tracks or trails, discovered the springs in 1846, they were just small seeps in what was described as a rabbit hole, thus the name. Later emigrants dug out the springs, but they "are actually wells, dug from 3 to 6 feet deep, and from 4 to 5 feet in diameter; containing cool, clear water but..." then described variously as "a stinking place," and a place with "water not fit to drink."

J. Goldsborough Bruff, *Rabbit Hole Springs.* This item is reproduced by permission of The Huntington Library, San Marino, California.

Several mentioned the stench of dead animals, and Bruff added, "Two of these springs were about 4 feet apart; in one was a dead ox—swelled up so as to fill the hole closely—his hind-legs and tail only above ground. Not far from this was another spring similarly filled."[10] He also counted eighty-two dead oxen, two dead horses and one dead mule within a tenth of a mile.

For a contrasting perspective, Edith A. Lockhart crossed the area in a train led by her husband, and wrote on August 16, 1861, "Pleasant day. Started at noon and went 18 miles to Rabbit Hole Springs, rested a couple of hours and went 18 more miles the next day to Hots Springs." *

From Rabbit Hole Springs, a sloping sage upland dropped to the Black Rock Playa or Mud Lake† as some called it, referring to the crusted, white, alkaline surface caused by water standing on it in the winter season. This was the hottest, driest, and most difficult section of the trail, and was arguably as difficult as the Forty Mile Desert on the other routes. Standing above the shimmering heat waves on the other side was the Black Rock, a landmark visible for miles.

George Edward Hayes wrote in 1849, "The first ten miles lay over a heavy sand road; the next twelve, over a white alkali plain...not a shrub nor even a bunch of wild sage was to be seen."

Bruff described this vista:

> *A very beautiful mirage in the S.S.W. on this plain, at the base of some mountains. In which appeared a long lagoon of light blue water, bordered with tall trees, small islands and their reflection in its delightful looking bosom. One of my men asked me if it was possible that that apparent lake was not water? I explained it, and informed him that not only was it such a plain as we here (stood) on, but that those pretty cedar-looking trees were only dusty dwarf sage bushes... He was astonished, and an uninformed person might well be. Oxen had stampeded for it, hoping to quench their burning thirst, and left their swelled-up carcasses over the plain in that direction, as far as we could discern them.*[11]

Many traveled this section at night to avoid the heat, and here Israel Lord wrote, "I write by candle light and think by starlight."[12] Many

---

* It should be noted that not only did the Lockhart train pass in 1861, long after the '49 Rush , but it also left the Applegate/Lassen Trail about a mile past Rabbit Hole Springs and continued on the Nobles Trail to Trego Hot Springs. There is good reason why Edith Lockhart found no "inconveniences" at Rabbit Hole Springs—2 July of 1860, Col. Lander's crew had excavated a reservoir, so emigrants could no longer complain.

† Fremont in 1843 referred to both Black Rock Playa and Smoke Creek Playa as "Mud Lake." This may have caused confusion, because Mud Meadows, farther north where Mud Meadow Reservoir now stands, has also been referred to as "Mud Lake." See Pardon Tiffany Journal entry for September 17, 1849, and the Applegate Waybill.

of them recorded large numbers of dead animals and commented about the resultant stench, the suffering of people from thirst, and abandoned wagons.

Lord continued:

> But to tell the truth, I am thoroughly disgusted with a sight so barren. So nothing but rock and sand and clay and ashes and dead animals—and who will object when they learn, if they will only believe, that I am traveling or standing in an atmosphere appreciable to all the senses. You ask, 'Do you hear the smell?' If you don't believe, try it. Why, even the wolves hear it. Nothing but ravens and crawling worms are here from choice. I taste it. I feel it. I smell it.[13]

Dexter Tiffany wrote:

> This has been the saddest day of my journey. Like us many have begun this route not knowing the distances for water and many have taken it because they feared they could not cross the desert of the sink of Mary's river with their weak oxen which distance by reason of the Emigration has become nearly 60 miles without grass. Consequently there has been a great loss in teams on this days march than any we have yet made. I counted 367 dead oxen, including 3 or 4 mules and horses. There are many wagons abandoned, some loaded and many men with their all on their backs... We saw men as we were going along unyoke their oxen and abandon them and their wagons. Most of the oxen I saw were shot in the head for as they had given out unable to travel their owners in kindness had ended their sufferings quickly rather than leave them to the slower and severer pangs of hunger.[14]

Near the center of this desert playa, the trail crossed the Quinn River channel, which led to a sink in the playa. The channel was filled with water making a muddy barrier to travel in winter, but it was usually dry in the later summer, as it was for the 49ers. After crossing this channel, the trail entered an area of low dunes before coming to Black Rock, where Black Rock Hot Springs provided water for relief after the long dry stretch.

In 1852, Tolsten Kittelsen Stabaek was traveling to California via the

LEGENDARY TRUTHS

Applegate/Lassen Road to Black Rock and then following the Noble's Road when he wrote, "In the evening we arrived in good condition at Black Rock Spring." He then added:

> *Remains could still be seen of oxen and horses lying in pairs and partly covered with sand; of wagons nothing was left but wheel rims and other iron work. The hides and hair of the five yoke of oxen and of several teams of horses lying there in the sand were surprisingly well preserved. The sight I saw there made so deep an impression on me that I can never forget it.*[15]

Applegate/Lassen Trail ruts going into Black Rock Desert.
Photo by Ken Johnston.

Black Rock to Mud Lake

From here, the trail continued north, passing numerous small hot springs for about five miles to Double Hot Springs. The water from the springs cooled as it flowed out toward the playa, watering a large area that provided grass for the starving animals.

Some diarists recorded people boiling coffee, beans, and other food, by immersing a kettle in the hot springs. Bruff mentioned having thoroughly cooked a grouse in Black Rock Spring. Care also had to be taken to prevent thirst-crazed animals from plunging into the scalding waters.

Arriving at Double Hot Springs on August 18, 1849, Delano wrote, "On looking around us we saw a beautiful plat of green grass, covering about an hundred acres which was irrigated by the water of several hot springs."[1]

On August 31, 1849, Isaac Foster wrote, "At the noon halt yesterday, were several boiling springs, two of which were great curiosities, like twins standing side by side....They are...about 30 feet in diameter.... Here we did our washing, and cooked our beans in the spring."[2]

About three or four miles north of Double Hot Springs another

LEGENDARY TRUTHS

49er, James Allen Hardin left the trail to go hunting. In a small ravine, he found some shiny objects he thought might be lead and could be molded into bullets. He took them back to camp, and then on to Petaluma, California, where he settled. An assayer identified some of the material as silver, which excited Hardin's return to search in 1858, a later silver rush, and the building of the present day ghost town of Hardin City, of which very little remains.

Ironically and tragically, news of silver in the area caused Peter Lassen, with Edward Clapper and Lemericus Wyatt, to prospect in the Black Rock area in 1859. It was here, only a short distance east of his trail and about twelve miles north of Double Hot Springs—in a canyon just south of what is now called Clapper Creek—where Lassen and Clapper were mysteriously murdered (allegedly by Indians).

Most of the trains rested and recruited their stock below the hot springs in preparation for another day of driving over desert and sage, on a sandy trail making its way between low dunes, to Mud Meadows (also referred to as Mud Lake in many journals).

Many interesting journal accounts of this section of trail referred to it as "… yet another dreary part of the desert to cross, over deep sand for twenty miles without water…we provided against the trials which we had already encountered, by cutting a good supply of grass with our knives, and filling our kegs with water."[3]

Whereas Dr. Caldwell, on September 5, wrote that when the moon was up they continued their journey, and with no other feed being available, they fed their animals corn shucks from their mattresses. Amos Batchelder wrote on September 18, "Men complaining of pain in the bowels and diarrhea, caused by drinking the water."[4]

Traveling at night and following the trail, as many did to avoid the heat, could be difficult due to the artemisia (sage) and greasewood. However, Israel Hale recorded a novel solution on August 25. "After the moon went down our men would go ahead of the teams and touch a match to the greasewood bushes that would burn although as green, as will dry oak leaves, which gave us a tolerable light to drive by."[5]

The trail followed up a wide valley with a white playa in the center, bounded to the east by the Black Rock Mountains, and to the west by the Calico Mountains, which derived their name from the rainbow of colors they display that proclaim their volcanic origin. Bruff wrote, "The main trail…on which others travel to Mud Lake, is deep sand and fine powder, with occasional stony places."[6]

Mud Lake provided good grass and water, and a place to rest and recruit the teams before proceeding on to Fly Canyon and High Rock Canyon. Here, Pardon Tiffany wrote on September 17, 1849, "Some think it is Mud Lake though it is all grown over with rushes and not more than half a leg deep…this lake is in a small valley and we found several warm springs perfectly circular fringed with rushes."[7]

Alonzo Delano on August 19 and 20 camped there and wrote:

Nearly all the trains which had preceded us were camped on the beautiful oasis, recruiting their worn-out animals, and cursing the hour in which they were tempted to leave the old trail. The first agreeable news we heard on getting in, was, that the Indians were very bold and troublesome…We kept a strict guard during the night, and all the companies were on alert; yet, notwithstanding all our caution, the Indians came down from the hills and drove off one cow and horse, and badly wounded two more horses.[8]

LEGENDARY TRUTHS

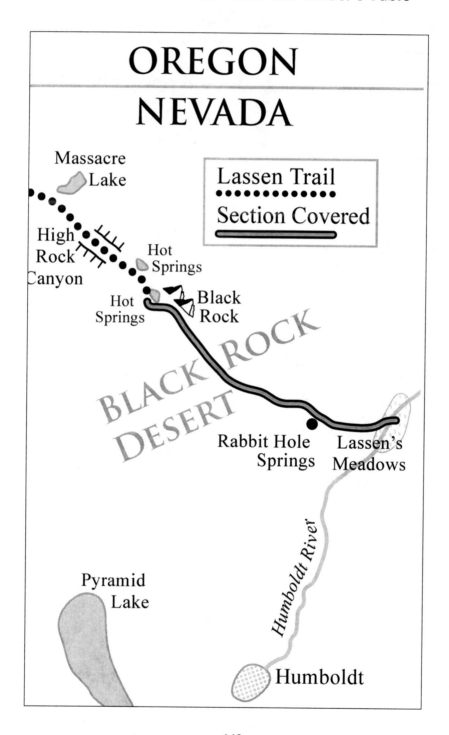

LEGENDARY TRUTHS

Mud Lake to High Rock Canyon

From Mud Lake, or Mud Meadows, the trail turned west and ascended a very rocky slope on the mountainous western side of the northern end of the long valley and basin containing the Black Rock Desert. At the summit of the slope, the trail dropped steeply for about two hundred yards into Fly Canyon. B. R. Biddle wrote on August 17, 1849:

> We started fro, camp with our road in full view, winding up a gentle acclivity, in a western direction. Near the summit, we came to an abrupt pitch where we had to use our big ropes to let down the wagons. This introduced us into a 'Kenyon' that opened into a pretty valley.[1]

Near where the trail entered Fly Canyon, Delano, on August 21, 1849, recorded seeing "an Indian snare for catching hares. This was sage bushes, set about four feet apart, propped up with stones, and extending in a line at least a mile and a half over the hill...The hares when alarmed, fled to the cover of these bushes, when the Indians shot them with their arrows." [2]

Howell wrote on August 28, 1849, "… passed an Indian sage fence for catching antelope." [3] And Bruff noted on September 25 that "…a distance of 2 miles from the road, was a very singular barrier, formed by the Indians, to pen in, probably, large hares when these hunt them (for there is no game here)." [4]

The trail then skirted north of the dry lakebed of High Rock Lake. Here some emigrants found grass and cut hay to take into High Rock Canyon, which provided a northerly cleft through otherwise impassable mountains. The canyon remains a remote and very scenic wonder that is singularly impressive, beautiful, and inspiring.

Elijah Bryan Farnham on August 27, 1849 wrote:

> … we came into a kanyon 21 miles in length. This a passage between 2 perpendicular walls of basaltic rock 3 and 400 feet 21 M long and in some places just wide enough to admit the wagon track between. Passed a cave of considerable size in the rocks. Tonight had all that was needful for camping. [5]

On the following day, August 28, Hale wrote:

> The canyon seems to have been formed by nature for a road. Its length I would say was fourteen miles, but at the out-come the mountains were not so high as at the beginning and center… I saw several caves as we passed but I thought it best to keep away from them as they might be the lurking places for Indians…. We drove two or three miles after we got through the canyon and camped on a branch with good grass and water and sage at a convenient distance. [6]

Bruff mentioned that the Cherokees "came up" when he was entering High Rock Canyon (he would later mention seeing the Cherokees farther up the canyon and also in Long Valley), and he camped in the canyon near some waterholes that had been dug by earlier emigrants not far from the caves mentioned by Hale. Bruff's description stated:

> In the face of the perpendicular wall of the right side, at base, is a singular cave…. The entrance is a low flat arch, 4 ft. high, in the centre, about 25 ft. spring; the chamber oval, and vaulted ceiling: 12 ft. high, (deepest) 35 ft. long,

LEGENDARY TRUTHS

High Rock Canyon looking north. *Photo by Ken Johnston.*

and 18 ft. broad. Much smoke inside. Level earth floor, much covered with fragments from the ceiling. Names and dates scratched all over the outer wall around the mouth of the cave, and numbers within. I wrote the name of the company and date passing, signed it, and pinned it up in the roof of this grotto. The part of the wall in which this cave is, gave name to the canon: as over the cave it rises in a vast spire, I judge to be 400 feet high; however not over 50 feet higher than the adjoining continuation. The rock appears to be basaltic.[7]

Andrew Soule traveled through the canyon in 1854 and, with humor of the era, recalled, "One had a large cave on the side. We went in, but did not find Saul in there asleep that we might cut off his skirts as David did."

After the spectacular high-walled narrows, the canyon opened out into a wider valley with camping places, water, and grass. The steep sides varied from palisades and eroded hoodoos to colorful layers of yellow strata, giving name to a large side canyon called Yellow Rock Canyon. Three and a half miles beyond Yellow Rock Canyon, a rock formation, according to Israel Lord's imagination, looked like a miner

Indian caves in High Rock Canyon. *Photo Ken Johnston.*

on his knees looking for gold. On September 22, 1849, he named the formation the "Californian," and described it as:

> *He seems to be kneeling at the south end of a long block of stone. His body thrown forward, elbows on his thighs and chin on his hands. A pretty large nose, and a decently long chin, but neither are unnatural. He has a pack on his back, and appears to be addressing a multitude of objects....*[8]

A short distance farther up the canyon, B. R. Biddle wrote on August 18, 1849, "We next came to a beautiful meadow of fine grass and well watered. It was indeed a cheering sight."[9] Continuing to gain elevation gradually, the trail ascended into a wide, rolling, open upland that afforded spacious views back over the mountains the canyon had cut through. The high peaks of the Granite Range to the south and west came into view.

To the north and west, more mountains appeared, and it was here that Upper High Rock Canyon also offered a way through. Most of the emigrant trains camped here and recruited their livestock before entering the canyon.

A small stream crossed the trail here, at the present site of a BLM cabin at Steven's Camp. It was fed by a spring, which Bruff wrote about in his journal of September 28, 1849:

I walked up to examine the spring—following its meandering streamlet up. The ascent was considerable, and about 400 yds. from the road. Tall grass and willows, with small cotton-wood, marked the line of this rill; and grantic (granitic) blocks were picturesquely piled about. When I reached the Mountain Spring I was delighted:—A pool, at the base of a large rock, circular margin of pebble-stones, pebbly bottom, and the clearest, coolest, and sweetest water I ever drank. The beautiful reservoir was supplied by a large fountain, gushing from a fissure in the large block above it, and delightfully shaded by a surrounding grove of willows and poplars.[10]

After slaking his thirst in what he referred to as a "limpid and romantic fountain," Bruff clambered higher up, following "hollows, filled with grass and wild rose bushes," until he reached the highest point of the nearly flat-topped mountain, "...on the edge of the deep narrow cañon, through which we had yet to wend our rugged and devious way; and looked down with astonishment—that such a pass could be prac[t]icable for wagons."[11]

Upon entering the canyon on September 13, 1849, Doyle wrote:

At this point we entered a narrow rocky Canyon 2 miles in length which is the worst and most dangerous piece of road yet passed. In some places barely wide enough for a wagon to pass, and over rock from 1 to 3 feet through. Two wagons were broken in passing through it which caused considerable delay. The broken axels were supplied from wagons otherwise damaged and left. 2 wheels were also supplied in like manner.[12]

Later, on September 17, 1849, Castleman reported the:

...most impassable canyon many places being blockaded with horses and cattle that had either perished in the mire or fallen over some stone and was unable to get up again. I think we passed more than fifty dead beast here in less than

two miles some had been left harnessed or yoked as there owners would become disheartened and would walk off and leave them.[13]

Due to the elevation, here temperatures could be extreme, and as early as August 29, 1849, Charles Glass Gray wrote, "Fires were absolutely necessary for the fingers, mine were never colder even during the riguors of an Atlantic winter. The thermometer at 6 oclock standing at 11 degrees above zero and by noon it was up to 90!"[14]

Although extremely rough, the trail passed between more towering and spectacular cliffs for a distance of about two miles, to where it opened out into a marshy area with grass and water, and continued northwest over a gently rolling mountainous area.

LEGENDARY TRUTHS

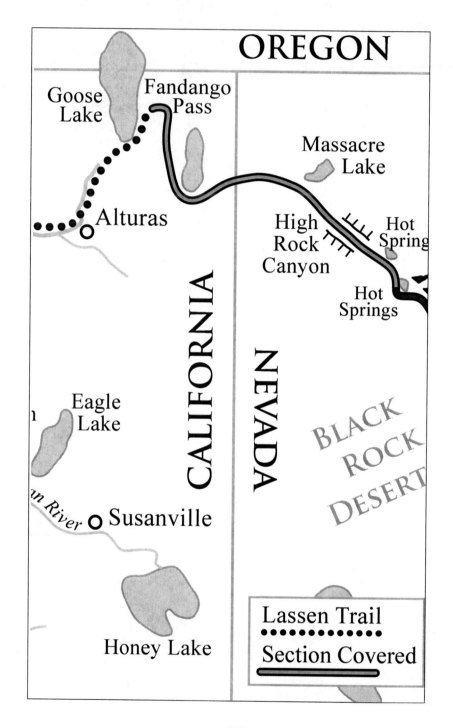

LEGENDARY TRUTHS

High Rock Canyon to
Fandango Pass

Alonzo Delano on August 23, 1849, wrote:

This last canyon was about two miles long, and just as we were coming out, we were greeted with the sight of a drove of cattle and a party of men and wagons going to the east. It was a strange sight to meet travelers going in an opposite direction, and we mutually halted to make inquiries. We found it to be a relief party from Oregon, going to meet the troops on the Humboldt with supplies; but it was with much satisfaction that we learned that there was a good and feasible wagon road, leading from Goose Lake, beyond the Sierra Nevada, to California, which was opened last season; that the passage of the great mountain was not difficult, and that now there was grass and water all the way. This ended all our doubt and perplexity on the subject, and lightened many a heavy heart. The best news of all was, that we should reach the gold diggings on Feather River in traveling a little over a hundred miles. Alas! How we were deceived, for 'the end had not yet come;' but the tale gave us infinite satisfaction for the moment.[1]

Beyond High Rock Canyon, Joseph Middleton described the area on August 4, 1849:

The horizon bounded by low flat hills—the road to the west or rather N.W. is over up and down country, some places rather steep but upon the whole good road so far...with reefs of black rock peeping out in places along on top of the flat hills in low squat form. Three miles on we cross another strip or belt of grass running from S. to N. similar to the one where we camped except in this there is a fine small stream running north in a black mossy bed—in the other no water ran; wells supplied water there in wet swampy place for watering cattle, and some good grass in season: 2 miles ahead they say there is grass where we will stop before entering on a desert of 16 or 18 miles...[2]

On September 29, 1849, Bruff sketched one of these "reefs of black rock," which he described as a "Singular Rock on left of road." This singular rock was a landmark near what is now called Massacre Ranch. Israel Lord described crossing the area on September 25, 1849:

Moved off just after sunrise over an undulating sage and greasewood plain; a most excellent road gradually descending directly west towards the highest and smallest table mountain peak which looks as if it sat upon a broad table mountain but in reality it is beyond it. The road goes through at its north base and a little south of some large, fine looking white bluffs or rocks. Two or three miles farther on I turned and looked back at the mountain we had left. On the west it presents a bold front of white rock, most singularly striped horizontally with yellow and orange. I never saw anything like it.[3]

Here he was describing where the trail crossed Long Valley and entered a canyon leading up to Forty Nine Pass,* as he was looking back at a prominent cuesta, now known as Painted Point.

Joseph Middleton described the formation on October 6, 1849 as:

> ...a high butment or bluff on the E. side of the valley. It is capped with a thick stratum of dark red rock (all this dark red rock is exactly of the colour and much of it, of the grain and hardness, of meteoric stones that I have seen) beneath its thin stratum light brick red; for a long way down yellow looking clay with some thin whitish strata interspersed in a few places, but near the bottom of the yellow...white predominates.[4]

Here he also described the road as they were entering Long Valley, which ran southwest toward Forty Nine Pass as "deep with fine sand before entering long valley but it is down hill and smoothe."[5]

Bruff also sketched the landmark on September 30, 1849, and noted, "On reaching the Wn side of this pass, we saw the evant couriers of the Sierra Nevada, close by."[6] Earlier, on August 20, B.R. Biddle wrote, "After passing a hill we saw, for the first time, proudly glittering afar, the snow peaks of the Nevada."[†]

Forty Nine Lake lies in Long Valley. It was mentioned in various journals as the emigrants passed to the north of its shallow water or crossed its muddy floor—depending on the lateness of their passing. Alonzo Delano wrote on August 24, 1849:

> We had gone on a desert about 12 miles, when before us we saw a pond of clear water, perhaps five miles in circumference, and we all hurried to the muddy beach to quench our thirst, and eagerly dipped our cups full. 'Salt.' Roared one—'Brine,' echoed another—'Pickle for pork,' said a third; and with thirsty throats we resumed our

---

* Today the pass is called Fortynine Pass, but in 1849, it was referred to as Forty Nine Pass and also as Little Mountain Pass.

† Here, another '49 diarist referred to the long awaited peaks of the Sierra Nevada as "the Real Simon Pure." But in truth, the snow covered peaks now appearing were in a range later to be named the Warner Mountains, and after crossing that range at Fandango (also known as Lassen's) Pass the emigrants still had miles of mountains in the Cascade Range to navigate through.

toilsome march.[7]

Simon Doyle on September 14, 1849 wrote, "A circuit of 3 miles brought us around it. Many men crossed the bed of the lake. Some were mired down and had to call for help to extricate them."[8]

Even though there was grass and water along the way, the animals—weak from the long journey, the extra stress of crossing the desert, frequently encountering rocky canyons and rough roads—continued to die along the roadside, and some were killed for food. On September 30 Bruff wrote, "Large timber greeted our eyes, on the mountains ahead. Passed to-day 14 dead oxen, 2 do horses, 2 do mules; 6 discarded oxen, 1 cart, several fragments of wagons."[9] He again mentioned meeting up with the Cherokees here. Also in this area, Indian attacks continued to be a concern, because sometimes at night they wounded some animals, which had to be butchered or left behind. The Indian danger would continue to increase as they crossed Fandango Pass and neared the Pit River area.

After Forty Nine Lake, the trail continued for another couple of miles of flat road across the last stretch of Long Valley, which Lord described as "... forty to sixty miles long north to south and of width varying from ten to fifteen miles. The north part seems covered with soda lakes, and others are scattered over it in all directions."[10]

Here, too, news of the remaining distance to the Sacramento Valley was causing concern. On September 30, 1849, Bruff wrote:

> *People here much alarmed, and I felt much concern, myself, from a statement, set up in camp, of distances on the route, on the western side, down to the settlements.—Showing it to be farther than I or any body else ever dreampt of. I felt confident that it followed Fremont's trail in:—striking the Valley of the Sacramento in 60 or 70 miles from the Pass, but this shows it to be otherwise.*[11]

Leaving Long Valley, the trail continued up through a beautiful canyon with springs and grassy meadows. The high mountains on either side had several interestingly shaped, conical rock formations. On the south side of the valley Joseph Middleton, on October 7, 1849, wrote, "On the face of the hills above the springs are a row of singularly peaked whitish pyramids all shaped very much like a bishop's mitre."[12]

Earlier, on October 1, Bruff had drawn a picture of them in his journal. About a mile on beyond the pass summit, there were some high volcanic dykes that Lord described, on September 26, 1849 as, "On the mountain side and a little to the left of the springs, is a very remarkable one. It is about sixty feet high and stands on a base about forty feet high, which has a smooth red face. On each side are two similar ones, but much smaller."[13]

Crossing a low passage over the mountains called Forty Nine Pass, the trail followed Forty Nine Creek into Surprise Valley. Hale, on August 30, 1849, described the pass and western descent as:

> *In the afternoon we drove through the little pass. It is nothing more than a gap or passage through a small mountain with a gradual slope to the hills and has several springs coming out some rods of the sides. We drove three or four miles after we got through and encamped in a valley surrounded by mountains. We had good grass and some water...I noticed as we drove along several mounds. They have the appearance of whitish hard clay. Some of them resemble stacks of hemp as it is put up after being cut or pulled....*[14]

Wagon Ruts on the Applegate/Lassen Trail entering Surprise Valley with the Warner Mountains in the background. Many emigrants believed these were the Sierra Nevada. *Photo by Ken Johnston.*

On one of these conical rock formations, someone used axel grease to write the number "49," and it is to this inscription that the names of Forty Nine Lake, Pass, and Canyon are attributed.

After the trail descended the pass and crossed some stony ridges, it dropped into Surprise Valley. Here, a Trails West trail marker quotes Elias Davidson Pierce's 1849 journal entry, "Brought us in full view of Surprise Valley and at first sight is apt to take the traveler by surprise to pass from a barren wilderness waste into a lovely valley lying at the eastern base of the Sierras."

The trail then descended a rocky ridge to the valley floor, where it crossed sandy Dry Creek, passed some hot springs, and traversed the wide flat-bottomed valley. From the hot springs (Leonard Hot Springs) on the east side of the valley, the trail continued west, to the south end of Alkali Lake (also known at the time as Plum Lake). It is shallow and at times dry enough to be crossed directly, depending on the year and amount of water.

When Hale camped at the hot springs before crossing the valley, he noted, "This has been a smoky day." B.R. Biddle found the atmosphere in the valley "so filled with smoke that we can see little that surrounds us." Many other journal entries of the year mentioned smoky days, fire scorched grass, and blackened trees. Some attributed the fires to Indians, others to "a very hartless Set of Beasts who try to distress the Emigrants behind them." Some may have been accidental, others intentional and malicious, and as mentioned before, one journal entry claimed sage and brush along the trail were set on fire to light the way for travel at night, in order to avoid the desert heat.

Along the Pit River, Swain wrote, "Evidences of a large emigration through here are seen in the blackened trees which have been set on fire, many of which we see burning every day, as well as in the condition of the road and the camping grounds." [15]

Pardon Tiffany also reported, "Large fires are burning all through the forest" [16] near the Feather River.

"The trail, here, turns to the left and courses around the lake. We saved four miles, by going straight across, the lake being dry." (Joseph Sedgley, September 1, 1849) On the western side of Surprise Valley, the trail turned north following the base of the Warner Mountains to the foot of Fandango Pass, earlier known as Lassen Pass. Along the foot of the mountains, there were clear streams with grass and good camping and recruiting areas, before the ascent to the top of the pass, which rose

LEGENDARY TRUTHS

1,700 feet in about two miles from the western shore of Upper Alkali Lake to the summit elevation of 6,155 feet.

In Surprise Valley, Alonzo Delano wrote on August 26, 1849:

> ...Yet the imagined difficulties were without foundation. Instead of losing our wagons, and packing our cattle; or, as some suggested, as a last resort for the weary, mounting astride of an old ox, and thus making our debut into the valley of the land of gold—we were unable to add a single page of remarkable adventure across the mountains more dangerous than we had already encountered.[17]

However, it should be noted that Delano was relatively near the front of the migration crossing the Lassen Route, and the hardships others later recorded were in part due to the lateness of their arrival.

Even ascending the pass, Delano portrayed the task of crossing "the back bone of the father of hills," with less difficulty than others did:

> ...For about a quarter of a mile the ascent was somewhat steep, and here was the only thing like difficulty. Even over this many wagons passed without doubling teams....At the steepest part our company doubled teams; but many did not, and the summit was gained without difficulty. The time actually spent in traveling from the base to the summit was not over one hour and a quarter, and the dread we had so long indulged of crossing this great mountain, died away at once on seeing the few difficulties of the passage....Once arrived at the summit, the view of mountain scenery is grand and beautiful. Below, on the west, at the distance of a mile, is a broad, green and grassy valley, abounding in springs. The valley is enclosed by high, pine-covered mountains, which seem to kiss the clouds.[18]

Hale, on September 3, 1849, wrote of a similar experience, "We drove about one mile and then doubled our teams. We got up without difficulty, although the last mile on the mountains was very steep." However, he also recorded more excitement:

> ...as my eye reached the Summit I saw a heavy laden wagon driven by ten yoke of oxen start rapidly down the mountain.

The chain attached to the tongue had broken just as they reached the Summit. It ran two or three hundred feet, taking the wheel steers with it and luckily turned bottom upwards. Many saw it and as many rejoiced to see it turn over, for had it continued to follow the road it must have destroyed considerable property, if not some lives. As it was, the chain and an ox yoke was about the amount. The wagon was not broken and the loading was provisions. The wagon was soon turned back, and the loading was partly packed to the Summit...The dust was so great that I did not discover oxen being fast to the wagon, and you can judge my surprise on his being let loose to see him jump up and run away; and how it was possible for a yoke of oxen to be drawn backwards that distance with so great velocity and for neither to be killed or crippled is something for which I cannot account.[19]

Bruff crossed the pass on October 3 and recorded, "10 dead oxen in or beside the trail and one on his knees dying in the trail. The dying ox was covered with an old gum coat, but to no avail, as the dust was suffocating and the following animals and wagons rolled over him in their haste to reach the top." [20]

LEGENDARY TRUTHS

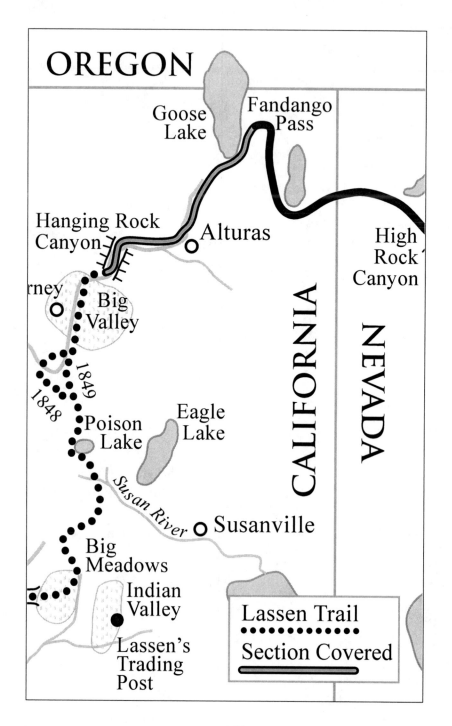

LEGENDARY TRUTHS

Fandango Pass to Pit River
and Hanging Rock Canyon

Fandango Pass was earlier called Lassen Pass, although Lassen was following the route pioneered in 1846 by Jesse Applegate and Levi Scott when he first crossed it in 1848. Bruff thought it rightfully should be called Myers' Pass because Myers claimed in a letter to Brig. General Jones, "...that he has personally been over every pass of the Sierra Nevada."[1]

However, Myers may have been in the area to the west of the pass in 1843 with Chiles, but there is no evidence he ever crossed it before 1849. Its name was supposedly derived from the celebration of emigrants having finally crossed what they mistakenly thought was the Sierra Nevada and dancing the "fandango," either from joy or else to ward off the cold. They cut up wagons to burn in their fires. The remains of these burned wagons inspired tales of an Indian massacre having occurred in the area. There is no documented evidence that a massacre ever occurred to support these "legendary truths."

Moreover, Jesse Applegate wrote in his Waybill of 1848 to "keep close watch here the Indians are very mischievous." Indian trouble, especially with the Pit River Indians, would continue for the rest of the '49 migration and into later years.

On October 12, 1849, the Wolverine Rangers had just pulled the last of their wagons over the summit. That evening they met E.H. Todd and six men with a government relief party, sent by General Persifor F. Smith in Sacramento to bring succor to the struggling emigrants. From Todd, they learned they still had "219 miles" (in actuality, it was more like 250 miles) yet to go to reach Lassen's rancho. On the next day, William Swain wrote that this information made "many of the company uneasy." However, the Rangers reportedly luxuriated on beef from the Todd relief party and were jubilant at believing they had just crossed the Sierra Nevada. Swain wrote, "This evening our boys and those of another train lying here joined with the Smith girls and had a tall time in the way of a fandango..." [2]

The trail followed down Fandango Valley passing "...trees hundreds of feet high and 4-5-6 feet in diameter," to the shores of Goose Lake. (Actually, the trail stayed on higher ground above the lakeshore). It then turned southward to the southern end of the lake, where the Applegate Trail rounded the lake and continued in a northwesterly course on into Oregon. Here, close to the present town of Davis Creek, the Lassen Trail branched off to continue south to the headwaters of the Pit River, then followed the river south and west to where Alturas, California is now located.

On September 24, 1849, Philip Castleman camped on a clear mountain stream about three miles south of Goose Lake, where he found "...tolerably good grass wood and watter."

He wrote:

> *...there was a company encamped a few hundred yardes above us on the stream. They said that they wer on a exploring expedition for Cal-under Capt Warner who was looking out a pass through the siera ne Vada for a railroad and that he had ben out ten days then with ten or 12 and his guide. they also told us that it was 260 miles into the valley when the road would lead us to Lawson's ranch this we tried to disbelieve for sometime as we wer hoping that we would be in the settlement in a few days and as our bread stuff was getting rather scarce we put ourselves on an allowance as*

we had only about eight days provision and there was little hope of getting any before we went to Sacramento City or Sanfrancisco.[3]

Two days later, on September 26, Captain Warner and his guide, Bateau, were killed when Indians somewhere in Surprise Valley north of the trail attacked their party. The mountain range would later be named in Warner's honor, and news of his death was recorded in several journals at the time.

On October 4, 1849, Henry Austin wrote:

Encamped for the night on a fine clear brook of pure water—On a tree by the brook we found a notice written by Lt. Williamson by order of Captn Warner to emigrants giving the distance to Lawsons, Sutter fort and the gold diggings with the prices of provisions at different places.[4]

Also, on October 4, Bruff recorded the mileages given on the sign and information about grass and water along the way, and the costs of provisions at Lassen's rancho and in Sacramento City. Lieutenant Williamson (second in command to Captain Warner) signed the notice. The sign also said, "Where the road leaves the Pitt Riv: it passes over the hills, and is very rough for 20 ms. Mr. Lassen recommends keeping to the right, and going around these hills, over a longer, but smoother road." *[5]

Bruff was a personal friend of Captain Warner, and when he heard of the Captain's death, he visited the camp of Corporal Sheckles, who related to him all the circumstances of the attack. He said that about "30 Inds Killed Warner and Bateau (guide) instantly—with 11 arrows in W. and 9 in Bateau—through calfs of legs body, thigh, mouth—lacerating mouths and jaws much. Wounded 2 men—1 severely with 4 arrows, the other slightly with 2." He also said the slightly wounded man was ahead, traveling with Lieutenant Williamson, who was pushing to the settlements with the party and effects.[6]

---

* It should also be noted that this reference by Lieutenant Williamson about Lassen's directions was a result of Lassen having been hired as a guide for the Warner Party; Lassen had traveled with the party as far as Big Valley. This would be the west branch by way of Willow Springs.

Following the river south, the trail passed some conical, beehive shaped rocks. A Trails West trail marker here reads: "L-3 - Conical Rocks. Striking the River this morning I noticed a cluster of singular shaped rocks sticking up in spires of conical shape 20 – 30 feet high. Andrew Lopp Murphy, Sept. 26, 1849."

Delano described them as "singular outcrops of volcanic sandstone." Near here, he joined the men of another train in making a fish seine, using:

> ...an old wagon cover, we proceeded to a beaver-dam, and while a party went above to drive the fish down, we waded in the deep water with the primitive net. In three hauls we caught fifty-five fine trout, and going with them to their camp, we had a delicious feast....[7]

The river and trail then turned in a more westerly direction and followed across a high table plain forming the wide Pit River Valley between rolling mountains, and passed by a tall, symmetrical butte, or isolated mountain that rose from the level plain shaped like a tent. Some called it Centerville Butte, but others named it Rattlesnake Butte and Rattlesnake Creek because of the rattlesnakes encountered in the area. It was in this area that the tall profile of Mount Shasta came into view. William Swain wrote on October 18, 1849, "Far to the west of us, solitary, rises to an immense height a gigantic mountain, [Mount Shasta], the top and sides clear to the base covered with snow—a magnificent sight."[8]

Alonzo Delano on August 31, 1849 wrote:

> The road led to a table plain above the valley, over Magnesia Hills, and then turned nearly west into the valley again, in about a mile. From the brow of the hill we had a charming prospect. The great valley extended many miles before us, and at the limit of our vision, perhaps eighty miles distant, a high and apparently isolated snowy peak lifted its head to the clouds, like a beacon to travelers on their arduous journey, and the clear water of the Pitt was sparkling in the morning sun, as it wound its way, fringed with willows, through the grassy plain. The high snow-capped butte was Mount Shasta; and though it appeared to us to be on a plain at the extremity of the valley, it was in fact surrounded by a

LEGENDARY TRUTHS

*broken and mountainous country, far from the course of the
river. We crossed the river twice during the day by easy and
safe fords, and found the volume increasing every hour.*[9]

The going was relatively easy here, but the cumulative stress of the
long journey was taking its toll. On October 6, Bruff mentioned:

*Wrecks of travel—wheels axels, and profuse ...Passed a dying
mule, just abandoned by 2 men....Many packed pedestrians,
4 dead oxen, 300 yds. E. of ford, we crossed a slew and rather
bad marsh, after passing over loose sand hills – more dead
oxen. – Continued over the bottom, a low stony ridge, down
into a meadow. – at the river; – forded, and S.S.W. ascended
and passed over a low plateau, or table-land, to a point ¼
mile between bends of stream, – 2 dead oxen, 1 do mule.* [10]

Also, by October 6, a government relief party, under the command
of Major Daniel Rucker, was arriving in the area to provide succor for
latecomers and to encourage them to hurry to the settlements before
the snows came. Several diarists recorded getting supplies from them.

About twenty-five miles long, the Pit River Valley narrowed on
its western end. The river entered a canyon between low mountains,
where it made a sharp bend toward the south and cut through Hanging
Rock Canyon. On the west side of the canyon about halfway through,
was a large Indian cave with a spring in it. This canyon was nearly as
steeply spectacular, if not as towering, as High Rock Canyon. Alonzo
Delano commented on September 2, 1849, "...had we not seen High
Rock Canyon, this would have been a curiosity in itself."

On October 8, 1849, Israel Lord described the canyon as:

*...passing some basalt walls on the right, nearly overhanging
the road, and almost crowding it into the river. Just at the
end of the section you pass a huge bluff, filled with fissures,
and having some immense caverns beneath. A hundred acres
of such country as surrounds this would be a fortune for any
man, near some great city in the east, but I have lost all
interest in these things. I am heartily tired of being shut up
among hills and mountains, with loose blocks of granite or
basalt hanging over my head; and I believe that there are
but few of my fellow-travellers who do not participate in the*

171

feeling. The only thing that makes it tolerable is the pine, which relieves the eye by its greenness, and the roar of the wind through its branches dispels the oppressive feeling of eternal silence and solitude.

Then, after having passed through the canyon, he added, "To one not thoroughly satiated, this might, nay, must be a scene of surpassing beauty. I can be astounded, or something of that sort, but to be interested, delighted; to admire is a long way behind me."[11]

On September 24, Simon Doyle wrote:

In two miles we came to the river at the head of the Canion, down which we traveled for the remainder of the day. Crossing the river (8) times and crossing over several points of ridges. Road bad...Today I had a fine dish of soup made of a large hawk commonly called a Pine Turkey in these parts. It was very palatable; the meat was white, tender and sweet. I thought equal to any chicken I had ever eaten. All who I could persuade to tast it pronounced it excellent, and general warfare was from this time on waged against hawks.[12]

LEGENDARY TRUTHS

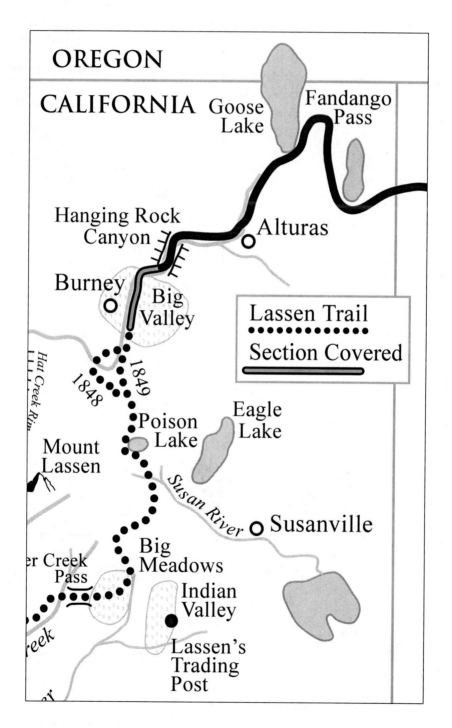

LEGENDARY TRUTHS

Hanging Rock Canyon to Big Valley

After the narrow confines of the Hanging Rock palisades, the route debouched into Stone Coal Canyon, which soon led into Big Valley. Here the Lassen Route joined with an old trail that early trappers had followed from Tule Lake to Pit River and the route Fremont, with Lassen, had followed in 1846. It was here where the Burnett Party from Oregon had come upon Lassen's tracks the previous year in 1848. The Burnett Party was under the guidance of Thomas McKay, who had been over the route when trapping with Ogden.

At the junction, Reverend Isaac Foster wrote on September 15, 1849: "After traveling 3 miles came to the Oregon road, coming in on the left hand, and about 11 o'clock met a government exploring party, who told us it was 170 miles to Lawson's...."[1]

Here a Trails West marker reads, "Lassen Trail—Oregon Road Junction, 'Today about noon we found the road leading from Oregon to California.... In the evening we met a train returning from the mines to Oregon.' Alexander Ramsay, Aug. 29, 1849."

175

Amos Josselyn wrote on August 29, 1849, "This afternoon got out of the Kenyon 5 miles back making 22 miles through the Kenyon. Drove 18 miles today. Weather cold in the morning and evening, pleasant in the middle of the day. We come into the road from Oregon City to San Francisco 11 miles back."[2]

On September 22, 1849, Delano wrote, "We crossed and recrossed the river at least a dozen times. Three miles from our noon halt, after passing over the point of a hill, the valley again expanded, and here we came to the junction of the Oregon and California road."

The next day after traveling a few miles he wrote, "... we entered a spacious valley, at least twenty miles broad, with a rich soil, which only required irrigation to make it very productive."[3]

In the Big Valley area, several diarists mentioned the ongoing problems with the Pit River Indians, and about meeting Captain Warner's Government Expedition. Peter Lassen was a hired guide for the expedition, and he accompanied it as far as Big Valley, but there, he apparently left to return to his rancho due to sickness.

Israel Lord wrote on October 10, 1849, "Papers in the P. Office* at the fork say that, 'The Wisconsin Train killed an Indian here four days ago and they are very troublesome.'"

Lord then added:

> We have found, every mile or two, deep pits close to the stream. They were originally of one shape and size, though some are now partly caved in and others almost entirely filled. The depth seems to have been ten feet, the length at the surface four, and the breadth two and a half, being oval in shape and growing gradually larger as they approach the bottom. They are probably root cellars or pits to catch animals or perhaps both. [4]

On October 1, 1849, Castleman noted:

> I have seen several pitts to day they are some 10 or 15 feet deep two or three feet in diameter at the top and eight or ten at their bottom for what these have been dug I can't imagine the dirt has ben carried off and I have noticed some being

---

* Information posted on the trail was often referred to as Trail Post Office or Trail Telegraph.

*neare trails which make me think they are traps to catch
some kind of game. I have seen no one that can give any
satisfactory account of them.*[5]

Swain mentioned "frequent deep pits" along the road being ten or
fifteen feet deep, and Joseph Middleton described them as "...10 feet
deep, and 3 or 4 feet wide at the mouth for 3 or 4 feet down, then
widening or swelling out at that distance down like the belly of a large
pot..."[6]

On September 13, 1849, before leaving Big Valley, Charles Gray
met a government train with pack animals under the command of
Lieutenant Williamson that was from California on an exploring
expedition. The packers reported that they:

*...were about 175 miles to Lawsons on Deer Creek, that
here were only 2 houses and nothing to be had in the way of
provisions that about 60 miles north of Lawsons and about
the same to the south would bring us to 'the diggings' and
that the road was rough and rocky all of which dampen'd
our spirits considerably.*[7]

The packers also said "...Lawson himself was with them, piloting
them through." Gray wrote:

*In the evening accordingly then Gen'l (being himself unwell)
sent 2 of our men to the packers camp to get some information
from him, he returned with the 2 men and around a large
camp fire he entertain'd us till a late hour, he was quite
unwell himself and and said he was emply'd by the Gov't
train at $10 per day and said their object was to survey the
country for a railroad route.*[8]

Lassen told them that the road ahead was not a bad one for a
mountain road. Then in the afternoon, Gray wrote:

*...started on a road which led over a high hill and thinking
we were on the wrong road, turned back and took up our
route through a canon and after driving a while found our
road completely block'd up, as it was only a 'turn off' so we
had to return again and take the road we took first....*[9]

Peter Lassen & His Gold Rush Trail In Fact & Fable

Note: as stated before, Peter Lassen was employed to guide the Government Exploration Party (under the command of Captain Warner with Lieutenant Williamson as second in command), from Lassen's rancho east through the mountains, in search of a suitable railroad route. He, therefore, could not have been at Lassen's Meadows on the Humboldt River luring unsuspecting emigrants to follow his trail to his rancho, as some of the legends suggest. Also, if he were trying to profit from emigrants coming by his rancho, why wouldn't he have stocked up on profitable items to sell, rather than, as Gray indicated, "that here were only 2 houses and nothing to be had in the way of provisions..."?

As noted, due to his sickness, Lassen gave up his guiding position with Lieutenant Williamson and returned to his rancho, where some of the emigrants arriving there noted his presence in journals.

The place where Gray commented about going up a high hill and thinking they were on the wrong route could have been the steep grade leading out of the Pit River Valley, where they "turned back and took up our route through a canon and after driving a while found our road completely block'd up..." Could the "canon" he was referring to be the Pit River Canyon south of Bieber? Were there tracks leading into that canyon? Could this possibly be the canyon Lassen wrongfully went down the year before, a trail which was later followed by Burnett? Had Gray actually traveled farther from the Pit River Valley (about 10 miles according to Burnett's recollection) and stumbled on the tracks left by the Lassen and Burnett wagons? And how far did Gray follow the tracks before coming to where they "found our road completely block'd up..., as it was only a 'turn off' so we had to return again and take the road we took first"?

This last description sounds somewhat similar to Burnett's description of following Lassen's tracks down a valley about eight miles, and finding "to our great mortification, we came to the termination of this lovely valley in front of a tall, steep mountain, which could not be ascended except by some creature that had either wings or claws," as stated earlier.

For years, trail enthusiasts had hoped that research in the area would clear up the questions as to where the place was that Burnett described; however, recently, Richard Silva discovered a promising valley going west about eight miles, as stated by Burnett, from near Willow Springs to the rim above the Hat Creek Fault. If Burnett were standing atop this

LEGENDARY TRUTHS

"mountain" and looking down, it truly "could not be ascended except by some creature that had either wings or claws."

For years, trail historians had looked in the area for "a mountain" with a sheer face Burnett could not go over, rather than looking for a mountain so steep wagons could not DESCEND, so steep only a creature with "wings or claws" could ascend. In the Hat Creek Valley below that point is "a lava bed some two miles wide," exactly as Burnett described. And across the valley from this point is where the Old Hudsons Bay Trappers' Trail crosses a low pass from Hat Creek into the Upper Sacramento Valley.

Was Lassen really "lost," as legendary truths suggest, when he brought his wagons here and was thwarted by the rugged topography from crossing to an easy route he had previously been over and knew about? Were McGee and Myers "lost" in 1849 when they too tried to get across here and couldn't?

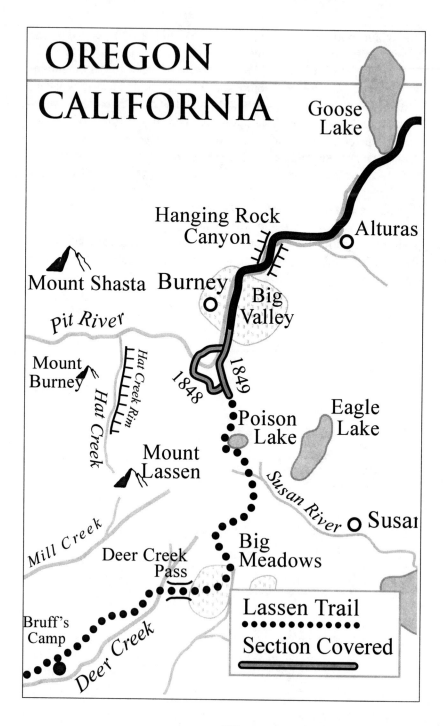

LEGENDARY TRUTHS

Big Valley Road Forks to Road Juncture

A few miles southwest of where the town of Bieber is now located, the Pit River entered the narrow, rocky, steep-sided, and impassable Pit River Canyon. At the head of the canyon, a railroad bridge now crosses the river where the Lassen Trail forked in 1849. The left hand route went up a steep and rocky slope toward Little Valley; whereas, the right fork crossed the river, went west through Muck Valley, again crossing the Pit River after it debouched from the impassable canyon. Then the trail turned south to Willow Springs and the headwaters of the Feather River.

According to the recollections of Peter Burnett, Lassen led his train along this route in 1848, and Burnett's train followed.

> *From the point where we struck the Lassen road...* [several miles west of Hanging Rock Canyon]...*it continued down the river in a westerly direction ten or fifteen miles until the river turned south and ran through a canyon* [where the

road went] *west for twenty or thirty miles, when it came to and crossed the river. ....After crossing the river, the road bore south; it being impossible to follow downstream, as the mountains came too close to it. Next morning we left our camp and followed the road south...*[1]

Doyle also described this stretch through Muck Valley on September 27, 1849:

Drove 18 miles to the last crossing of the Pitt River. At our encampment of last night the road forks, the left hand leaving the River, the Right crossing and running over ridges 18 miles and striking again at our encampment of tonight. We found no water in the distance and the road verry rough and some places dangerous. A great many broken wagons lay scattered along the last 10 miles.[2]

On September 13, 1849, Jewett wrote, "...camped here last night and lost five of their cattle to the Indians...We left Pitts River and struck S.E. for the waters of the Feather River."[3]

At Willow Springs, the emigrants found grass, water, and a good resting place after having passed a very rocky stretch. Doyle wrote on September 29, 1849:

For 7 miles our road was over a solid, or rather attached, mass of rocks, the roughest I ever saw a wagon taken over. After that we had a good road...At the Willow Springs we saw some packers who had been out 6 days trying to get through to Sacramento Valley. They found the way impassable for mules and had just returned to the road. 9 foot men also started out for the same purpose. They had not returned but those who had come in expressed doubts of even them getting throug (sic) the country is so rough. Many narrow gorges, they say, are impassable for man or beast.[4]

From Willow Springs, the road continued about three miles south to where it joined the left fork beside Beaver Creek, about two miles east of the present site of Jellico.

The left hand fork, or the road in Big Valley, was opened in 1849 and cut off a few miles, but was considered steeper and rougher.

LEGENDARY TRUTHS

We here leave the river it forks one road crossing the river to the right the other keeping to the left over the hill the right hand road is 15 miles the longest and a little the smoothest. At a distance of 20 miles by the left hand road they come together again we took the shorter left hand road and the roughest and rockiest I ever traveled. Anonymous.[5]

This left hand route went up a steep, stony hill, which Bruff described as:

...very elevated. –A magnificent prospect from the top. The Snow Butte (St. Joseph) about 50 ms. below Tschastes, being S. about 40 ms. distant, clothed with snow, and truncated with clouds....What a scene, from here! The Snow Butte, and his blue neighbors, deep vales. Silver-thread like streams, near mountains, dense forests, bright deep valleys, andc. in every tint of one of natures most extensive landscapes! Pshaw! –enraptur'd with a landscape! --how ridiculous! I have seen many. And some nearly as grand; besides I must look out for the train, or there will be some accidental capsizements, maybe a broken neck or leg!—No time now for the Fine arts, we must patronize the rough ones.[6]

On October 21, 1849, Pratt wrote, "We nooned at the foot of a mountain; here are two roads; the one to the left we took, as we saw a Gov't train with provisions come that way."[7]

Alonzo Delano arrived here on September 5, 1849, and wrote:

We Bid farewell to the fine valley of the Pitt, and took our course in a west-of-south direction over a long hill, the precursor of a hard, rocky road. It was twelve miles to the first water, and fourteen to the first grass. The day was too smoky to obtain an extended vie, but what we saw showed us a rough, mountainous country all around.[8]

The road went up and down hills, crossing ravines, and following a rough, stony route to Clark Valley. It was in this area that Israel Lord found and copied the following note in a trailside "post office."

C.H. Bush.
I past hear tha third day at 8 oclock
I am not well I hope that yo ar well
Indians war githered ennto large crodes.
Be watch ful. At nit, Jonh E. Bush.
Mean near about 30 Indians saw yh
near last nit.

Lord then added, "There you have it verb. et lit. et punct. 'Lo the poor scholastic.'" [9]

After Clark Valley, the road crossed Horse Creek by going down a steep and dangerous incline. Then the emigrants had a steep pull up out of the canyon to get to a good camping area where they found plenty of water and grass. Bruff, on October 10, 1849, described the crossing:

> *...then an awful descent...Broken wheels, capsized wagons, tires, hubs, and broken wagons, profusely strewn all the way down...and steep bank to ascend on the other side...we had to double-team each wagon successively, and bang and shout the mules up.*

Later at the evening camping place, Bruff noted that there was "an abandoned wagon, and pieces of others; discarded clothing and. 3 dead oxen, and 1 horse." [10]

At Little Valley, many trains stopped to camp for the good grass and water. Then it was about fifteen miles to where the road re-joined the right-hand fork. In this distance, the road passed to the north of Mud Springs and continued to Beaver Crossing,* both important watering spots. Grass was generally plentiful, but the road was rocky in places, and wagons and teams continued to fail from fatigue and hard use.

Elisha Preston Howell wrote:

> *In this valley (Little Valley)....several other smaller companies encamped here, and, what to us is of far more importance, Capt. (William H.) Warner of the U.S. Army,*

---

* Recent discoveries by Richard Silva have shown this route to be more accurate than in previously published guides, and Trails West has recently relocated some of its trail markers as a result.

with a corps of Topographical Engineers, and Mr. Lawson (Peter Lassen), all direct from the Sacramento valley. We got a correct Waybill here and instead of being within a few miles of the end of our journey, we find it is 140 or 150 miles to the sacramento (sic) valley.[11]

Bruff mentioned the woods being "alight and crackling with many fires, burning the huge dry pines." He also described an interesting, different type of wagon:

Passed a house–wagon, drawn by 3 yoke of oxen and 2 small cows—3 ladies with them—This wagon was termed by the emigrants—the 'Steam-boat'—the pipe sticking out of the top—A family of the name Alford, were the proprietors...A lady in the 'Steam-boat' wagon, an infant born a month since in these mountains.[12]

Another interesting account in this area involved an Irishman named Pat, who was seen in this vicinity with a large hencoop attached to the rear of his ox-wagon. It was filled with chickens and roosters he and his wife had brought all the way across the plains and mountains, speculating on their value in California. Pat, it seemed, had his wife along to share in "all the programme of the route, assis[t]ing to drive, yoke and unyoke, water, feed the chickens, cook, etc." When questioned about the chickens, he was reported to have replied, "...by the howly mother of Moses, I'd rather starve than kill one of them."[13]

Somewhere south and a little west of Little Valley, a couple of miles to the east of what is now known as Jelly Spring (Jelly Camp on the map), Howell's party overtook the Myers-Hudspeth company that had started on the Applegate/Lassen Trail four days before them. Howell wrote:

Here we overtook Myers and Hudspeth's Company, and the St. Joseph, Mo. Company. Myers had been here a day or two trying to find a way through to the right, to the Sacramento valley. Hudspeth had gone ahead, and Myers heard at this place that he was returning on this rout to meet his Company, he gave up his right hand road.[14]

Hudspeth had gone on to Lassen's and returned with a report of the road ahead.*

Myers was familiar with this country, having been here with Fremont and Lassen in 1846 on their return to the Sacramento Valley from Klamath Lake, and he thought he could find a more direct wagon route to the Sacramento Valley. However, Myers' desire defied him, as it had other emigrants who had tried but, due to encountering impassable terrain, had been forced to return to the Lassen Trail.

When Bruff came to this area, he expected the road to go west to the Sacramento Valley where Fremont had crossed the mountains north of Lassen Peak. He wrote, "My ideas, and so expressed, were, that I had been in favor of this northern route, and as described by Meyers, in his letter to Adjt. General, but coming into the valley at its head…"

Later, at his camp in the snow, he reminisced, "Had the road been found, as I know it might, 200 miles back from Lassen's to run W., our company would now be at work in 'Redding's Diggings,' some 50 or 60 miles N. of this camp [Bruff's Camp], at the head of the Sacramento Valley."[15]

Finally, to confirm this conviction, sometime after Bruff reached Lassen's rancho, on August 3, 1850, he wrote, "J. J. Meyers, and a small party returned from prospecting…He met Capt. Lyon on Pitt river, on the 3rd, from thence they traveled in to the settlements in 5 days." [16]

Later, on August 10, 1850, Bruff met Captain Lyon and wrote:

> *The Captain described to me the route…He said that the trail laid along a series of beautiful valleys, without any rugged or steep to cross, and where wagons can travel easily. This is where I thought the road ought to strike into the Sacramento Valley, from the Pit river, below the Pass of the Sierra Nevada when I crossed last fall.* [17]

Again, Bruff noted the short route into the valley, which he knew existed when he was traveling south of the Pit River in 1849 on the Lassen Trail. According to Lyon's map, he traveled up Cow Creek and

---

* The author wonders if Hudspeth hadn't returned with road information, would Myers have persisted in exploring his route to the west and maybe would have found a connection to the route followed by the old trappers. Myers had crossed there in 1843 with the Chiles' Party.

reached the Lassen Trail at or near the Horse Creek ford.[18]

In their notes Read and Gaines added, "This is where Lassen, in '48, struck west 'through a beautiful valley,' to be defeated by a 'mountain which could not be ascended except by some creature that had either wings or claws.'" Was Lassen lost, or was it just that, as Read and Gaines speculated, "He did not thread the needle's eye"? [19]

This area roughly matched the description given by Burnett where his party followed the tracks of the Lassen train west and met impassable terrain, causing them to have to retrace their steps and assume that Lassen was "lost." Likely, Lassen, too, was searching out a more direct route, and he likewise failed. In 1846, when Lassen was with the Fremont Party returning from Klamath Lake, they crossed the Pit River and came south to somewhere in this area before turning west and crossing the mountains just north of Mount Lassen. Therefore, is it fair to pass judgment that he was lost any more than Myers was? In this case, "legendary truths" leave reasonable doubt—Lassen was probably trying to retrace the earlier route.

Road Juncture to Feather River

About fifteen miles south of Little Valley, the two branches of the Lassen Trail reunited. On September 30, 1849, Simon Doyle wrote, "We came to the junction of the roads which separated at the lower end of Round (Big) Valley. The left hand road nearer but the worst so the report sais."

On October 3, he described the area as "Road through pine forest, mostly down hill, country broken, stoney, and verry poor. Day cold enough for December weather." [1]

From the juncture of the two roads, the route followed around the western base of the volcanic cone of Blacks Mountain, and passed a couple miles to the east of Jelly Spring. It then swung eastward through Patterson Flat to Aspen Well and Dixie Spring in Harvey Valley, where there were numerous springs that were visited by the emigrants. Here the route turned southwestward, again to pass through Gray's Valley and on south through Bogard and Pine Creek Valley, where James Pratt, on October 26, 1849, wrote "We got into camp by moonlight—A stream of excellent water near...We found encamped near two men who were almost dead with the scurvy." *

This route to Dixie Spring was needlessly circuitous and it was later shortened by a direct route, south from Blacks Mountain straight to Poison Lake, and then south to Pine Creek. According to Tom Hunt, Peter Lassen discovered this shorter route in 1850, when he was prospecting for the mythical Gold Lake.†

Feather Lake was so named because of the large numbers of feathers on and around it.‡ Here, Andrew Lopp Murphy, on October 8, 1849, wrote, "The road this morning led across the valley a S.E. course 2 miles. Rocky in places then through scattering of pine 2 miles to Feather Lake. A small lake to the left." §

Charles Glass Gray, on September 19, 1849, wrote:

> *Stop'd near a small lake call'd 'Goose Lake' and noon'd there were a large number of wagons camp'd here and most of them like ourselves out of provisions, everybody seem'd to be on the look out to buy something and almost all of them without success. We did make out to get 2 quarts of beans, which were delicious. They however and a pipe of strong tobacco made me quite sick, so that I passed a poor night of it.*[2]

The trail continued south through Norvell Flat, which was "finely wooded with magnificent pines," and on one of the trees several notices were posted advising following emigrants to take the side trail, which forked to the west and south of the main trail and offered more grass and better camping.

> *...when we came to Little Goose Lake here we filled our caggs fearing we would have to travel some distance without watter we had not traveled more than 4 or 5 miles from this*

---

* Inscription on Trails West Marker L-31. Lassen Trail to Pine Creek Valley.

† Personal conversation with Tom Hunt on April 14, 2011.

‡ Feather Lake was also referred to as Goose Lake in some journals, as was Goose Lake north of the Pit River. Tule or Rhett Lake in the Klamath Basin was also sometimes referred to as Goose Lake.

§ Inscription on Trails West Marker L-32. Lassen Trail to Feather Lake.

lake when we came to a new road   here wer a note on a tree stating that there was good watter and grass 1½ miles distant so we took the right hand road and found it to be true to the great gratification of our company.[3]

In this area, Bruff mistook the Susan River (which flows southeastward to Susanville and Honey Lake) for one of the numerous sources of the Feather River and mentioned "...Axels, wheels, and other parts of broken wagons, old clothes...dead oxen." He also recorded several graves. The stress of travel, the great distance and shortage of food, the effects of scurvy, and the lateness of season were beginning to be of considerable concern to the emigrants still in the area, and to those following.

Many diarists, along with Bruff, recorded the hardships, hunger, numbers of people abandoning their wagons and starting to pack their remaining belongings, and their bedraggled appearances. The need for government relief was becoming urgent.

Near Swain Valley, Bruff wrote on October 14:

...on a neighboring hill Maj. Rucker, U.S.A. was camped, with his wagons, provisions, and men, of the Relief party, sent out by Gen' Smith. He was surrounded by begging emigrants, men, women, and children. The Maj. had killed an ox the day before, and he had to serve out the fresh beef, pork, flour, bread, etc. as judiciously as possible—subject of course, to much imposition.—The importunity of the begging emigrants, was annoying some greatly in need, some meanly bent on an increase of stores, and others, who would steal a dying man's shoes. His stores were insufficient to serve those actually in want, but how was he to discriminate? Then he had to contend with impudence, etc. from the disappointed and rude applicants. It was one of the most delicate, and troublesome duties ever entrusted to any one![4]

From Swain Valley, a west branch of the route followed Dry Creek to Clear Creek and turned west, following the Hamilton Branch of the Feather River westward until it joined with the North Fork of the Feather River at Big Meadows. An east branch continued south through Norvell Flat. The river was dammed in 1917, and the meadows, now flooded, are known as Lake Almanor.

LEGENDARY TRUTHS

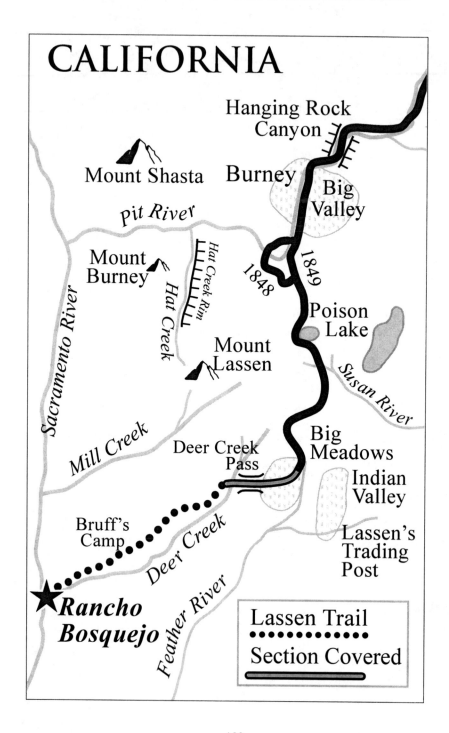

CALIFORNIA

Hanging Rock
Canyon

Mount Shasta   Burney

Big
Valley

Pit River

Mount
Burney

Hat Creek Rim

1848   1849

Poison
Lake

Hat Creek

Mount
Lassen

Susan River

Mill Creek

Deer Creek
Pass

Big
Meadows

Indian
Valley

Bruff's
Camp

Deer Creek

Lassen's
Trading
Post

Rancho
Bosquejo

Feather River

Lassen Trail
••••••••••••
Section Covered

LEGENDARY TRUTHS

Feather River to
Deer Creek Crossing

From the headwaters of Feather River, it was still some seventy miles to Lassen's rancho. It was also many miles downstream to the mines or "Gold Diggins." However, due the presence of the Feather River here, distances from Lassen's Meadows on the Humboldt to the source of the Feather River were reportedly much shorter than to the "mines," which were farther downriver. This gave a misrepresentation of travel expectations, and it may have contributed to the "legendary" mislabeled appellations of "Lassen Cutoff" (Cherokee Cutoff).

The Feather River received its name from the Spanish *Rio de las Plumas*, which was bestowed upon the stream by a Spanish exploring expedition, headed by Captain Louis A. Arguello in 1820. It was so named because of "the great numbers of feathers from wild fowl floating on its bosom." His party continued north to Fort Vancouver, passing to the east of what is now called Mount Lassen, which his padres named San Jose, and emigrants referred to as Snowy Butte or

Mt. St. Joseph.*

Delano wrote of expecting "to find auriferous indications" in the river, but he was disappointed to find "neither quartz nor slate." This was because the river arose in the volcanic soils and rocks of the Cascade Range, not geologically conducive to the formation and crystallization of quartz and gold. The river then had to flow many miles southward before cutting into the intrusive granites and quartzes of the Sierra Nevada, where gold was found.

The juncture of the two forks of the river flowed through Big Meadows. Here emigrants camped, recruited their stock, and cut a supply of hay to sustain their livestock on the last leg of the journey, which would take them down the crest of a high, barren, rocky ridge between Deer Creek and Mill Creek, until they reached the valley of the Sacramento River.

In the Big Meadows, which now are inundated by the waters of Lake Almanor, Alonzo Delano described their appearance on September 10, 1849:

> *...From the indications along the edges, this valley is overflowed by the rains of winter and the melting snow of spring—thus making a broad but shallow mountain lake, of from sixty to eighty miles in circumference. Ducks, swans and wild geese covered its waters, and elk, black-tailed deer, and antelope were numerous on the bottoms; while the tracks of the grizzly bear, the wolf, and cougar, were frequent on the hills. We halted for the night on this beautiful bottom after a drive of sixteen miles.*[1]

Other diarists described the approach, having to ford the streams, and the beauty of the area. Castleman, on October 10, 1849 came to the Feather River and wrote, "We traveled some two or three miles in a Western direction acrossing several streames which ran into the river."[2]

Henry Austin, on October 16 wrote, "...we struck the river we crossed one of its tributaries—a most beautiful stream—water clear as

---

* Various sources differ as to whether the date was 1820 or 1821. Arguello is also credited with the naming of Rio de los Osos (bear) and Rio de los Uva (egg). As the Spanish pronunciation of the word was "Ooba," it is easy to see how it was Americanized into "Yuba" by the heedless miner.

a crystal and rushing over a bed of long grass and pebbles. The ford the finest I ever saw."[3]

Also on October 16, Bruff described the area as, "The water of Feather river, a half mile below, as clear as crystal, bottom small pebbles, and beautiful plants and long choralline looking grass in it, adhering to the flat rocks. Numerous fish swimming about as leisurely as gold fish in a vase...."[4]

He went on to describe the activities of the emigrants camped there: "Women in groups, sitting by their wagons, children playing about, in the grass. Mowers busy cutting hay, others tinkering on their wagons, clothes drying on the green grass; stately pines and furs, with their dark green foliage and bright brown trunks..."[5]

Today, Lake Almanor fills the valley where the Feather River flowed and where many emigrants camped and cut grass for the last stretch over the mountainous ridges to Lassen's rancho. Large springs flowed into the lush bottomlands called Big Meadows, which not only provided grass for hay, but also had marshy areas that had to be avoided, since many animals reportedly got mired there.

Israel Lord, on October 20, 1849, wrote:

> *Cold morning. Had to haul a great many cattle out of the mire...Camped on the west fork of Feather River, where it comes in from a valley on the right...Here we cut grass... The grass here is coarse and not very good. The river is thirty yards wide, and ten to fifteen feet deep, with a strong current and clear cold water. There is a detachment of the government relief party here, camped with a depot of provisions, and McClure, of Elgin, has hired to them until they return at $150 a month.[6]*

The lush meadows and timbered slopes were a refreshing sight to emigrants who had spent the last couple of months in the treeless plains, the bleak wastes along the Humboldt, and the barren desert. The increase of game in the area was not only welcomed, but needed, to supplement their waning larders. On October 22, 1849, Lord wrote:

> *Coming up the broad spring brook, on the last section, I saw a wild goose, and off went his head, at 100 yards. This is a god-send for we are hard up for something fresh. Bacon is a*

drug and goose is a rarity, especially a young one like this.
We have Ball and McAuley ahead these four days after deer,
and hope to come up with them tomorrow on Deer Creek.[7]

Doyle, on October 5, 1849, wrote:

Our grass was soon cut down and then we spent the
remainder of the evening looking about us at the beauties of
nature. In strolling down the stream I chanced to see an old
Indian Canoe laying upon the bank in some brush. On closer
inspection I found that it contained two Indian carcases, two
sets of Bows and Arrows, a fish net and two Goos eggs. Each
of the carcases bore the mark of a bullet; one in the brest
the other in the back, and were lying as though they had
been sitting in the canoe when shot, one falling backwards
the other forwards. Some time had elaps since the deed was
done.[8]

Somewhere in this area the previous year, Lassen and his train had
stopped to recruit their animals. They, too, were out of provisions and
he was contending with mutinous members when the Burnett Party
arrived to help. Is it not ironic that this year, it was Lassen, himself,
who arrived with information and advice for the struggling emigrants?
Going north as guide to the Warner Expedition, his passing by was
noted by Delano on September 11, 1849:

...there was an encampment of a hundred wagons, laying
over to recruit their cattle, for it was known that it was
seventy miles to Lawson's, in the valley of the Sacramento,
and also, that fifty miles of the distance is over a rough,
mountainous desert, destitute of grass and water. Lawson
himself had passed the day before with an exploring party,
and left directions what course we were to take to reach the
valley, as well as a table of distances to water, which was
posted on a tree by the roadside above our camp.[9]

A couple of weeks later Lassen was returning to his rancho and
again passed through the area, when Gray noted on September 22:

Last night Lawson, whom we saw about a week ago
[September 13, in Big Valley] arrived, having given up

LEGENDARY TRUTHS

his place in the exploring expedition and returns home on account of his bad health, he interested us much by his accounts of California, even at his account we shall have a rough time of it and he puts as favourable a view of it as he can and at the same time have regard for the truth. He says there is much sickness in the mines and that our late arrival will be no detriment to us on that score.[10]

It is interesting to speculate that if Lassen had not been in bad health and if he had continued to accompany the Warner Expedition, he may have been killed with Warner. If so, would the "legendary truths" have continued to accuse him of luring the 49ers over the trail to his ranch? Or would they recognize that he was only a guide who had pioneered a route the year before, and that many, who knew the hardships of the alternate routes, willingly chose to take it? Those not in the "know" blindly followed, and they were the ones who started the rumors which led to the "legendary truths." Others, like Captain Warner, would hire the man, Lassen, for his knowledge of the area, and emigrants, like Delano and Gray, would respect his advice.

The previous year, Lassen's train was in dire straits—destitute of provisions and manpower for road building—until Burnett's Oregon party came to the rescue. Likewise, this year's migrating emigrants were in the last throes of their journey, especially the ones trailing behind at the end of the emigrant trains. As was generally the case any year in the history of the trail, the emigrants at the end of the migration were the ones to suffer most. Fortunately, this year, government relief was sent out in order to prevent a repeat of the Donner tragedy of 1846.

On October 6, 1849, Doyle wrote:

...The entire train had been out of meat for some 10 days and in fact everything else except flour and coffee. Not withstanding the many signs of wild game our hunters has as yet been unable to kill any, and not knowing that they would meet with better success in the future we took the poor old steer as a last and only resort to avoid a visit from lank, lean, old Monster starvation; for money was too scarce to depend upon buying provisions at present prices—if they could be found for sale—which was from here on impossible. I am truly glad we have got away from the Meadows, for

*the scenes of distress and privation sickened me and my
inability to relieve the distressed caused me deeper regret
and sympathy.*[11]

The road left Big Meadows where Prattville now stands. It traveled
in a westerly direction, then in a northwest direction, following up
Soldier Creek, passing through Soldier Meadows and then Deer Creek
Meadows to Deer Creek Crossing. Earlier in the summer, there was
good grass in these meadows, but by October, what with the large
numbers of emigrants and their livestock passing through, grass in the
meadows was scarcer. Bruff overheard a little girl say to her brother,
"Never mind, Buddy, tàint far to grass and water." [12]

LEGENDARY TRUTHS

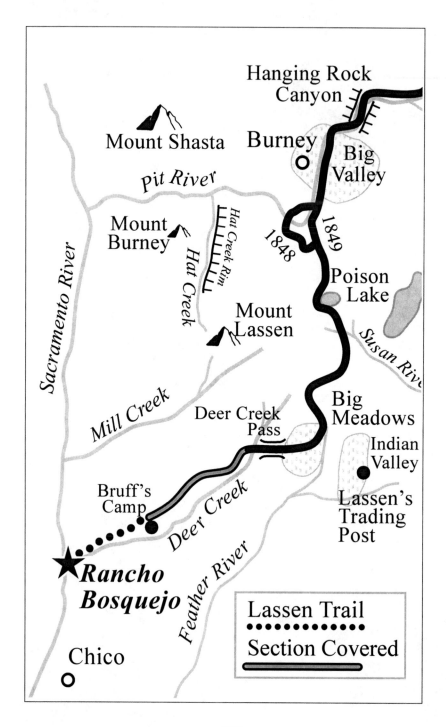

LEGENDARY TRUTHS

Deer Creek Crossing to
Bruff's Camp

Game was becoming more numerous, and many journals mentioned various forms of wild meat supplementing the emigrants' larders. Gray mentioned not having any luck fishing, but "...the crow meat was much better than I had imagined." Others reported ducks and geese being shot on the lakes or streams in the area. Doyle wrote on October 8 and 9, 1849:

Deer in the mountains here in great numbers and every man who can rais a gun is out hunting. A perfect rore of guns may be heard in all directions and great numbers of Deer are being carried in. Everybody has forgotten the probabilities of starvation and a smile is on every countenance...4 fine fat deer were brought into camp. I think there was at least 200 deer killed here today. Day cloudy and cold. The mountains to the South are covered with snow. A man was chased by a

*Grizzly Bear...From this point in the valley the road leads
over or along rockey ridges without grass; water scarce.*[1]

Perhaps Bruff recorded the most interesting hunting report of the
year on October 20, 1849, when he wrote, "Shot a very dark brown
Vulture, measuring 9 feet from tip to tip." Bruff was very precise in his
documentation, and the only bird with a nine-foot wingspan was the
California Condor. Condors were much more numerous and had a far
wider range in the 1800s than today. (The Lewis and Clark Expedition
shot one near the Columbia River at the beginning of the century.)
Whether Bruff shot the condor for food and cooked it, or what he did
with it, he didn't report, but the fact that he recorded shooting it in this
area is of ornithological interest—if not historical significance.

After Deer Creek Crossing, the road followed the creek southwest
for a couple of miles to where the valley constricted, forcing the stream,
road, and mountains close together. There were thick willows along
the stream, and the canyon sides were heavily timbered with pines,
cedars, and a few oaks. Bruff noted on October 19, "...tolerable grass,
but much marsh—some dangerous for animals. Numerous camps here.
Children laying and playing on the green sward, happily unconscious
of the troubles of others." [2]

However, two weeks later, weather conditions had changed, and
emigrants at the rear of the migration were severely affected. On
November 3, Orson Pratt wrote, "Last evening a large train passed.
Women and children passed us with packs on their backs!" Then on
November 4, he wrote, "The snow covers the ground. Some of our
cattle are frozen to death! The rest of them are unable to move."

Without oxen, they were forced to abandon their wagons, and he
said, "...we all pack our clothing. We have to leave about everything."
He also reported there was distressing news from the rear of the
emigration: "They say there are 40 women and children behind yet;
some sick men also that must perish..." [3]

Near Alder Creek, the road branched off to the right of Deer Creek
and followed the ridge separating the drainages of Mill Creek and Deer
Creek into the Sacramento Valley. Doyle wrote on October 10:

Drive 12 miles to Spring in the road [Round Valley Spring]. ...
Last night snow fell on the mountains to the depth of 4 inches.

LEGENDARY TRUTHS

Day cloudy and cold and everybody is pushing forward as
fast as possible, fearing that winter has set in and they may
be caught in the snow. God help the hindmost. About dusk
snow commenced falling quite rapid and continued until I
went to bed.[4]

In about three more miles, the road entered Round Valley, "One
of the few places along the ridge where even a little amount of water
could be obtained." *

Amos Batchelder wrote on October 11, 1849, "Stopped once in
a small opening in the forest, where there was but little feed for our
animals. We obtained our water from springs around the margin of
their opening." †

Following the divide through wooded terrain, the road climbed to
a high ridge where some emigrants were obliged to double team to
ascend it, and where Bruff reported many dead oxen, scattered wagon
parts, clothing, and deer heads, horns, and skins.

Along this same ridge, Delano wishfully referred to "auriferous,"
or gold bearing rocks, but he mistakenly reported, "The country around
is a confused, broken mass of mountains, to the utmost limit of vision,
and is highly auriferous, with stupendous outcrops of slate and white
quartz." [5]

Perhaps if he had reported, in more understandable layman's terms,
seeing "veins of gold" (in the spectacular and highly non-auriferous—
non-gold bearing—volcanic palisades) rather than "auriferous outcrops
of quartz," this "legendary truth," or optimism, could have incited a
"Rush" like the mythological "Gold Lake" would later in 1850!

From this high viewpoint, the road descended to The Narrows
where:

> *...(military men call it a 'ridge' and the mountaineers 'the*
> *back bone' for there is an immense abyss on each side) we*
> *could look down thousands of feet, the side of the ridge*
> *seeming almost perpendicular. Large trees at the bottom*
> *look'd like shrubs, and immense masses of rocks like pebbles*
> *and together it was one of the grandest sights I have seen on*

---

* Inscription on Trails West Marker L-48—Round Valley.

† Inscription on Trails West Marker L-51 Lassen Trail—Round Valley

the whole route.[6]

Henry Austin on October 21, 1849, wrote, "The view below and before us Truly grand – the lofty mountains, the stupendous rocks with deep but magnificent vale below...Renders this one of the finest and most picturesque views I ever beheld." *

Israel Lord described the ridge on October 29, 1849:

> *We are inexorably bound to this ridge as is a locomotive to its iron track. Have nothing but acorns to feed our cattle. They are abundant. A man can gather a bushel in a few minutes but if he picks them up clean and fit to feed it takes one half to three quarters of an hour or longer.*[7]

Today from the Narrows one can look down, as Gray said, and see the volcanic formations and the rugged canyons of Mill and Deer Creeks. A short distance farther down the grade, a dirt road—Ponderosa Way—winds its way down the canyon to a volcanic plug on Mill Creek called Black Rock. It was a sacred site for the Yahi Indians, who lived in Mill and Deer Creek Canyons. On October 29, 1849, Bruff hiked down to the rock from Bruff's Camp and sketched it.

---

*   Inscription on Trails West marker L53. Mill Creek Overlook.

LEGENDARY TRUTHS

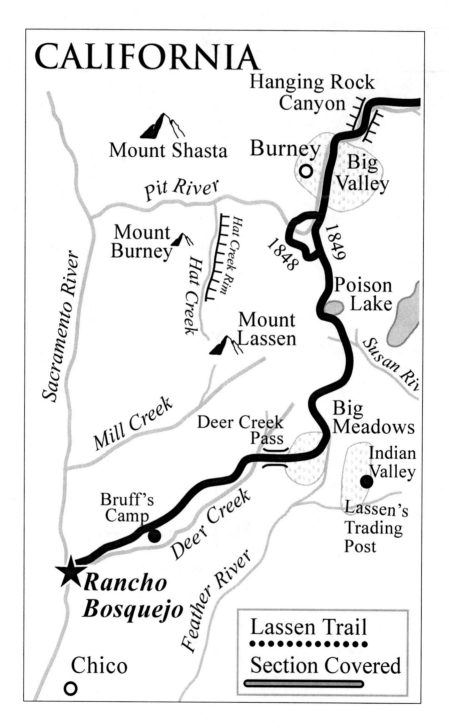

CALIFORNIA

Hanging Rock
Canyon

Mount Shasta

Burney

Big
Valley

Pit River

Mount
Burney

Hat Creek Rim

1848

1849

Hat Creek

Poison
Lake

Sacramento River

Mount
Lassen

Susan Riv

Mill Creek

Deer Creek
Pass

Big
Meadows

Indian
Valley

Bruff's
Camp

Deer Creek

Lassen's
Trading
Post

★Rancho
Bosquejo

Feather River

Lassen Trail
••••••••••••
Section Covered

Chico

LEGENDARY TRUTHS

Bruff's Camp to Lassen's Rancho Bosquejo

A stone marker erected beside the road in June 1984, marks the site of Bruff's Camp. It has a bronze plaque inscribed:

> *J. G. Bruff, Leader of the Washington City Mining Co., camped on this site from Oct. 21, 1849 to Dec. 31, 1849. While here guarding company goods, at what he called 'his Mt. Lodge in prosperity,' he aided, fed and cheered many weary, hungry, and sick Emigrants struggling to the gold fields.*

This was a natural campsite, and from what Burnett wrote in his recollections, it is thought that he camped there with Lassen in 1848, "That evening [after passing the Narrows] a large portion of our party encamped on the summit of a dry ridge, among the intermixed pine and oak timber." [1]

Arriving on October 21, 1849 Bruff wrote:

Here we have to cut down oak trees and browse our animals on the leaves and tops. A great many travelers camped here. Found a large corral of wagons, and accumulation of property, by a party of men who were ostensibly engaged in felling timber and getting out pine shingles, for Lassen.[2]

One would conclude that the shingles for Lassen's ranch buildings also came from this place, and that Lassen had scouted the area before his 1848 journey. If so, this would explain his knowledge of the need to keep to the ridge top between Mill and Deer Creeks, which he imparted to Burnett and the other emigrants of the year. The previous year, Lovejoy in his recollections said Lassen had been over the route "three or four" times.[3]

Bruff reported that these woodcutters, who allegedly worked for Lassen, would tell emigrants that there were still fifty to sixty miles to travel over "...the most rugged and difficult road ever traveled by Christians," and that the emigrants should entrust their goods and livestock to them for safekeeping.

J. Goldsborough Bruff, *Rear of the Author's Camp*. (Bruff's Camp) This item is reproduced by permission of The Huntington Library, San Marino, California.

LEGENDARY TRUTHS

The poor emigrants were at once disheartened, and in despair, left their wagons, cattle, and all their effects, except such as they could pack on their backs, and pushed on. These men had been emigrants themselves, yet they were determined to prey on the misfortunes of the brethren; and make a harvest of their calamities.[4]

Because Bruff was captain of the Washington City Mining Company, he felt compelled to stay with the company's holdings and watch over them until the members of his company could reach the valley and send help back. But they, in effect, abandoned him. He spent the winter guarding the wagons and property, and recording his experiences and news of passing emigrants in his journal.

For the three or four weeks after October 21, a steady procession of men, women, and children, with wagons of every kind, horses, mules, oxen, bulls, cows, and packers carrying the only possessions they could manage, passed by Bruff's camp.

One of the visitors, a fourteen-year-old named Henry Ferguson, later remembered the pleasure of reaching Bruff's camp, where his family's friends, the Alfords, had arrived and camped earlier. The Alfords had killed three deer during the day and shared a nice venison dinner with them when they arrived. Then:

About midnight, in gloomy darkness, the storm broke upon us, hurricane like winds twisting the trees in its fury, and breaking off near the ground the great black oak tree under which our tents and also the tents of our friend Alford were stretched. The body of the tree fell on the Alford tent, killing the old man and his oldest son (William, age nineten) (sic) instantly, and fatally injuring the younger son (Lorenzo, age fifteen) and their hired man, a Mr. Cameron, who both died the next day....The great concussion and falling tent poles left three of our children badly hurt, but none fatally so, but no one can imagine a darker scene than came upon us.[5]

Documenting that night of October 31, 1849, Bruff wrote:

...we were awakened by a man, crying at the top of his voice —'Hallo, here! Turn out and assist, a tree has fallen on a couple of tents, and killed and wounded several persons!'...

We raised the bloodstained tent, cut it off from the chords, and extricated the broken tent poles, etc. And there lay a shocking sight! –An aged, grey headed man, and his grown son, with their hips buried in the ground, and their eyes turned up in death! Next another son, and beside him, a young man, his comrade, slowly dying in agony, with broken legs and mutilated bodies... [6]

The bodies were buried at the site, and their epitaph reads:

Their journey is ended,
their toils are all past,
Together they slept,
in this false world, their last:
They here sleep together,
 in one grave entombed—
Side by side, as they slept,
on the night they were doomed!

As the bronze plaque states, Bruff stayed here until "Dec. 31, 1849," when he, with the help of a couple of friends, constructed a sled and moved his books, journals, and some possessions and food a couple of miles farther down the road to Obe Fields, where the Robert's makeshift cabin was located. He set up a new camp near the cabin and remained there until April, 1850.

When he finally staggered out of the mountains, sick and weak from hunger, and after believing, "I fear I have suffered all this travel for naught," he wrote on April 10, 1849:

Thank God!—I have safely passed a trying ordeal! My extreme sufferings are terminated, I trust. The people here, particularly Col. Davis' family, are exceedingly kind and friendly, and do all in their power to alleviate my misfortunes, and make me comfortable. A hearty breakfast—Pan-cakes and molasses, rolls and fresh butter, stewed and broiled beef, coffee and milk. [7]

Bruff later moved down to Lassen's, where he was employed in Lassen's store, did some survey work for Lassen, and accompanied Lassen's party prospecting for gold.

LEGENDARY TRUTHS

The author, recently retracing the trail and Bruff's journey, stopped near Obe Fields and noted:

The view from here is magnificent and exhilarating. One can see a hundred miles up and down the Sacramento Valley. The mountains of the Coast Range lie beyond, and the expansive vistas across the canyons extending to snow covered mountains, with Mount Shasta far to the north, emote the sense of a big wide open, rocky, rugged and lonely place where one can feel the 'lonely.' It's a tangible, numenal presence but not an emotion. I'm alone but not lonesome; No, this 'lonely' is the essence of solitude, peace, and quietude which I feel.

The earlier wagon trains, arriving without the difficulties experienced by the later trains, probably shared the same feelings of grandeur and satisfaction as they descended from the mountains and saw these vistas, as Lord did on October 29, 1849, when he wrote, "The view of Sacramento Valley from here is magnificent. You can see it this morning for at least 100 miles up and down and the mountains beyond roll up like a wall in the morning sunlight." [8]

J. Goldsborough Bruff, *Straggling Emigrants*. This item is reproduced by permission of The Huntington Library, San Marino, California.

211

Earlier, on September 29, 1849, Gray wrote:

We then went on for about 3 miles and just at sunset had a splendid view from the high ridge we were on, looking down upon the tops of hundreds of peaks color'd blue and green and black and some of them just tinged with the golden rays of the setting sun! [9]

Later emigrants were abandoning their wagons and packing or walking on to Lassen's. Major Rucker and his government relief party were encouraging all they met to abandon everything and make haste to the valley. Hunger, fatigue, and filth were troubling to some, if not most, as mentioned by William Steuben, on September 20, 1849, "Could you see me I would not be recognized. Dirty, filthy and fully equal in appearance (to) the natives excepting Being in an entire state of nudity…" *

By November 6, when Orson Pratt was nearing Obe Fields, winter had set in, and he wrote in his journal:

The road was then entirely obliterated by the snow; but we had the advantage of a footpath made by some just ahead of us…We have descended far from the mountains, and are now, we suppose, near Big Hollow [Steep Hollow]…It was perceptible how much had been our descent to-day, when leaving the heavy snow we came to where it was scanty, and sloppy, and where rain instead of snow was falling. We learn that the government relief train was bringing up the rear emigration about 13 miles behind our camp last night. Great is the aid thus afforded, if only to keep open the trail, for the deep snow very soon obliterates traces of the road, and one is as it were in the dense forest without guide or chart. [10]

A couple of miles below Robert's cabin and Bruff's last camp at Obe Fields, the road dropped into Steep Hollow, which was extremely difficult to descend into, and was described as a veritable "sarcophagous of broken bones and wagons." According to Gray, the area was "cover'd with ox chains, and yokes and wagon bodies and fixtures, axel trees and broken wheels and tongues and enough old

---

* Trails West Marker L58 Lassen Trail—Unrecognizable Emigrants

irons to set up a foundry…" [11]

A Trails West Marker, #L-58, Lassen Trail—Steep Hollow, placed beside the road here is inscribed: "There were several trains encamped in this hollow and it reminded me of a small village as all wer up…to make an early start as there was a verry steep hill to climb before we could get out of this hollow." P.F. Castleman, Oct 20, 1849

As the road lost elevation, the tall Jeffrey pines, sugar pines, incense cedars, and large black oaks gave way to a more open live oak and digger pine cover, interspersed with the short, dry, straw-colored grass so typical of late summer and fall in the California foothills. Everywhere the ground was covered with rocks varying from small pebble sized to large boulders—the Tuscan Formation—which extends from Lassen Volcanic National Park westward over the foothills to Palo Cedro, and south nearly to Chico.

It is a *Laharic* formation caused by volcanic eruptions from ancient volcanoes pre-existing the later eruptions and formation of Mount Lassen and the surrounding peaks. These ancient volcanoes spewed forth lava, which melted snow on the shoulders of the mountains, causing large mudflows to rush downward and outward across the lowlands. The mud carried rocks and boulders incorporated in it, and when the mud eroded away, it left the landscape littered with the exposed rocks and boulders.

The Lassen road crossed this formation and dropped off the high ridge. It gradually leveled out onto the floor of the Sacramento Valley, where it crossed Dry Creek, Onion Creek, and finally Deer Creek before arriving at Lassen's rancho.

At Lassen's Rancho Bosquejo

Lord described the approach to Lassen's rancho on October 31, 1849:

Next course S.W. to Antelope Creek [Dry Creek?], *road descending and good—along the stream bordered by live oak, through which lies our road. This stream has a deep rocky bed, covered with boulders and furnishes abundance of good water, but the grass is everywhere fed down...*

Then he wrote:

After resting the cattle a while and congratulating and being congratulated on our safe arrival, we moved off south three miles, rising a few feet from the creek bottom to the broad level red land, which stretches off with an even surface to the next stream, south and south east. Our course nearly south. This stream is very shallow, and its bottom covered with smooth round pebbles, from the size of a pea to a large pumpkin.

This was Onion Creek, and, "...Next course S. S. W. two miles to Deer Creek. The last mile sandy and a dead level. The oaks along here are the largest, by all odds, we have yet seen." [1]

LEGENDARY TRUTHS

Lord then crossed Deer Creek, which he described as having a swift current, about twenty-five yards wide, eighteen inches deep, and lined with various kinds of trees draped with grapevines. He went on:

Lassen's establishment consists of a couple of houses built of sun dried brick and covered with logs and shakes or long split, oak shingles. He has a large enclosure south of it, irrigated by water taken down in a ditch from the creek...but I did not see anything growing in it.[2]

Delano described Lassen's rancho on September 17, 1849 as:

...two or three small adobe buildings, one of which was called by courtesy a store, having little flour, whiskey, and a few groceries for sale. Around the trading post were lounging gangs of naked Indians of both sexes, drunken Mexicans, and weary emigrants, enjoying respite from excessive fatigue in the flowing bowl; and take it all in all, it did not give me a very flattering impression of the morals of the citizens of the first establishment.[3]

On October 22, Castleman wrote:

...the country over which I have traveled today is leavel and many oak are seen scattered here and there all of which are heavy laden with acorns the grass seames to be dead but it is bright as new hay and I think equally as good   there is a great many wagons tents and half faced camps on deer creek and neare Lawson's house there seems to be some person sick in almost every one of them the [there] is a great deal of travel to and from this place flour is worth 60 cts per pound beef 35 and 40 [unreadable] $16 pr lb tea $2 lb coffee $1 pr lb   the teames came in late this eavening.[4]

Jewett, on October 8, 1849 wrote:

Went up to Lawson's ranch which consists of several buildings, built of adobe and a yard or Korel, the fences constructed of logs. This is for the purpose of branding cattle which run wild in great numbers requiring no care from their owners except to get them up and brand them once a year by a party of men on horseback.[5]

Castleman also commented on the use of horses on the rancho. On October 24, 1849, he wrote:

Lawson killed a beef this morning which done in a singular way from what I have ben accostoum to the band was driven up in 1 mile of the house and here a Buckaroo caught the [?] with a reata and he threw him an cut his throat with as much care apparently as one wowld lead a dog with a rop this was performed on horse back the animal seemed to understand his business perfectly well.[6]

Lassen's rancho was considered the long awaited end of the journey—the "Promised Land" on the banks of the "Sacred River"— "the stream of the Holy Waters," as some of the journalists referred to the Sacramento. Although the rancho and countryside were beautiful and a welcome site to the weary travelers, Lord gave a more graphic and grisly description:

There is plenty of liquor here. No lack of drink or drunkards, regular bloats, There are some dilapidated out buildings and a log house in course of erection. The whole establishment is on the bank of Deer Creek, which (the bank) is here 15 or 20 feet high and lined with alder, sycamore, willows, etc. Quarters and parts of beef hang on the trees and lie around on logs. The whole place is surrounded with filth. Bones, rags, chips, sticks, skulls, hair, skin, entrails, blood, etc. etc....The steep bank of the creek, down which all must go for water, is paved with this offal.[7]

Thousands of emigrants with the wagons, livestock, and property they were able to bring through, were arriving and passing by on a daily basis throughout the latter part of summer, and extending into the winter, when the last stragglers would arrive. Most would rest awhile, recruit their livestock, convalesce from sickness and/or scurvy, and buy what few supplies were available or that they could afford. Then they would continue on to Sacramento, San Francisco, or to the gold fields.

Major Rucker, upon hearing of the suffering of emigrants accompanying the relief party of John Peoples, returned to Lassen's

216

rancho and discovered that many of the stragglers had made it through the snow and wintry ordeal. However, John Peoples didn't arrive with the last of the emigrants until two days later on November 26, 1849. Rucker wrote in his report to General Smith:

> *A more pitiable sight I never beheld as they were brought into camp; there were cripples from scurvy and other diseases, women prostrated by weakness, and children who could not move a limb, be lifted off the animals, so entirely disabled had they become.*[8]

John Peoples was more compassionate of the women and children, but more intolerant of the men. He wrote in his report to Major Rucker:

> *I must take occasion to remark that had the men of the rear emigration thought less of their property and more of the lives of their families, I could have brought them all to the (Sacramento) valley before the storm. ....I am now well convinced that had there been no relief party, and some one...to assume command of men, women and children, that most of them would have perished in the snow.*[9]

Perhaps it is here fitting to mention again that 1849, in addition to being the "Year of the Gold Rush," was also known as the "Year of the Greenhorn." The men referred to by Peoples were the ones who left Independence at the rear of the migration, thus predisposing themselves and their families to future time restrictions and problems. They remained in the rear until the grass from the other routes was depleted, and even in the face of imminent winter danger, they continued to delay and lag behind, despite People's warnings and urgings. These were the ones, too, who would suffer the most, and shift the blame to Lassen for developing the trail in the first place.

Even after observing the hardships experienced by the emigrants on the Lassen Trail, Major Rucker evaluated reports from the relief parties under his charge on the Carson and Truckee Routes. He wrote in his report to Colonel Hooker, Assistant Adjunct General:

> *...Although the distance is much greater than by the old routes, and some of the emigrants were much longer in getting in, I cannot but think it a fortunate circumstance they*

did so, for the loss of property would have been greater on the old trail, as the grass would all have been eaten off long before they could have arrived.[10]

Doyle noted in his journal:

At the Ranch everything is a regular jam. Men going hither and yon, whiskey, some a meals victuals, others to get the meal without buying for they have nothing to buy with, some to pore forth curses and abuse upon Lassin for his rascally deceitfulness in making the Northern road. In this all hands join and the Old Dutchman is in eminent danger of losing his life and makes himself as humble as possible.[11]

In this, Doyle, along with the previous quotes, showed the vitality and importance of Lassen's rancho as an entry into California, but he also revealed the bitter feelings of many emigrants who arrived after suffering hardships equal to, and maybe greater than, those using the Carson and Truckee Routes.

It is interesting, though, to note that Doyle said they blamed "Lassin... for his deceitfulness in making the Northern road." There is no mention of Lassen or his emissaries intentionally deceiving or luring them on the route as the "legendary truths" that followed would claim. One may wonder why it was "deceitful" for him to have made a road the previous year to his own rancho. Obviously, these tired, disgruntled emigrants were scapegoating Lassen, rather than taking responsibility for their own choices for being late on the trail and for following others who knew (or didn't know) the distances involved.

If Lassen's "rascally deceitfulness" was true, then one wonders where the generosity and hospitality came from for the "others" who got a "meal without buying for they have nothing to buy with." Doyle and his "all hands" should have joined to laud rather than blame "the Old Dutchman" for this. And, surely, with thousands of emigrants pouring in, there must have been limits to that hospitality. But when Bruff straggled in to Lassen's early the next spring, he reported, "Capt Lassen pressed me to stay, and I slept here....Certainly many a starving emigrant had cause to thank him." [12]

Reports of Lassen's hospitality, and the fact that the government survey party employed him that summer, spoke as to his character and also his activities and whereabouts during the summer. This gives one cause to wonder why the "legendary" charges against him, suggesting profiteering motives for laying out the trail, and accusing him (or his representatives) of misleading emigrants at the turnoff on the Humboldt, kept recurring.

If he had anticipated the great surge of emigrants using his trail and had profiteering motives, he undoubtedly would have laid in a large supply of merchandise in preparation for their arrival. Instead, word on the trail was, "…that here were only 2 houses and nothing to be had in the way of provisions," as reported by Gray when he was in Big Valley. Yet the high prices prevailing at Lassen's rancho (as they were throughout Northern California) for what things he did have for sale, probably led most 49ers to assume they had been duped, and to charge Lassen with deliberate misrepresentation of his cutoff in order to "make money out of the emigrants."

Even John D. Unruh, in his book, *The Plains Across*, mistakenly wrote, "That Lassen profited greatly from the sale of foodstuffs and other materials to the forty-niners is clear from the letter of John Wilson to Thomas S Shackleford, Apr. 12, 1850, at San Francisco." [13]

Quoting the letter, Unruh wrote:

Wilson, who had traveled over the Lassen route in 1849, wrote, 'Last year 20 000$ worth of potatoes turnips and cabbage and pumpkins could have been sold there, besides shoes boots, clothes, beef more than 3 times that much if they had been there to be sold. Indeed, Wilson had been so impressed with the profit potential of Lassen's enterprise that he and an Oregonian purchased two-thirds of Lassen's holdings, agreeing to pay $15,000 each within five years. [14]

Note the wording "could have been sold if they had been there to have been sold"! Reading this letter correctly as Wilson wrote it, one could readily see Unruh misread it, and Wilson was touting the potential the rancho could have had if those things could have been made available for sale.

It was not only the length and difficulty of the trail that precipitated its unfavorable reputation. But, as stated before, the high prices for commodities in California, especially at Lassen's rancho, led most 49ers to believe they had been taken advantage of, and they thus wanted to blame Lassen for misrepresenting his cutoff in order to fleece them. In addition, anyone who had recommended or suggested the route, as well as some of the guides who took the route from their own experience and choice, were thought to have been emissaries of Lassen.

LEGENDARY TRUTHS

The Forty Mile Desert
And Other Routes

For a more accurate assessment of the difficulties of the Lassen Route and the criticisms, curses, and "legendary truths" assigned to it, one must consider the alternatives—compare the other routes, with their difficulties, hazards, hardships, and dangers—to those of the Lassen Route. The first two thirds of the 1849 emigration went over the Truckee and Carson Routes. Journals from the 49ers, and emigrants using these trails in successive years, gave a more balanced assessment of the deaths of animals, the loss of equipment, and the sufferings of people crossing the Black Rock Desert and the Forty Mile Desert.

It may be assumed that about a third of the 1849 emigrants went over each of the alternate trails. The Carson Route and the Truckee Route presented approximately equal difficulties ascending the Sierra Nevada. However, once over the summit, the Carson Route had the advantage of a much easier descent into the Sacramento Valley, whereas, the Truckee Route was rougher. The Carson Route did not offer an advantage in crossing the desert and, in fact, it may have been worse.

As early as July 28, 1849, Vincent Geiger was on the Humboldt and reported, "Already the grass is so scarce that we will not be enabled to get through, if at all, by merely the skin of our teeth, and what the seven thousand teams behind us are to do—God Almighty only knows." [1]

By the time the emigrants approached the desert, "they had plodded and slogged and climbed and descended nearly two thousand miles. Their animals not lost to Indians, thirst, starvation, sickness, accident, or killed to feed the poorly provisioned, were worn and thin." [2]

"Brother, the great difficulty about crossing that desert is getting to it in a condition to cross it," [3] was sound advice to the western traveler. The earlier trains to follow the Humboldt and arrive at the desert, generally arrived in better condition to cross the dry stretch and the steep mountains that followed. Later emigrants were not so fortunate, and one anonymous emigrant was quoted as saying, "Our cattle are getting so poor that it takes two of them to cast a shadow."

Fortunately, the Humboldt Sink provided a resting place where the animals could be recruited and hay cut for crossing the desert. Wakeman Bryarly, on August 9, 1849 described the scene:

This marsh for three miles is certainly the liveliest place that one could witness in a lifetime. There is some two hundred and fifty wagons here all the time. Trains going out and others coming in and taking their places, is the constant order of the day. Cattle and mules by the hundreds are surrounding us, in grass to their knees, all discoursing sweet music with the grinding of their jaws. Men are seen hurrying in many different ways, and everybody attending to his own business. Some mowing, some reaping, some carrying, some packing the grass, others spreading it out to dry, [or] collecting it for transportation. In fact the joyous laugh and familiar sound of the whetted scythe resounds from place to place and gives an air of happiness and content around that must carry the wearied travelers through to the 'Promised Land.' [4]

On July 15, 1849, William Johnston was near the front of the migration and recorded in his journal:

A march of five hours brought us to the vicinity of the Sink of the Humboldt River, at about nine o'clock; and continuing over a well beaten sandy trail until noon, we encamped on

LEGENDARY TRUTHS

*the edge of the Great Desert. Of late the region through which
we journeyed had been growing more and more desolate;
but there was reached what might be aptly termed 'the valley
of the shadow of death,' and over its portals inscribed: 'Who
enters here, leaves hope behind.'*

*Towards the south—for in that direction the road bent,
was a vast solitude covered with loose sand, which the
wind heaped in hillocks, like waves of the sea. Scarce any
vegetation existed; at long intervals might be seen a stalk
of sage or greasewood, gnarled, blackened, and looking as
if well nigh exhausted in its hard struggle for life....Where
we encamped, we found it necessary to dig wells for water.
These wells, about four feet in diameter and of a trifle less
depth, furnished an abundant supply of water, but intensely
brackish, bitter with salt and sulphur. Some mules, and men
also refused to drink of it; but with nothing else to quench the
thirst, we were painfully conscious that all would eventually
use it, before better could be found.*[5]

Beyond the Sink:

...there was found a mud lake [known as Humboldt Lake;
in some years it was a dry lakebed], *ten miles long and four
or five miles wide, a veritable sea of slime, a 'slough of
despond,' and ocean of ooze, a bottomless bed of alkaline
poison, which emitted a nauseous odor and presented
the appearance of utter desolation. The croaking of frogs
would have been a redeeming feature of the place, but no
living thing disturbed the silence and solitude of the lonely
region.*—Reuben Shaw, 1849 [6]

From here, the desert hardships began. Struggling in the deep sand
and heat, Edwin Banks was prompted to write on September 2, 1849,
"Some think they see the elephant. If fatigue, weariness, constant
excitement, and awful distress among cattle make the sight, he is
surely here."

It was here where "The mules were in a tremble of lather most of
the time—as though they smelled 'the Elephant'! Probably it was the
stench of dead cattle which affected them so." [7]

Numerous other writers recorded the intense suffering and loss of livestock and property that "the Elephant" exacted on the Forty Mile Desert in 1849 and subsequent years.

E.S. Ingalls wrote on Aug. 5, 1850:

> ... and all hurry away, leaving behind wagons, property and animals that, too weak to travel lie and broil in the sun in an agony of thirst until death relieves them of their tortures... Morning comes and the light of day presents a scene more horrid than the route of a defeated army; dead stock line the roads, wagons, rifles, tents, clothes, everything but food may be found scattered along the road; here an ox, who standing famished against a wagon bed until nature could do no more, settles back into it and dies; and there a horse kicking out his last gasp in the burning sand, men scattered along the plain and stretched out among the dead stock like corpses, fill out the picture. The desert! You must see it and feel it in an August day, when legions have crossed it before you, to realize it in all its horrors. But heaven save you from the experience. [8] And "William Kelly saw men delirious with thirst, 'howling for water,' and throwing themselves down, 'in a fainting state under the shade of the wagons.'" [9]

As early as July 22, J. D. Breyfogle predicted the problems later emigrants would have by writing:

> Our horses are failing very fast and I am doubtful whether we get them through. Times are getting very precarious. If grass does not get better very soon our horses must give out and then we must shoulder our knapsacks and foot it. Still, even at that, we are still better off than hundreds of others behind us. I think there must be a great many perish for want. There are four hundred wagons about three days behind all jambed (sic) together and must necessarily camp together and in that case their stock must perish and they must suffer. [10]

He then went on to describe the difficulties his own train was experiencing:

LEGENDARY TRUTHS

*Arrived at our camping ground about dark within six miles
of the end of the river and remained overnight without
supper as there was no wood and we dare not use the water
nor give it to our horses on account of the alkali. Travelled
25 miles. (This is truly a gloomy time. We are yet some three
hundred miles from our destination. Our horses nearly all
giving out. No grass nor much prospect of having any for
some sixty or seventy miles. If we don't, we must leave our
wagons and pack our horses, and if they give out, we must
foot it the balance of the way, and if we are detained on
the road, our provisions will run short. We hear dreadful
accounts of the sufferings in crossing the dessert (sic), but
hope it is not so bad as represented. We start at four to try
our luck.)*[11]

Later Breyfogle's predictions became manifest as he wrote on
July 26:

*...From twelve o'clock to sunrise the emigrants are passing
in crowds, nearly perishing for water, and are leaving mules,
horses and oxen to starve on the plains for they can't drive
them on. I don't know what will become of the back trains.
Hundreds must perish in crossing the desert.* [12]

Edward C. Harrow arrived at the sulphur spring three miles beyond
the Sink. On August 14, 1849, he described, "...the spring, which is
now surrounded with dead cattle, mules and horses, from which there
comes an almost unbearable stench. The water is very bad, but we have
no choice, this or none, and the greater part of the desert before us." [13]

Later, crossing the desert to the boiling spring, Harrow wrote,
"Dead and dying teams line the road and there is one continuous
stench which is almost unbearable..." And when he reached boiling
spring he reported:

*Large quantities of dead cattle are lying about, wagons
and everything we can mention is left here, presenting to
the worn out traveler the wildest wreck of destruction he
probably ever saw, and when he arrived by night or day
nearly choked with thirst, to hide[his?] horror he finds that*

225

*the water is undrinkable until it is made coffee of. Cattle too
arrive almost dead for want of water have to wait for hours
before it is cold enough for them to drink, during which
many often die, and the next traveler that comes has to step
over their stinking bodies to get some water to drink....*[14]

The Boiling Hot Springs on the Truckee route made the crossing
easier than that of the Carson Route, but deep sand bogged down the
wagons for the last seven to ten miles on both the Carson and Truckee
routes. Despite being "salty, brakish, sulphurish, and not palatable,"
the water was a lifesaver to men and livestock. Some emigrants made
it more palatable by making coffee with it, and members of the Bryant
Party "drank copiously of it."

Schallenberger, in 1845, wrote that it made his oxen sick. Later in
1852, Andrew Child, wrote, "nearly all who drank from it suffered
from its effects." Another emigrant, referring to the hissing, gurgling,
and rumbling sounds coming from the springs and geyser said, "Let us
be off: All Hell is firing up." [15]

Many journals testified to the grim scene of desolation where the
bodies of dead beasts of burden, wagons and discarded goods lined the
route, and animals were driven to the utmost limits of endurance, until
they died by the hundreds.

Bennett Clark on August 5, 1849, wrote, "All along the desert
road from the very start even the way side was strewed with the dead
bodies of oxen, mules, and horses and the stench was horrible. All our
travelling experience furnishes no parallel for all this." [16]

David Lavender's statistics, in *The Great West*, reported:

*Because the Forty-mile Desert on the familiar trail between
Humboldt Sink and Carson River was more heavily traveled,
it produced even more shocking statistics. 'I should think,'
wrote one man, 'I passed 1,200 head of cattle and horses
and a great many wagons–Harness, cooking utensils–tools
water casks etc. that cost in the United states $50,000.' On
this stretch and on all the trails, skulking Indians further
shattered morale by killing many animals from ambush,
although they killed few people.*[17]

It was said that there was $43,000 worth of wagons to be had, free, within ten miles of Carson River.

A year later, in 1850, Franklin Langworthy wrote:

> *The destruction of property upon this part of the road,*
> *is beyond all computation. Abandoned wagons literally*
> *crowded the way for twenty miles, and dead animals are*
> *so numerous, that I have counted fifty carcasses within a*
> *distance of 40 rods. The desert from side to side is strewn*
> *with goods of every name. The following articles however,*
> *are particularly abundant; log chains, wagons, wagon*
> *irons, iron bound water casks, cooking stoves and utensils,*
> *boots and shoes, clothing of all kinds, even life preservers,*
> *trunks and boxes, tin bakers, books, guns, augers, and*
> *chisels, mill and cross cut saws, good geese feathers in*
> *heaps, or blowing over the desert, feather beds, canvas*
> *tents and wagon covers.*[18]

Mrs. Margaret Frink also traveled to California with her husband in 1850 and kept a diary in which she described the horrors of what she saw on the desert:

> *Friday, August 16 [1850] ...We set forward again at ten*
> *o'clock and soon began to realize what might be before us.*
> *For many weeks we had been accustomed to see property*
> *abandoned and animal dead or dying. But those scenes were*
> *here doubled and trebled. Horses, mules, and oxen, suffering*
> *from heat, thirst, and starvation, staggered along until they*
> *fell and died on every rod of the way. Both sides of the road*
> *for miles were lined with dead animals and abandoned*
> *wagons. Around them were strewed yokes, chains, harness,*
> *guns, tools, bedding, clothing, cooking-utensils, and many*
> *other articles, in utter confusion. The owners had left*
> *everything, except what provisions they could carry on their*
> *backs, and hurried on to save themselves.*[19]

James Bennett painted a disturbing picture of the sights he, too, observed crossing the desert:

> *...The destruction of property here [the desert near Carson*
> *River] is immense. For forty miles the road is strewn with*

abandoned wagons and sometimes the whole of their contents except provisions. Whole caralles (sic), numbering five or six wagons, were found deserted and the place literally covered with dead cattle; many of them still tied to the wheels of the wagons. The whole air throughout the desert was tainted with the smell of carrion. The night was unusually cold and we passed several encampments where persons were burning wagons to warm themselves. At four o'clock a.m. we came to a halt by two or three old wagons which we used as fuel for cooking. During our journey in the night we had left two cows and an ox on the desert, unable to travel any further. At nine o'clock one entire team gave out and we were compelled to leave a wagon within six miles of the river and drive the cattle onto water....[20]

Elisha Perkins crossed the desert in 1849 and reported:

On the last desert as on others we saw great numbers of dead cattle mules, horse etc. We passed in our two nights march somewheres near 130 or 140 oxen. Killed mostly by the sulphur water and hunger. 15 or 20 were lying about the hot springs, some still alive and dying by inches, poor things I could but pity their hard fate. No possible chance for them to escape. Nothing to eat or drink. The country in the vicinity of the springs and in fact all the way for the last 100 or 150 miles is certainlly (sic) the most dreary—desolate, God forsaken region that can be imagined—sand—sand from our hill mountains and valleys nothing but sand, with a scattered growth of miserable brown stunted sage…giving the landscape an ashy hue. May I be delivered from ever seeing such another tract. It is enough to shrivel a man's soul into assimilation with the products of the soil. Soil? There is no soil of pure sands of Araby.[21]

On the Truckee Route, after crossing the desert, the Truckee River provided water to save the ones who made it across, but it also became an obstacle in itself, being a swift, cold current, having to be crossed many times on the way to the fearfully steep and rugged pass.

William G. Johnston was a member of the first wagon train to enter California in the memorable year of 1849. Even being at the front of the migration, he commented about the difficulties of the route and the shortage of grass on the pass:

> *...The stream in its precipitous course dashed furiously against great rocks, which lay in its way, foaming and fretting madly; scarce more so than did we when having got over the ridge, we found the road frightfully steep, quite narrow and beset with rocks. Had not others preceded us we might have questioned whether such difficulties were not insurmountable. Within the narrow gap which we ascended the sun never enters, and the air had the chilliness of an ice house. Our night camp at seven o'clock was made alongside the mountain torrent. Grass was scarce, and the mules were obliged to subsist on the recollection of excellent pasturage enjoyed in the morning; a fodder not very fattening...*[22]

On the way to the pass, the trail passed the gruesome remains of the Donner tragedy, where Elisha Perkins described the situation and its difficulties so well:

> *I gathered some relics as curiosities and left, thankful that late as my journey had been prolonged, I was still safe from any such catastrophe as befell those unfortunates (speaking of the Donner Party).*[23]
>
> *Up, up we toiled wondering every five minutes how 'the dickens' ox teams and wagons can get over here, and it is a wonder indeed, until at 3 p.m. we arrived at the foot of the terrible 'Passage on the backbone.' For half an hour before arriving we could hear the shouts of teamsters urging their cattle up the steep and when we were near enough to see through the forest we could look up nearly over our heads and see wagons and cattle looking like pigmies, and as if almost suspended in the air. The 'Pass' is through a slight depression in the mountains being some 1500 or 2000 feet lower than the tops in its immediate vicinity. As we came up to it the appearance was exactly like marching up to some immense wall built directly across our path so perpendicular is this dividing ridge and the road going up to its very base turns short to the right and ascends by a track cut in the side of the mountains till two thirds up when it turns left again*

and goes directly over the sumit.

The distance to the top of the pass I should judge to be about ½ mile, and in this short space the elevation attained is somewhere near 2000 feet! The mountain is mostly rock. Where the road is cut tho' it is red clay and stone, which by travel and sliding of animals feet has been much cut and powdered up making a deep dust on the first half of the steep. At the foot of the ascent we found the Missionary Train from Indiana, preparing for the Enterprise. One wagon had already started with 13 yoke of cattle attached, the load in the wagon not exceeding 600 lbs, and they could get but a few yards at a time stopping to rest their team. They were about half way up when in an inclining place the wagon began to slide over the precipice! The men seizing hold at all points stopped its progress to destruction, and by some management it was placed upon the road again. Had it got a fair start over the hillside it must have dragged all the cattle with it down upon the rocks below. We leading each his mule, began to scramble up sometimes upon 'all fours' like our animals, and glad enough were we to stop 'to blow' several times before reaching the top. [24]

On the Carson Route, those emerging from the desert came to Carson River, which likewise provided water but didn't require the river crossings the Truckee did:

Ragtown here on the Carson River is named from the interminable piles of wind-strewn rags discarded by the emigration. And, despite all that has been left behind on the plains in the way of iron, it might just as well be called "Irontown.' Hundreds get this far with wagons, but have broken their animals down in the process; the iron remains of burned wagons strew the plains and river shore. And for that matter, Feathertown is a suburb of Ragtown—for, back up the trail a mile or two, someone ripped up a feather mattress to get the ticking, and an acre or two meets the eye on arriving here. [25]

Keep in mind that these emigrants, who suffered so and lost so much in livestock, wagons, and property, were the earlier arrivals—ahead of the seven thousand plus emigrants who chose the Lassen Trail as an alternate route. What would the toll have been had they, too, come this way? In addition, the mountain passes still remained ahead, to cause more delay, suffering, and loss.

Before going over the mountains, James Bennett wrote:

> *Leaving Carson Valley the road for six or eight miles passes over a range of high and barren bluffs and enters Carson River Canyon. I shall not attempt a description of this mountain pass but simply remark, that for the passage of wagons, this is as difficult, perhaps, as the imagination can conceive....* [26]

Then came the pass, which was supposedly as difficult as the Truckee Route. James Bennett described it in this way:

> *...we commenced the ascent of the third and last range. This was the worst day, dead horses and cattle strewn the road from end to end. It is sufficient indication of the terrible hardships to be encountered by those less fortunate than ourselves. Two of our best horses died during our encampment, before reaching the summit. We were also for a time in the region of eternal snow.* [27]

1849 Rescue Party

With the arrival of the early emigrants into the Sacramento Valley came news of the thousands who followed, of the lack of grass on the route, and hardships they would undoubtedly experience. Letters were arriving, carried by messengers, with pleas for help. People in California, especially citizens of San Francisco, began to grow alarmed. Fear of a repeat of the Donner Tragedy caused them to take action at the reports of thousands of emigrants, some including women and children, remaining on the trails as winter was approaching.

General Persifor Smith, in his capacity as commander of the Pacific Division of the U. S. Army, decided to send relief parties to aid the incoming emigrants. He ordered Major Daniel H. Rucker, Assistant Quartermaster—supplied with a hundred thousand dollars out of the Civil Fund—to purchase supplies and hire men and mules to send out and meet the emigrants on all trails. Citizens of San Francisco supplemented this amount with donations equaling twelve thousand dollars.

The fact that General John Wilson (who was a kinsman of President Zachary Taylor and had been appointed by him on March 30, 1849 as Indian Agent to California) was among the emigrants at the end of the migration, was probably a significant factor in the decision to allocate government funds for the rescue.

LEGENDARY TRUTHS

Major Rucker performed his duty efficiently by sending out pack trains to the many routes by which the emigrants were known to be approaching. He, himself, went with one of these trains and remained in the mountains until the last emigrant had been brought in. The expedition undoubtedly saved many a life. The selection of Rucker to head this effort was only one example of the dependence always placed upon the army in cases of emergency and illustrated the concern of Californians for those caught in the mountain snows, such as members of the Murphy-Townsend-Stephens Party in the winter of 1844-45 and those of the Donner Party in the winter of 1846-47.

When Milton McGee arrived at Sacramento on September 17, 1849, after having just crossed the Lassen Trail, he wrote:

> *Maj. Rucker Sir: I have been informed that you were, on the part of our government, sending out provisions to relieve the emigrants now on their journey to this country. I have just come in from the northern route, and can assure you from my own knowledge, that many are now entirely destitute of provisions, while others will not have a sufficiency to bring them within many days travel of the Sacramento Valley.*
>
> *Since I have piloted the foremost wagons on the northern route, many, in fact nearly all of those in the rear have followed; and I would most respectfully suggest the propriety of your sending them such relief as their present situation requires.*
>
> *Very respectfully, your ob't servant,*
> *Milton McGhee** [1]

By mid September, Major Rucker had relief teams on each of the three overland trails: the Carson, Truckee, and Lassen routes. The teams were to backtrack on each route to dispense provisions, oxen, and mules to those in need. And they were to ensure that those in the rear would cross the mountains before the winter storms struck.

Charles Kilburn had orders to leave Sacramento in September with relief for the emigrants on the Truckee route, and camped about thirty miles from the summit.

---

* Most historians spell his name McGee. Pierson B. Reading in his journal spelled it McGhee, as it is spelled here.

As we were now approaching the rear of the emigration on this road, I endeavored to obtain accurate information of our road, the actual condition of the emigrants on it. On consultation with Dr. White, he informed me there was but one other train behind. This proved to be true; and as I found I was at the time but about fifty miles from the Carson line, where we could dispose of our relief to better advantage, I concluded to change over to that route.

Reaching the Carson line in about sixty miles, he reported:

On the summits we found a fall of snow; and in many places it had drifted to four or five feet in depth. In a short report of this kind it is impossible to detail the amount of suffering relieved by my party on the two lines. The energy and generosity of the government in thus relieving the needy was openly expressed and commented on by the whole of the emigrants. After passing the two summits on our return, we found many in utmost need.[2]

John Chandler who had originally been sent to the Carson route wrote:

I then proceeded with my train to the canon, on Carson River, which I reached on 12th October. There I found some twenty wagons, the emigrants owning them having passed by my trail, and directed to advance to that point where relief would be given them. On the next day I distributed amongst the persons accompanying said wagons, about forty-four mules; finding them persons in a very destitute condition, and wholly unable to proceed without immediate and extensive aid.[3]

What if, rather than taking the Lassen Trail, seven or eight thousand more emigrants had followed this route?

Robert Hunt, with orders to provide help on the Carson River road, wrote:

On the 14th we met Captain Kilburn, of the U.S.A., returning who informed us that the emigration was not so large as we had been led to expect, as much the greater portion of those who were behind, had been induced by Lieutenant Hawkins and several others to take the extreme northern or old Oregon route, which, owing to the lateness of the season, was considered the safest; he also Informed me that Dr. P.B. Brown, of St. Louis, was entirely out of provisions, and was in a perfectly destitute condition, as he had all his mules and cattle frozen to death in the snow-storm of the 11th, and had been compelled to abandon everything, with his wagons, near the second or last summit. I immediately despatched two men with provisions to his relief....On the following day we met the Pioneer train in quite a crippled condition, having lost thirty of their best mules the night before, by Indian ...

A couple of days later, farther east on the trail, and after helping several destitute groups, he reached Lick Springs:

...and then found the family and train of Dr. B.B. Brown [before, he had written "Dr. P.B, Brown"], *waiting for the return of the Doctor who had gone back after his wagons with the government cattle furnished him by Colonel Foreman. We then learned the particulars of the storm of the 11th. His wagons had just commenced the ascent of the last summit when they were overtaken by the storm; the wind blew so strong, the snow and hail fell so thick and fast that they found it utterly impossible to proceed any farther, and were compelled to wait till the following day for it to abate; several of his train were frosted, and all of his stock, but two mules that were tied close to a large lire* [fire], *were frozen to death.*[4]

According to George Stewart:

Near the summit on the Carson Route, the altitude was over eight thousand feet, and the storm of October 10 was severe. One party was caught just as its wagons had started the last ascent. Hard-blown hail and snow flew so thickly that no one could proceed. The party encamped and built fires. During the night several people were frostbitten. Two mules, which kept close to the fires were saved. All the other stock, mules and oxen, froze to death. Fortunately the storm was of short duration.[5]

Last on the Carson Trail was Sarah Royce, with her husband, Josiah, and daughter. In her diary, she wrote of meeting with the relief party.

Presently at the head of [a] steep incline appeared two horsemen....As they came nearer, they smiled, and the forward one said (to my husband), 'You and your wife, and that little girl, are what brought [us] as far as this.... We belong to the Relief Company sent out by order of the United States Government to help the late emigrants over the mountains. We were ordered only as far as Truckee Pass. When we got there we met a little company that had just got in....There was a woman and some children with them; and that woman set right to work at us fellows to go on over the mountains after a family they met on the desert....She said that there was only one wagon, and a woman and a child in it; and she knew they would never get through them canons and over them ridges without help....And she kept at me so, I couldn't get rid of her. You see I've got this man to come with me and here we are, to give you more to eat, and let you have these two mules, and tell you how to get right over the mountains, the best and quickest way.[6]

Leaving their wagon behind, the Royces packed their belongings on one mule. Sarah and her daughter rode the other, and Mr. Royce walked beside them. Sarah was afraid of falling with her daughter, so in rough areas had her husband ride and hold the girl. But getting accustomed to riding, she wrote, "…on the second day of our new style of travelling I rode twenty-five miles…A week later, we crossed the highest ridge, viewed the 'promised land,' and began our descent into warmth and safety." [7]

With relief activities concluded on both the Truckee and Carson routes before snow blocked the passes, the focus turned to the Lassen Trail, where the last of the migration was trailing in. But again, consider the problems that would have occurred if the seven to eight thousand emigrants behind the Royces had continued to follow them from Lassen's Meadows, rather than take the Northern Route (Lassen Trail).

As early as October, snow was reported on both the Carson and

LEGENDARY TRUTHS

Lassen Routes. However, of the two, the higher altitude, temperatures, and snow conditions grew worse because "hard-blown hail and snow flew so thickly that no one could proceed" on the Carson Route.

Whereas, on the Lassen route, Doyle wrote, also on October 10:

> *Last night snow fell on the mountains to the depth of 4 inches. Day cloudy and cold and everybody is pushing forward as fast as possible, fearing that winter has set in and they may be caught in the snow. God help the hindmost. About dusk snow commenced falling quite rapid and continued until I went to bed.*[8]

By October 28, Charles Kilburn wrote on the Carson Route, "On the summits we found a fall of snow; and in many places it had drifted to four or five feet in depth."[9] But it wasn't until November 4, that snow became a real concern on the Lassen route. As recorded by Orson Pratt, "The snow covers the ground. Some of our cattle are frozen to death! The rest of them are unable to move."[10]

The last of the emigrants reached the Sacramento Valley on November 26, and the lateness was partly due to the extra miles required on the Lassen Route. However, this was a full month later than when freezing cold and drifts of snow "four or five feet in depth" were troubling the emigrants on the Carson Route. Even if the last of the migration in 1849 had saved time by choosing the shorter route, they would still have been behind Dr. Brown and the Royces, whose sufferings and losses were equal to those on the Lassen Trail.

The Lassen Trail had the advantage of not having the high passes to surmount, as did the Truckee and Carson Routes. Major Rucker, who was in charge of the rescue efforts on all the trails, evaluated reports from the relief parties under his charge on all the routes. He concluded that it was "…a fortunate circumstance" that the later emigrants chose the Lassen route rather than the others, " for the loss of property would have been greater on the old trail, as the grass would all have been eaten off long before they could have arrived."[11]

PART 4

Lassen 1849 and Beyond

1849–1850
Dealing with the Wilsons

But all these evils became insignificant in comparison with the swollen torrent of shysters, who came from Missouri and other states of the Union. No sooner had they arrived than they assumed the title of attorney, and began to seek means of depriving the Californians of their farms and other properties...these legal thieves, clothed in the robes of the law, took from us our lands and our houses without the least scruple enthroned themselves in our homes like so many powerful kings.
—Mariano Guadalupe Vallejo

Among the emigrants to receive help from Peter Lassen were General John Wilson and his family, who were some of the last to get out of the mountains. Wilson had sent requests ahead for help from Lassen, stating that he was a representative of the U.S. Government and that the government would reimburse Lassen by for any supplies and services he rendered. Wilson also received help from the government rescue party, but according to John Peoples, he was difficult to deal with, and through his stubbornness, he lost livestock and brought undue hardship upon himself and his family. Moreover, his arrival in the Sacramento Valley would also (as stated in the above quote from General Vallejo) bring undue hardship and ongoing financial ruin to Peter Lassen.

A kinsman of President Zachary Taylor, John Wilson was a Missouri lawyer with "more than ordinary ability," and he had a "large practice." From July 5, 1827, to July 25, 1828, he was editor of the *Missouri Intelligencer.*[1]

> *In politics Wilson was strongly pro-Adams and bitterly anti-Jackson. One writer notes that he was of 'violent prejudice and temper.' A letter of July 14, 1827, in the Leonard Collection, describes a near-riot that took place at the scene of a barbecue held at Fayette on July 4th, because of an unauthorized political oration, which 'teemed with abuse of Adams and laud of Jackson'; and that 'then Wilson got up and spoke bitterly.' While other man (and some women) tried to pacify the crowd, Wilson 'stood surly as a bore, wielding a three-foot cane around his head.'*[2]

Before leaving for California, Wilson had been a guest at the home of his kinsman the president, Zachary Taylor, and conferred with him about a cabinet appointment to which he aspired. On March 30, 1849, Taylor appointed Wilson Special Agent for the Indians of what was then called the Deseret-California region, perhaps to assuage his disappointment at not being given a cabinet position. However, Read and Gaines suggested that perhaps Zachary Taylor's major purpose for sending his kinsman to California was to form a Mormon liaison for establishing the state of Deseret as a non-slave state.[3]

By combining the two free (Deseret and California) territories into one, it would have had the desirable effect of decreasing the number of free states entering into the Union, thus preserving the balance of power in the Senate.

Nevertheless, in 1849 President Zachary Taylor, eager to avoid disputes as much as possible, sent his agent John Wilson westward with a military escort of the Mounted Regiment under the command of Brevet Captain R. M. Morris. A week after Wilson's arrival in the Great Salt Lake Valley, claiming to represent the U.S. Government, he had a crucial conference with Brigham Young and the leadership of the Mormons. Wilson assured them that President Taylor had commissioned him to inform them that the President "fully appreciated their situation," and was favorably disposed toward the Mormons. Later, when he arrived in California, Wilson was a signer of the Deseret Petition, which never came to fruition.

The sixty-year-old Wilson, traveling with his wife and family, had great trouble with his military escort, and continually disagreed with Captain Morris. Finally, at Goose Creek he dismissed the captain and his army escort. Wilson then procured the guidance of General Joel Palmer (who had been with Lieutenant Hawkins' military supply train going east) to take him on to California.

Morris and the army escort continued on the Carson Route, where Morris lost his wagons and mules on the desert, and General Persifor Smith sent out one of the government relief expeditions to aid him. Palmer guided the Wilson Party on to the Lassen Trail, where they suffered the theft of twenty-two mules by Indians, and in Fandango Valley, Wilson, out of necessity, "caached" half his goods—among them his "Law Books." They were also aided by another government relief expedition sent out by General Persifor Smith.

On November 1, the relief expedition under John Peoples reported he had:

> *...reached the upper Feather River valley, where I found all the rear of the emigration with General Wilson, family, and escort....I urged the emigrants to move on, and also General Wilson. To the General I gave two mules to haul on his family carriage, and argued the propriety of his abandoning his wagons and packing his mules lightly. He did not agree with me, and that night he lost all his mules in the storm, whilst mine were safely sheltered in the valley.*[4]

General John Wilson sent the following letter, addressed to Peter Lassen, ahead with his son, William, reminding Lassen of their past association, proclaiming his status and importance as an agent of the government, asking for help from Lassen, and promising payment. As stated, Wilson was being guided by Joel Palmer who had accompanied Burnett in helping Lassen come in to his rancho the previous year from Lassen's Big Meadows. Therefore, Lassen was also familiar with Palmer.

Is it any wonder then, that Lassen's confidence in them was swayed into accepting them as partners in his business? And, is it fair for historians, like Ruby Swartzlow, to assume that he probably had "poor business ability," or for John Unruh, David Lavender, or Will Bagley to describe him variously as "incompetent," "sly," "wily," or as "an affable but inept Dane"? Wilson was convincing and disingenuous, as we shall see, in his dealings with Lassen and others.

> *Feather River 4th Nov 1849.*
> *Peter Lassen Esqre.*
> *Sir,*
> *One of your old acquaintances (the writer) is in a considerable of a fix. I send my son and drivers of my men to you for aid: they will tell you all our circumstances and our needs.*
>
> *I rely on your aid and kindness and hope if you can aid me you will do so and if not, that you will help my son Wm. and the men with him to obtain the needed relief. You will remember me as having many years resided at Fayette, Howard Co. Mo. I am appointed Indian agent and also Navy Agent for all California.*
>
> *Any arrangement my son and you make I will fulfill. I shall I hope be on in a day or two after him but if possible he will like to return with the needed relief if he can before I get there. In the meantime please to supply him and the men with him, with provisions and such quarters as will make them comfortable till I come and if any of them want to go ahead without waiting for my arrival give the provisions to take them on to Sutters and I will pay you for it.*
>
> *Your attention and kindness to these matters and to them will lay me under great obligations to you for which I hope in person to thank you in a few days as well as pay you for them. If Mr Lassen is not at home this note is addressed to any gentleman who may be in that neighborhood and they may rely upon my doing to them the proper thing:*
> *Your old friend*
> *John Wilson* [5]

Wilson himself reported:

*All died when we were overtaken by the snow…leaving us on
foot with part of our train 80 miles apart…and we were left
on foot and had to encamp till I sent my son (Wm. Henry)
through the snow and rain to the settlements for animals to
carry my wife and daughters. Here in a second cache was
left the 'balance of our goods.'[6]*

His son traveled with William Swain, carrying Wilson's letter
to Lassen. When they passed Bruff's Camp on November 5, 1849,
Bruff wrote:

*Hear that General Wilson's family consists of 2 young ladys,
the mother, 2 sons young men, and a little boy, and that they
have been compelled to abandon every thing, even their
carriage, for want of animals.—That they have cached, in
Pitt and Feather river valleys, an extensive and valuable law
library, and many valuable goods, including silks, etc.—and
the relief party, are assisting them forward, having furnished
the females and children with mules. In one of the wagons at
my camp, is a large circular tent; this I shall pitch, and with
pine branches and old clothes, bags, etc. can make them a
comfortable lodging place, when they come up.[7]*

William Henry (young Wilson) arrived at Lassen's rancho with
Wilson's plea for help on November 8, 1849,[8] and Lassen later
confirmed this with his court testimony,[*] stating that Wilson, his wife
and family, and Joel Palmer were detained by snows in the mountains,
and requested assistance and provisions. Lassen said he sent mules,
horses, (many of which were lost on the journey) and provisions, by
which they were enabled to reach his rancho in safety.

Lassen said Wilson represented himself as being an agent for the
government of the United States and that he was traveling at the expense
of the same. Wilson promised that the government would pay Lassen
for his assistance, provisions, etc.[9] However, Lassen claimed he never
received any compensation from Wilson, Palmer, or the government.

The General later wrote to a Mr. Abiel Leonard in Missouri, saying
that it commenced snowing and raining in the mountains for fourteen

---

[*]   In 1853, The Wilsons would sue Peter Lassen and Henry Gerke
over ownership of *Rancho Bosquejo.*

days and nights, and:

> *As for the animals brought back by Wm. Henry from*
> *Lassen's, the roads being impassible they were of little use*
> *as travelling out there exhausted them so that out of 8 we*
> *lost 3 before we got to the settlement, and my whole family*
> *had to walk on foot, ...some of us not having a 'change of*
> *raiment' to put on wading through snow 2 ½ feet deep, and*
> *roads with no bottom that a mule could reach, and remain*
> *head above ground.*[10]

On November 12, 1849, Bruff welcomed them to his camp:

> *Near Sun Set Genl. Wilson's family and company came up,*
> *and I accommand(at)ed them with lodgings—circular tent*
> *for the ladies, large square one for General and soms (sons),*
> *and wagons for the others, though several preferred sleeping*
> *around the camp-fire.*[11]

Wilson's party left after breakfast the next morning on the thirteenth. Wilson went on to spend a couple of days at the Davis Place, as the creeks were running deep and difficult to cross. While there, Wilson mentioned to Davis his interest in purchasing a portion of Lassen's rancho. It is pertinent to note that, while in Missouri, Wilson became interested in land speculation and at one time wrote to Abiel Leonard that he had purchased a half-interest in a claim for fifteen million acres of land, and claimed that the heirs were pressing him to buy the other half.[12] (Perhaps this was a foreshadowing of what would transpire between him and Peter Lassen in 1849. One wonders what happened to the fifteen-million acres in Missouri, and how the other partners fared—or suffered.)

During Wilson's stay at Lassen's rancho, he and Palmer advised Lassen that it would be better, and advisable, for him to take into partnership some active young man to assist in managing his rancho, "to protect and keep the emigrants from stealing his stock etc." Wilson proposed himself and Palmer as such partners, and as an inducement to accept his proposition, he presented his qualifications to Lassen. Lassen later testified in court:

> *...that by reason of his official Character and position under*

the general government he [Wilson] *could influence the sale of a large portion of the lots of said City of Benton** on said rancho and by his capital and influence would then build up a large town while the defendant* [Lassen] *and said Palmer, with the assistance of said Wilson's name, capital and influence and by proper and energetic management would be able to raise and sell a larger amount of produce and vegetables by means of all which they would make a large fortune for each of them; and defendant further says that trusting to the representations of said Wilson and having a great respect for and confidence in the Government of the United States and its agents, he was induced to listen to the persuasions of said Wilson and Palmer and finally it was arranged between them and defendant that defendant should enter into an agreement with said Wilson and Palmer each one third part of four leagues of the lands of said Rancho and Stock and of defendants interest in said Benton City, upon their each paying to him the sum of $15000.00 (making altogether the sum of $30,000.00) of which sum $6000.00 (being $3000 by each) was to be paid in one year in Cash and the balance in five years during which time said Palmer was to live upon and personally assist in conducting and managing said rancho, and said Wilson was to sell the lots and build up said City of Benton; And when said Wilson and Palmer had performed their agreement and made said payments in full defendant was to convey to each of them one third part of said four leagues of said Rancho, Stock and of his interest in said City of Benton. Said Wilson thereupon drew up a writing which he informed defendant was to the effect of the above statement, the defendant not being able to read or well to understand or speak the english language, and having at that time great confidence in said Wilson, trusted to his representations respecting said writing and signed the same.*[13]

---

* Ironically, Wilson was an inveterate enemy of Thomas Hart Benton. Wherever Benton spoke in Missouri, Wilson would counter with a scathing rebuttal, as Wilson was an avid hater of any members of an opposing political party, which he called *"Locofocos."*

LEGENDARY TRUTHS

Because General Wilson, United States Indian Agent and Naval Agent for all California, was so influential, Bruff had earlier made special efforts for the Wilson's comfort at Bruff's Camp. And, Wilson's arrival in San Francisco was awaited with interest in both military and government circles. His influence also gained Lassen's confidence, but Lassen's inability to speak and read English fluently made him vulnerable to misinterpretations and misunderstandings.

Lassen had a store on the rancho for the sale of goods and merchandise. John Young had an interest in the store, and Wilson and Palmer wanted Lassen to buy out Young's interest, saying he could make a better "arrangement" with Young than they could. They then inventoried the store and goods at $1,100.00.

William Myers, who had a comfortable home on the rancho, later testified that:

> *Palmer had a problem with the ownership of the stock in the store and Palmer was about to fly off. Wilson wanted me to go into it in Palmers place. I said I had not means enough to do so, and Wilson said they had a credit of five years and could make it out of the Stock in that time I then asked Wilson why he did not buy the half of it himself, he replied it was better to have three, as a majority could govern and he and I could control Lassen. I then said in that case I would have nothing to do with it and the conversation then ended.[14]*

Later in the trial, Peter Lassen testified:

> *Wilson and Palmer agreed that they together would advance or furnish to defendant goods or money to double the amount of said inventory, about the sum of $2,200.00. Soon after said agreement said Wilson and Palmer left said rancho by a boat for Sacramento City as they declared to purchase a stock of goods and supplies for said Rancho and store and requested defendant to meet them there with teams and wagons to take said goods to said Rancho; defendant immediately proceeded to Sacramento City with four or five of his teams etc. but could not there find or hear of said Wilson and Palmer except that they had left that place for San Francisco without purchasing goods or leaving any message for defendant.[15]*

247

According to their agreement, Lassen:

...then purchased goods for said Store and rancho to the amount of about $4,557, but by reason of the same and, overflow of the Sacramento river and its tributaries he was unable to return by land to said rancho and found it necessary and did purchase for the sum of $8000.00 a small steamboat to transport himself and said goods to his said rancho and with the expectations of using said boat in forwarding the objects and designs of said partnership all which was afterward approved by said John Wilson; And defendant says he paid to Smith Bensley Co of whom he purchased the same for said goods and Steamboat about the sum of $12,557, excepting therefrom about the sum of $3,000 for which he gave them his notes for all which said Wilson and Palmer by and under their agreements with him were equally liable with defendant; that said defendant took said goods to said rancho where many of them were sold and disposed of by William Wilson a son of said John Wilson and whom he had left at said rancho. No part of the proceeds of which were ever paid over to or received by defendant.[16]

At this point in the history of Lassen's life, the "legendary truths" spin fact into fable. *Fairfield's Pioneer History of Lassen County* quoted the *Red Bluff Beacon,* saying:

In the spring of 1850, Peter Lassen having disposed of one half of his ranch to Palmer, took several teams of oxen to Sacramento City to purchase some provisions and while there conceived the idea of selling his cattle and buying a steamboat, the most unfortunate speculation of his life. Mr. Palmer sold his interest in the concern to General Wilson, and while Peter with his purchase (the little steamer Washington) was cordelling up the river with his Indians, other parties were taking away and selling his cattle.[17]

Franklin Scott wrote that:

Lassen had bought the Lady Washington, a small steamer built at Sutter's embarcadero in the fall of 1849; perhaps he had even helped to build it. More likely he had been involved in some sort of partnership in the venture of owning the steamboat.[18]

However, we know that Lassen couldn't have helped build it, because he was busy during the summer and fall guiding Lieutenant Williamson, and he was at his rancho until the last emigrants, including Wilson and Palmer, arrived in November.

On January 3, 1850, John Wilson wrote the following letter to Lassen.

> *Peter Lassen Esqre. Sir,*
> *I was glad to hear from Capt. Peoples that you had bought for us a small steamboat; it will add greatly to the prospect of doing a good business. I hope you will keep all the force you can sowing wheat, barley and be sure to have a very large Store of vegetables put in.... I feel that we ought to [be] very anxious to have a large crop of vegetables and indeed everything that we can raise for accounts have reached us here perfectly satisfactory to show that the emigration next year will far exceed that which came in by your road and if no more than what came in this year comes next we can sell all we can raise and more...I have been told by experienced persons they would bring very high prices and that contracts might be made before bringing them down. I only mention this for your Consideration for you know about these matters better than I do.*
> *I am with great Respect*
> *Your Old Friend*
> *John Wilson*[19]

Interestingly, Bruff mentioned other steamers. On May 15, 1850, he wrote, "The little steamer (not named) passed down stream this morning. I went down, 2 miles, to Meyer's house (on town site)." Then on June 8, he wrote, "At dusk the Steamer Lawrence, Capt. Chadwick, arrived at Lassen's Landing." Bruff had slept onboard.[20]

Swartzlow, in *Lassen His Life and Legacy* wrote, "It is reported that Lassen purchased a steamboat in the fall of 1849 to haul supplies up the Sacramento to his ranch and that it was wrecked." She continued,

"…Lassen did have a keen interest in ships. Ownership of a steamboat would have had great appeal to him."[21]

Read and Gaines, who edited Bruff's diary, noted:

> *However, Hutchings' Illustrated California Magazine (IV,4) contains an interesting statement in connection with this 'little steamer Washington.' It says that the 'Lady Washington,' a sternwheeler, was built at Sutter's embarcadero in Sept., 1849, that it ran on the upper waters, being the first to ascend above the mouth of the American River. According to this account the little steamer struck a snag, sank, was later raised and renamed the 'Ohio.' If Peter Lassen purchased the 'Lady Washington,' and if, as Hutchings' Magazine states, it struck a snag, this might explain why Peter's steamboat venture was unlucky.*[22]

Read and Gaines also found:

> *In an obituary of Charles Lincoln Wilson,* * The Themis, Dec. 20. 1890, stated: 'in the spring of 1850 [he] brought the first steamer that traversed the upper waters of the Sacramento river, to a point above the Feather river and as far as Deer creek, where Peter Lassen had located…'* They then later suggested, *Since Lassen and Colonel Charles Wilson were partners, why not suppose this first steamer north of Sacramento City to have been jointly owned by the two men, or to have been owned by Lassen and underwritten by Wilson?*[23]

To dispel the "legendary truths," Lassen's court testimony said he paid $8,000 as agreed by John Wilson. He successfully returned to his rancho with the provisions and goods and did not sink the boat, as some legends imply. It seems that Lassen's voyage was the first as far upriver as his rancho, but other steamboats followed. The ownership

---

* Charles Lincoln Wilson was not related to General John Wilson. Swartzlow said he was born in Maine, arrived in San Francisco in December 1849 aboard the steamship *Oregon*. He apparently acquired Palmer's interest in the three-way partnership with John Wilson and Lassen. In 1850, he tried to hire Bruff to survey and lay out Red Bluff. In 1851, he built a plank road in San Francisco. In 1855, he was one of the developers of the Sacramento Valley Railroad.

of boats, their names, which one sunk, and by whom, becomes unclear in the shadows of history.

In the same court case, Augustus Easton testified that he:

> ...was employed in Sacramento City as engineer on a steamboat up to Lassen's Ranch, He took a note for his services and presented it to Charles Wilson, who claimed 'it was a matter with which he had nothing to do.' It was signed J. Palmer and Co. and signed by young Wilson. Lassen later paid part of it and Gerke gave him a note, part of which has been paid. He testified that he had heard of Charles Wilson trying to run a steamboat up to Tehama and sunk it.[24]

Captain Thomas Lyle testified he was commander of the steamboat *California* for Wilson and others. He recognized Charles Wilson as one of the owners, and in the winter of 1850 and 1851, he took charge of the steamboat with the understanding that it was to run to Benton City. "Previous to this and early in 1851, Wilson and myself chartered California to go to Benton with goods and freight, but we could not get there." Later, on cross-examination, he testified, "I was permanently engaged to run the Steamboat to Benton on wages and that was my first trip. The house of Belknap and White paid me for my services."[25]

Henry L. Ford testified he was on board Charles Wilson's steamboat when it sank below Benton City. He said Mr. Belknap was on board and appeared to exercise acts of ownership. Cross examined, he said he didn't know if Charles Wilson owned the steamboat.

Augustus Belknap testified that Charles Wilson chartered a steamboat from Belknap and White and later bought a large interest in the steamboat, which he sank and lost on running it up to Benton City.

The purchase of the provisions for the rancho and the cost of the steamboat put Lassen deeply in debt, while at the same time John Wilson's son, William Henry Wilson was managing the rancho and selling off cattle and goods—the profits of which were not returned to Lassen, nor used to dispel the debt. Thus, Lassen was forced to find a buyer (Henry Gerke) for his rancho so he could pay off his debts. He later (in 1853, in the court case mentioned above) testified that the Wilson-Palmer deal had cost him $100,000 in goods and property.[26]

Incredulously, Swartzlow stated a "legendary truth" that, "The reason for Lassen's lack of financial success was probably poor business ability." [27] However, he was respected and considered industrious by his neighbors, wherever he lived. Earlier, John Sutter was so impressed with Lassen's ability that he wrote in a letter to the U.S. Consul, Thomas O. Larkin, "P. Lassen is building a water saw and griss mill. He have already a good horse mill. He will be rich in a few years. He is a very industrious man."[28] Lassen was very successful, accumulating a sizeable wealth in land and stock until the Gold Rush brought problems.

René Lassen wrote in *Uncle Peter:*

> *They arrived to* Bosquejo Rancho, *rested here for a while—and to thank Peter Lassen for his helpfulness, they sometimes stole his cattle and other belongings. Many of the people who robbed his ranch were people who had been visiting there before—and whom Lassen had been helping in difficult situations.* [29]

Although he (René Lassen) didn't say so, this could have referred directly to General John Wilson and his son, William Henry, and maybe even to Joel Palmer, "who had been visiting there before."

In General John Wilson's defense, it has been previously noted that he became interested in land speculation and purchase while in Missouri. In 1851, after taking a prospecting voyage to Gold Bluffs, north of Trinidad, California, General Wilson became president of the Pacific Mining Company, a developing association. The company claimed:

> *In the spring of the year, after a succession of calms, the entire beach is covered with bright and yellow gold. Mr. Collins, the secretary of the Pacific Mining Company, measured a patch of gold and sand, and estimates it will yield to each member of the company the snug sum of $43,000,000 (say, forty-three millions of dollars!) and the estimate is formed upon a calculation that the sand holds out to be one tenth as rich as observation warrants them in supposing.' ...General John Wilson and Mr. Collins, both of whom had been among the number of discoverers, frankly testified to the truth of these wonderful statements. The beach, they said, for a great distance, was literally strewed with pure gold...No wonder people raved....The ancient excitement of Mississippi and*

LEGENDARY TRUTHS

South sea schemes was a bagatelle in comparison. [*][30]

The author's defense of General John Wilson hereby rests his case!

Lassen was at his rancho on April 9, 1850, when Bruff struggled out of the mountains after remaining with his company's goods and wagons all winter. When he arrived at Lassen's, he wrote, "Capt. Lassen pressed me to stay." On April 20, Lassen took some neighbors, six Indians, and forty oxen, and accompanied Bruff back to his camp to see what they could salvage. Bruff mentioned that on this trip Lassen prospected a ravine for gold. He also noted some irritation with Lassen because he had not brought along enough feed for the oxen.

Lassen believed that Benton City was going to be developed into a growing settlement, and when they returned to the rancho, he hired Bruff to help survey it. On May 2, 1850, Bruff noted that "Mr. Eastman—steam-boat engineer; and Colonel Woods and Wilson [Charles Wilson]—the latter gentlemen wish me to accompany them to the 'Red Bluffs,' about 30 miles up the valley, to lay out a town there."

However, Lassen didn't release Bruff from his agreement, and insisted that he finish the survey of Benton City. Bruff admitted that Lassen had pre-engaged him for the survey and added that he was engaged "'for the company'—Gen. John Wilson, Col. Wilson, and Lassen—to lay out Benton City." [31]

Lassen attempted to help Bruff with the survey work, and disagreements developed. Bruff considered Lassen "an honest old man," but "ignorant and stubborn." Swartzlow, in *Lassen His Life and Legacy*, wrote, "The term stubborn was applied to Lassen by others, too, and he seems to have deserved this description." [32]

Lassen then hired Bruff to manage his store while he was prospecting. Lassen returned from prospecting with some samples of gold. Bruff continued to manage the store until July, when he followed Lassen on a prospecting trip into the mountains.

While Bruff was working at the store, on July 9, 1850, Bruff mentioned they were "told that 10 miles back, on Dry creek, there was a party of 20 emigrants, perfectly destitute, and unable to proceed. Lassen sent them bread, fresh meat, liquor, and a horse to bring a sick man in upon." This is another example of Lassen's charity to incoming

---

[*]   They reference Soulé, Gijon, and Nisber, *Annals of San Francisco* (1855),   pp. 311-314, quoting a reporter for the *Alta.*

emigrants in need.

Earlier in the spring of 1850, rumors of a "Gold Lake," "whose shores were covered with lumps of purest gold," were bringing prospecting parties to Lassen's rancho on their way to search for the fabled lake somewhere north of the Yuba River, east of the Feather River, and south of the Pit River.

The lure for gold was in the air, and these stories caused Lassen to organize a large "company, beef cattle, indians and squaws, pack horses, mules, etc. and started at 10 a.m. on the 'Gold Lake' hunt." Bruff claimed that he didn't believe in the "Gold Lake" story, but that he was interested because "the excursion will be over a country very little if any known; and we may be so fortunate as to find a rich gold place, if not a Gold Lake." [33]

For a non-believer, it is interesting that a year later, in San Francisco, Bruff would be enticed by General John Wilson to take a steamer north to Trinidad in search of the Gold Bluffs. Bruff recorded in his January 9, 1851 entry:

> There is considerable excitement here, amongst adventurers, about a golden discovery, recently, on the coast. These auriferous cliffs have accordingly been called the 'Gold Bluffs.' And a company formed, called the 'Pacific Mining Company,' to work it—or more correctly, to sell shares. Every idler is now talking of going there. [34]

General Wilson was continuing to hoodwink others, as he had Lassen.

LEGENDARY TRUTHS

1850
Prospecting in the Mountains
and Discovering Honey Lake Valley

*It is one thing to show a man that he is in error. And another
to put him in possession of truth.*

—John Locke 1632-1704

Since Lassen had turned over the controlling interest in his ranch
to Wilson and Palmer, who had agreed to manage and improve it
and develop Benton City, Lassen was free to guide a prospecting
party, including Bruff, Battis, Young, Brittle, Meyerowitz, Burton, a
Frenchman, and several others. They prospected around the Feather
River Valleys, searched around the base of Lassen Butte (Mount
Lassen), and explored Indian Valley, where Lassen would later build a
trading post. Later in the summer and fall, Lassen led his party as far
north as the Pit River, east to the area where Alturas is now located,
and then they went south to discover, explore, and name Honey Lake
Valley and Honey Lake.

Being ill with various complaints, Bruff tended to stay in Lassen's
base camp recording the various comings and goings of different groups
joining and leaving the party. He recorded interesting observations of

wildlife and the dangerous encounters various members experienced with the Indians.

On August 10, 1850, he wrote, "Lassen's squaws went out to dig roots. Pedro, one of these Indians, is very ill, and his squaw, not over 15 years of age, is exceedingly attentive to him, day and night."[*1] On the night of August 20, Bruff laid in bed listening to talk around the campfire. In his journal, he recorded some of the details of that evening:

A lank long-haired, loquacious Oregonian—a very noisy bragging fellow, swore by G-d that Lassen was a d-d fool! Knew nothing about the mountains, nor how to hunt gold; and that if the party contemplated joining L., after they reached him; he, for one, would not go!...the opposition to joining Lassen, now spread, among those who were too lazy, or afraid of arrows, and thus the contemplated force was reduced to a few staunch determined men...The conduct of the opposition is ungenerous, when it is well-known, that every man on this ground, came here either to go out with Lassen, or await his successful researches, and then realize the benefits of it.[2]

On August 26, Bruff wrote:

All the parties are camped and close by, are awaiting the return of Lassen, to go out on the big and final hunt, this season, for the igneus faatius Lake. The time is wiled away, by reading, conversing, smoking, shooting, playing cards— uchre and monte, and drinking.[3]

---

* Although Bruff mentioned "Lassen's squaws" here, earlier on July 28, he wrote "Lassen's indians, with their Squaws, and the Squaw of a half-breed Frenchman are here." Nowhere does he specifically mention an Indian woman of Lassen's or indicate a connubial relationship. However, "legendary truths" indicate that Lassen may have had an Indian woman and may have even sired a son with her. These stories still persist in Susanville. It is said that an Indian by the name of Isadore Jim Lassen claimed to be the son of Peter Lassen.

LEGENDARY TRUTHS

J. Goldsborough Bruff, "Repose of Tired Adventurers." This item is reproduced by permission of The Huntington Library, San Marino, California.

On September 20 Bruff wrote:

A consultation now ensued about the leadership of the party, as there were several aspirants to that honor. So a vote was taken, those in favor of Lassen rode over to the right, and those in favor of Jones, to the left; resulting in the election of Lassen.[4]

They rode north to the Pit River and then east to where Bruff noted that at places both "Mount Tschastes" (Mount Shasta) and the "Snow Butte" (Mount Lassen) could be seen in the distance. He noted that "Tschastes" was "W.S.W." so they must have traveled some distance to the north. When Bruff and Meyerowitz were shot at by Indians and escaped, they later reported to Lassen. "…Old Pete said we might 'tank' our 'Got'." [5]

They traveled south to Honey Lake on October 25, 1850. Lassen had visited and named Honey Lake Valley earlier that year; he named Honey Lake because of a sweet dew on some of the plants found there.

Read and Gaines pointed out that Fariss and Smith were correct in claiming that Lassen was "...not only the pioneer of Honey Lake and Honey Lake Valley—he was perhaps their white discoverer." They also stressed that Fairfield was wrong in questioning Fariss and Smith's claim, stating that "Very few, perhaps none of the pioneers of this county went through Honey Lake valley before Roop came here in [June 1853]..."[6]

When they returned to the Feather River Valley, Lassen and some others resolved to obtain provisions and to winter there. On October 15, 1850, Bruff wrote, "Old Pete expressed a strange desire, to return at this season, to one of the Feather river valleys we passed through, to prospect, and pass the winter. He seems to entertain a great repugnance to returning to the old ranch."[7]

Bruff returned to Lassen's rancho and while there heard of an Indian who had been whipped and later shot by McBride, a friend of one of Davis's sons. Bruff visited the Indian and sent laudanum to ease his pain. Later, Lassen also returned to the rancho, and when Bruff told him of the Indian's suffering, Bruff wrote:

> When I related the incident to old Pete, he was deeply affected, and shed tears, observing to me, in a sorrowful tone, 'Captain Bruff, that's his reward for speaking in defence of his murdered brother!' and told me that he knew the lad well, and he was an inoffensive clever fellow.[8]

At the same time, it was discovered that a German guest of Lassen's had robbed one of Lassen's trunks. When Lassen was told he had been robbed, he replied, "Well, robbed again, of my honest gains, and hard work!—I owe debts, and don't care for myself, if I had not one dollar; but I do care for them I owe!"

Later, the culprit was apprehended. He confessed when confronted with a noose, and was sentenced to be stripped to the skin, secured to an oak tree, and lashed twenty times with a rawhide *riata*. "As the rascal's feelings were much hurt, Lassen, kind hearted fellow, gave him a big horn, to soothe him."[9]

On November 15, 1850, Bruff noted:

> At 10½ A.M. Lassen, Burton, Isadore Jones, Hough Sr. Campbell, and two others moved off, to winter in the mountains.—They drive a horse and an ox wagon, and

are all mounted. They contemplate packing the oxen, etc. when they have drawn the wagons as far as practicable, and reserve the oxen for meat. They have stores on packed animals, as well as in the wagons.[10]

Present day marker on Hwy 395,
near the spot where Lassen and Bruff passed in 1850.

1851–1852
Nobles Emigrant Trail

*All truths are easy to understand once they are discovered;
the point is to discover them.*—Galileo Galilei

Nobles Trail was promoted to the merchants of Shasta City in 1852 by William Nobles as being "a good wagon road from this place to the Humboldt river…which will be shorter and in every respect more practicable than any other overland immigrant route into California." Nobles claimed credit for the discovery and was paid $2,000 by the merchants of Shasta City for revealing the route to them. However, Peter Lassen also claimed he knew the route long before Nobles came to the area. Speculation and controversy persist to this day.

According to Robert Amesbury, William H. Nobles "…came into Honey Lake Valley or was guided by Peter Lassen with a band of 80 men in the spring of 1851. He probably heard and believed the story which Bruff recorded."

That story in Bruff's account revealed:

> *There were amongst us an individual who knew a man, who not long since traveling to California, started with 5 companions from somewhere about Mud Lakes (Black Rock*

LEGENDARY TRUTHS

*Desert) leaving the emigrant road there to reach California
by a cutoff—a diagonal beeline—and he found a lake deeply
basined in the mountains with plenty of golden pebbles and
hostile Indians near the headwaters of the Yuba.* [1]

Was Nobles interested in the gold when he went to Honey Lake
Valley, or was he more interested in the "cutoff"? At any rate, Tim
Purdy, Susanville historian, wrote, "At that point, Nobles and Lassen
parted company."[2] From there, Nobles must have explored the route
through Smoke Creek to the "emigrant road [Applegate/Lassen] at
Mud Lakes." Thus, he would have scouted and confirmed the true
"cutoff" that so many 49ers and Bruff had expected.

However, according to *Hutching's California Magazine*, Nobles'
proposed route at this time would have met the Lassen Road at Lassen's
Big Meadows. These meadows were just to the west of what was to
become known as Nobles Pass.* Nobles then continued to Lassen's
rancho, following the Lassen Route. He did not yet know of the pass or
route north of Mount Lassen that his road would later follow—the road
that Lassen would claim he knew first.

Swartzlow in *Lassen: His Life and Legacy,* wrote:

> *Lassen's interest in emigrant roads into California continued.
> In Hutching's California Magazine for 1856-57 an article
> entitled "A Jaunt to Honey Lake Valley and Noble's Pass"
> gives a description of the country and newer trail from the
> Humboldt River to the Sacramento Valley by way of Honey
> Lake Valley, known generally as Nobles' Road. The author
> states that Peter Lassen discovered Honey Lake in 1850 and
> that he was the guide for William H. Nobles in 1851 on the
> first exploration of Nobles route. He traversed, then, a good
> portion of the National Park which now bears his name.*†[3]

---

*   According to *Fairfield's Pioneer History of Lassen County, California*, in reference
to the *Hutching's Magazine* June, 1857 article "'Lassen's Big Meadows' was the west
end of Noble's pass; and that the old settlers of Indian Valley claimed that to Peter
Lassen is due the honor of having discovered the Noble's pass route, having known it
long before Noble saw it."

†   In the Court Transcripts, Pomeroy testified that Lassen and Nobles left on an
expedition in February of 1852, and "The business of the party was to explore a new
route through the mountains."

Lassen had previously been over the area north of Mount Lassen (then known as Snowy Butte) twice in 1846 when going after John C. Fremont, and then returning with him to *Bosquejo*. According to Bruff on August 12, 1850, "Lassen's expedition, rode in [to Lassen's base camp near the headwaters of the Feather River]...They had traveled to Cow Creek, found a lake at its head, and several others; been around the Snow Butte..." [4]

Perhaps, this was when, according to "legendary truths," Lassen was the "first person" to climb the peak that was to later bear his name, although there is no documentation to support this. None other than, "Grove K. Godfrey, who ascended the peak in the summer of 1851, states in an article he wrote in *Hutching's California Magazine* in 1860 that Peter Lassen was the first white man to climb the peak." [5]

Swartzlow went on to speculate that Lassen may have claimed that honor when, as she wrote, "It is reported by Godfrey that he and his group met Peter Lassen between Indian Valley and the North Fork of the Feather River. He [Lassen] had with him a small pack train carrying provisions and merchandise to his store in Indian Valley." [6]

In *Fairfield's Pioneer History of Lassen County, California*, he questioned that Nobles Trail went through Lassen's Big Meadows, which he was correct in questioning. Nobles' discovered route ended just east of the meadows, but later would follow the Lassen Trail north, to where it branched west and continued over the mountains north of Mount Lassen. In referring to *Hutching's Magazine* article, Fairfield wrote:

> *A part of the foregoing, at least, is certainly a mistake. The Noble route never went through Big Meadows and down Deer creek; and if Lassen knew that route, he must have found it after he made the Lassen Trail. It doesn't seem reasonable to suppose that if he knew of the Noble's pass route, he would take a party of emigrants up to Oregon and back, just to get from the Black Rock peak to Mt. Meadows. If he did, he should have been punished for it.* [7]

Interestingly, Tom Hunt's essay in *A Guide to Nobles Trail*, edited by Richard K. Brock and Robert S. Black, also quoted the June, 1857, *Hutching's California Magazine:*

> *Most persons are well aware...[of] the emigration on what*

LEGENDARY TRUTHS

is known as Noble's Route (Peter Lassen however it is claimed by the old settlers in Indian Valley, is entitled to that honor, having known it long before Mr. Noble ever saw it, and moreover was his guide all through this route, Mr. N. being entirely unacquainted with it.) This Mr. Lassen himself solemnly affirmed in our hearing, and so to us; and we make mention of it now that honor may be given where honor is most due.[8]

However, Tom Hunt went on to question:

Was Lassen here taking credit with the writer of this article for something he hadn't done, that is, taking credit for opening yet a second historic trail into California? Or was this just an example of "Old Pete" embroidering the historical record by playing loosely with the facts, simply because he knew that there was nobody around some five years after the opening of the Nobles Trail who could challenge his claim? Or then again was it possible that Lassen had, indeed, piloted Nobles along the basic Nobles Trail route in conjunction with one of his own journeys of exploration through the country in question?[9]

Hunt referred to the transcript of trial testimonies from the court ruling on a lawsuit filed against Peter Lassen and Henry Gerke by John Wilson and Charles Wilson, dated October 5, 1853. From the testimonies, Hunt concluded, "The doubt raised by the above-cited 1857 *Hutching's California Magazine* article can finally be laid to rest. 'Old Pete' was, indeed, coveting more than the honor that was due him."[10] Thus published, it adds to the "legendary truths" about Peter Lassen, but in this case, as in others, are they more "true" than the truth itself?[*]

Nobles claimed to have hired a couple of men at $8 each per day for eight months to assist him in finding a better route over the mountains. He wrote:

In February ... I commenced at a point from 80 to 100 miles of

---

[*]   At the time of publication of this book, Tom Hunt and some historians still question whether Lassen guided Nobles or whether Nobles showed Lassen the route.

Walkers Pass in the Southern end of the Sierra Nevada's and passing through the summits thoroughly explored the whole range to the Columbia River, which resulted in the discovery of a pass [Nobles Pass] in that range of mountains.... [11]

Considering that snow depths linger on the Sierra passes long into the summer, coupled with the distances Nobles would have had to travel to meet his claims of "passing through the summits thoroughly explored the whole range to the Columbia River," as well as the time it would have taken to cover these great distances—even over some passes that hadn't yet been opened—his claims for travel and expenses seem so preposterous, that one historian wrote "...the complete letter is quite self-serving," and "...being a promoter at heart, Nobles was prone to exaggeration on his behalf." [12] The cost to Nobles for two men at $8/day for eight months would total $3,840 just for their wages, not including other expenses.

Later, Nobles asked the merchants of Shasta City for $2,000 as a payment for showing them his newly discovered route. Tom Hunt wrote that Nobles, "was one of the smart ones who saw the advantages of mining the miners, and his payment of $2,000 was undoubtedly more than most gold miners accumulated from their mining activities." [13]

According to an editor's comment in *A Guide to the Nobles Trail*, Nobles' payment of "$2,000 in 1852 was the equivalent of $49,280 in 2007." [14] So this was indeed a large amount of money, as Hunt pointed out. But using the same equation of $1 in 1852 = $24.64 in 2007, and using Nobles' claim of paying $8/day each to two men for eight months, his cost, as stated above, would have come to $3,840, or in 2007 dollars, $94,617.60, just for wages, not including costs for equipment, food, animals for transportation, and other desiderata and incidentals.

It isn't surprising, therefore, when Nobles returned back East to promote his road that it didn't take Nobles long before he was embroiled in accusations of misappropriating federal funds and property, land speculation, extravagance, and procrastination. Historian W. Turrentine Jackson concluded that: "Nobles, on the other hand, had at least proved himself utterly incapable of mastering the necessary technical details associated with the administration of a federal government project. At

---

*   Referring to statements by William Nobles in a letter from Nobles to Jacob Thompson, Secretary of the Interior, April 16, 1852. (Letter found by Tom Hunt.)

times he appeared not only unfit, but belligerent and insubordinate."[15]

In contrast to Noble's reputation, one should consider some of the testimonies toward Lassen's integrity and honesty. The June, 1857, edition of *Hutching's California Magazine* article states that Lassen was the discoverer of the route as claimed by the "old settlers of Indian Valley," and "solemnly affirmed" by Mr. Lassen.[16] A *Red Bluff Beacon* article on October 27, 1858, states, "Whoever shakes the hand of Peter Lassen shakes the hand of an honest man."[17] Swartzlow's tribute states, "There is no indication that he [Lassen] was morally less than circumspect" and "...Peter Lassen was an honest and forthright man.[18]

It may still be controversial as to who discovered the route. However, considering Nobles' character and predilection to exaggeration and self-aggrandizement, as opposed to the testimonies toward Lassen's integrity and honesty, one would conclude that Lassen was the one who should have received the credit.

It therefore seems likely that the reports were true that either Lassen guided Nobles over part of the way or Nobles at least consulted with Lassen before he met with the proposed "company" at Gerke's in the fall of 1851. In the words of Ruby Swartzlow, "He [Lassen] was consulted by soldiers, travelers, and emigrants because they relied on his familiarity with the terrain."[19] So, if at the time Nobles were looking for a new route, he surely would have sought out Lassen.

Tom Hunt wrote, "Furthermore, both men had to have been active in the same geographical area in the early 1850's. It is hard to imagine Nobles, who was determined to open a new and better route into California, not searching out Lassen and availing himself of that trail pioneer's store of knowledge."[20]

Indeed, if one scrutinizes the transcript of the Wilson/Lassen trial testimonies more carefully, one reads that in the fall of 1851 (probably after having explored the Nobles Route from the Mud Lakes [Black Rock] to Lassen's Big Meadows), a group of men met at Gerke's home in San Francisco. In this group were Nobles, along with Lassen, Henry Gerke, C.C. Catlett, General A. Hudson, I. L. Van Bokelyn, St. Felix, Messersmith, and others. Their purpose was to form a company to promote the new, shorter route, develop ranches along it, and monopolize trade with incoming emigrants.

In the court transcripts, there is no mention of Nobles asking for a "certain payment," as he would later, at Shasta City. There is only mention of establishing ranches. Tom Hunt added that in doing so, they "might be able to turn a tidy profit," and since Lassen's rancho was at the terminus, it would "effectively give the proposed company a complete monopoly of trade along the route."[21]

Lassen produced papers to this company about his ranch, supposedly to get the company's help in clearing his entanglement with the Wilsons. Messersmith later testified:

> *Was at Gerke's home at the time St Felix, Van Bokelyn, Lassen and others were there in the winter of* [1851 and] *1852. I remember Lassen wished to join our Company and produce papers there about his Ranch which were read over; ...The Lassen Ranch had nothing to do with the matter of our Company at its origin. The object of the Company was to explore Nobles pass and locate Ranches on the line of it...I never heard of the Lassen Ranch until after the Return of some of our party from up Country. Then heard Lassen had made propositions to Nobles to come in and join our Company. Have no interest in the Lassen Ranch.*[22]

Note, the "Nobles pass" referred to here was the area west of Susanville along the Susan River, east of where the Nobles route joined the Lassen Trail east of Mount Lassen. Nobles was seeking help in "locating Ranches on the line of it." He wasn't asking them for a monetary payment.

Apparently, at this time, Lassen was interested in trying to enlist their help in ousting the Wilsons from his rancho. Tom Hunt wrote that Nobles and the others could not satisfy Lassen's request to get rid of the Wilsons, so the deal collapsed."[23] Because of this or some other reason, Nobles decided to further his explorations and take his road around the north side of Mount Lassen and end it at Shasta City, rather than at Lassen's rancho. To do this, he met with Lassen at *Bosquejo* to explore the route.

Pomeroy testified:

> *I think he* [Lassen] *left again in February and was gone only a few days he was to explore a new pass* [not to be confused with Nobles Pass, which was east of Mount Lassen and

ended near Lassen's Big Meadows].* *The party consisted of Lassen, Noble, Gerke, Hudson, Van Bokelyn, Smith and St. Felix. This was February 1852. The business of the party was to explore a new route through the mountains. I never heard any dissatisfaction* [presumably dissatisfaction with the Wilsons] *on the part of Lassen until after this party arrived at the ranch it was about the time that Gerke and Noble arrived. I think Gerke came up on the second trip of the Comanche* [?].[24]

When Pomeroy was cross-examined, he referred to his bookkeeping at Lassen's rancho and expenses for the exploration on the pass over the mountains:

...Mr. Lassen was charged at his own request with the board of the exploring party with the exception of Gerke. He said he did not want Gerke charged anything as he was a particular friend of his and that he always stopped at his (Gerkes') house when down at San Francisco with out any charge being made for it.[25]

If Nobles already knew of "the new pass," why hadn't he gone directly to Fort Reading and Shasta City rather than going all the way to San Francisco to meet with Lassen and men associated with him and his rancho? (Lassen's rancho was at the end of the established road Nobles probably followed from Nobles Pass and Lassen's Big Meadows directly into the Sacramento Valley.)

If, as some historians maintain, Nobles already had discovered the route north of Mount Lassen, why did he go out of his way and waste more time with Lassen and the others, who could not "satisfy Lassen's request to get rid of Wilson" or "locate Ranches on the line of it [Nobles Trail]"?

Later in the spring of 1852, after the "exploring party" found the "pass" through the mountains, William Nobles convinced the merchants of Shasta City, California (near present day Redding), that he had discovered a viable wagon road to their thriving town. As stated

---

* "Lassen's Big Meadows was the west end of Noble's pass," according to *Fairfield's Pioneer History of Lassen County, California,* referencing the *Hutching's Magazine* article.

before, for the consideration of $2,000, Nobles agreed to show the businessmen of Shasta City the new wagon route that initially branched off the Applegate Trail at Black Rock, and headed southwest across the Black Rock and Smoke Creek Deserts to Honey Lake Valley and Susanville. From there the trail continued westerly through forested and volcanic country, crossing the mountains on the north flank of Mount Lassen, finally descending into the upper end of the Sacramento Valley near Fort Reading, and terminating at Shasta City.

The Nobles Trail became one of the easiest of all the wagon routes into northern California, and it received heavy use in subsequent years.[*][26]

To date, the only resolution to the controversy as to who discovered the route depends on what we can deduce from the following:

- Written records (listed above) of their movements and explorations preceding 1852

- Lassen's "solemn affirmation"

- Many testimonials as to Lassen's honesty

- Claims of "old settlers"

- Newspaper articles

- Interpretation of testimonies in the Wilson/Lassen Court Trial, as opposed to Nobles' claim, based on a self-aggrandizing letter he wrote

---

[*]   The Nobles Trail was designated as part of the California National Historic Trail by Act of Congress in the 1992 Pony Express and California National Historic Trails Act.

LEGENDARY TRUTHS

1851–1854
Indian Valley

...Another great story ruined by the facts!—Fred Eckhardt

Continuing the story of Lassen's activities in the years from 1851 to 1854, we find that Lassen wintered in Indian Valley in 1850-1851. In 1851, he and Burton built a cabin at a site selected the previous year by Lassen and Meyerowitz. They raised vegetables, which they sold to miners and prospectors passing through the valley, for 15 cents per pound—turnips, beets, lettuce and other vegetables. In the spring and summer, Lassen continued his prospecting.

In March 1852, after showing Nobles the pass over the mountains, Lassen returned to Indian Valley with Meyerowitz and George Edward St. Felix. They opened a new trading post at the cabin Lassen and Burton had built the year before. They improved the cabin by putting a good roof on it, thus completing the first house in Indian Valley.

They planted a much larger garden of vegetables to sell, as they hoped to serve emigrants coming to California on the recently opened route over Beckwourth Pass. Lassen also engaged in blacksmithing. Rosaline Levenson, in *The Short-Lived Explorations of Isadore Meyerowitz*, noted, "Of the Lassen-Meyerowitz partnership, W.H. Hutchinson commented, 'So...the Dane and the Pole, lived their daily lives and were more self-sufficient than their counterparts manage to be to-day.'" [1]

By now Lassen was thoroughly disgusted with the General John Wilson/Joel Palmer deal, and considered the contract invalidated because they had failed to pay him anything or to live up to their agreements. Joel Palmer had returned to Oregon, and had not fulfilled his contract obligations. Colonel Charles Wilson allegedly assumed Palmer's position in the three-way partnership, but Lassen denied the validity of the change. From the testimonies, it seemed that Charles Wilson had taken over the ownership, or at least part ownership, of the steamboat, and was on it when it sank.

Lassen considered the Wilsons crooks who had deceived and defrauded him by stealing and selling off his stock, and not fulfilling their agreements to properly run and promote the rancho. So in order to pay off debts accrued as a result of his agreement with Wilson and Palmer (to purchase increased provisions for the store and the investment in a steamboat to transport the goods) Lassen sold his rancho, including his claims against the Wilsons, to his friend, Henry Gerke, on July 2, 1852, for $25,000.

As a result of the sale, on the 21st day of August 1852, Lassen was served a warrant by Sheriff's Deputy, George Pierson, of Butte County. "I certify that I served the within summons on Peter Lassen at the North Fork of the Feather River in Butte County…" [2] Gerke was served a warrant in San Francisco on the 16th day of August. Charles L. Wilson and John Wilson brought a suit against them, claiming the sale to Gerke was illegal because of the interest held by John Wilson and Joel Palmer in 1849. Charles Wilson claimed he had assumed Palmer's position in the co-ownership of two thirds of the rancho.

On June 14, 1853, the court ordered the venue of the trial be moved to San Francisco, and after several postponements, the trial took place in September. On October 5, 1853, the court ruled in favor of Lassen and Gerke, vindicating them and confirming the disingenuousness of the Wilsons.

During the winter of 1852-1853, Lassen and Meyerowitz stayed in Indian Valley. "The winter of 1852-53 was unusually harsh and long. Heavy snows started in November 1852, blocking the mountain trails and making it impossible for the emigrants to receive expected shipments of supplies. Some left the area, Meyerowitz and Lassen remained." [3]

According to Swartzlow, little is known of "the Danish pioneer's activities during the years of 1853 to 1855." However, Fairfield stated that Lassen and Meyerowitz continued to live in Indian Valley in 1853 and 1854. From the court records, we know Lassen had to travel to San Francisco for his trial defense against the Wilsons, as described above. For the rest of the year they probably continued raising produce for sale, doing blacksmith work, and possibly, prospecting.

Swartzlow wrote:

> *Two letters written to John Bidwell and signed by Lassen request supplies of flour. One was written October 27, 1853, from Charley's Ranch and ordered 600 pounds of flour. The second, dated October 21, 1854, was written from Indian Valley and requested 6,000 to 8,000 pounds of flour.*[4]

In 1854, Meyerowitz procured a liquor license with William T. Ward, who in 1857 became the first Plumas County judge. Meyerowitz and Ward listed their occupation as tavern owners, but since Lassen was reportedly temperate, it isn't clear whether they intended to sell liquor at the trading post.[5]

1855
Finding Gold in Honey Lake Valley

Rather than love, than money, than fame, give me truth.

—Henry David Thoreau

Early in the spring of 1855, Lassen prospected in Honey Lake Valley near the present town of Janesville in Elysian Valley. Common tales said Lassen was so taken with the beauty of the site that he told those around him that he would like to be buried there. Fairfield wrote, "Some of the earliest settlers say that they came over Diamond Mountain, and camped under the tree where Lassen was afterwards buried."[1]

Getting satisfactory results in finding some gold, he returned to Indian Valley for supplies and men to help. Later, in June, he came back to Elysian Valley with a mining outfit. He had his men dig two miles of ditch from Hill Creek to bring water to his claim. The ditch is still called Lassen's ditch. The claim reportedly paid well until the water supply dwindled. He returned to Indian Valley for more provisions, blacksmith tools, mining tools, and livestock. He surveyed a site, including the mining claim, but he never recorded his claim to the land.[2]

During the summer, Lassen cut twenty tons of hay from the valley's bunch grass to provide feed for the winter. In October 1855, Lassen and Meyerowitz moved their residence and possessions from Indian Valley to Honey Lake. With them, they brought some cows, horses, blacksmithing and mining tools, a plow, and other things.[3]

That fall Lassen, and his companions, Isadore Meyerowitz, Joseph Lynch, Newton Hamilton, Marion Lawrence and John Duchene, built a log cabin on the south side of Lassen Creek and spent the winter in the Honey Lake Valley, becoming, what some claim, the first pioneers of Lassen County. The cabin continued to be used until 1896, when it was destroyed by fire.

Fairfield wrote:

> *The next thing required was a shelter for himself* [Lassen] *and men during the winter. They then erected the long, low, log house, which has never been without a pioneer tenant to this day... The cabin, or house, is nearly fifty feet long, sixteen wide, six logs high, and covered with a shake roof. At either end is a room sixteen feet by twenty. One of these Lassen used for a general storeroom, and the other for an apartment to live in, and which he floored with lumber cut with a whipsaw. At one end of this room was built a rock fireplace, with sufficient capacity to admit cordwood. The openings to the outside world were a door and a three-foot square window, over which barley sacks were nailed to keep out the cold. The small room in the center was used by Peter as a sleeping apartment, and where it is said he always kept a bed for a traveler or a friend.*[4]

Fairfield also wrote that:

> *During the winter, Lassen and his companions busied themselves in sawing out lumber with a whip-saw for sluices, and splitting rails for fencing. About five thousand rails were gotten out, and in the spring were used to fence a portion of his land. The weather was so mild and pleasant, that the stock passed through the winter with but little need for the hay he had provided.*[5]

All throughout his tenure in California, Lassen had been friendly with the Indians—living, working, and traveling with them. Levinson wrote:

After he settled at Honey Lake Valley, Lassen became friendly with the Indians and was known for his competence in dealing with them. 'He trusted them implicitly' states Leon Whitsell, 'and was known everywhere as a personal friend of Chief Winnemucca of the Piutes. He even gave them powder and bullets for their firearms so they could hunt.'[6]

Lassen and Chief Winnemucca were both Masons; however, Fred Kingsbury later recalled:

Peter and Father [William Kingsbury] *were both Masons. In fact they were both members of California's first Masonic Lodge, whose charter Lassen brought overland from Missouri before the Gold Rush.*

To the surprise of my father, and other white men, Young Chief Winnemucca and his council displayed an unexpected knowledge of Masonic grips and signals.

My father could never determine where or when Winnemucca and his braves had become acquainted with Masonry, or how the aboriginal inhabitants had acquired the grips and various other indications that they were well versed in Masonic lore.

There was a possibility that Indians from the Cherokee Masonic Lodge, or Masons who associated with the Piutes, taught them the ritual.[7]

LEGENDARY TRUTHS

1856
Honey Lake Valley Politics

In a time of universal deceit, telling the truth is a revolutionary act.—George Orwell

According to Fairfield, news of Lassen's finding gold in the valley set off a great rush of miners to the area in the year of 1856. Some miners did quite well, but the gold resources weren't extensive. In the spring of 1856 Meyerowitz with his Indian wife and other companions, who had been living with Lassen at his cabin, began to stake out land claims of their own in Honey Lake Valley.[1]

Because of problems arising from land claims of settlers and squatters in Honey Lake Valley, on April 26, 1856, Meyerowitz met with Lassen and eighteen other settlers at the home of Isaac Roop to draw up laws for the area, as they didn't believe they were in either Nevada or California. Stories of the time said the residents refused to pay taxes to California, claiming that they were in Nevada; and that they refused to pay taxes to Nevada, claiming that they were in California. As a result, they proposed to establish a new territory.

From all accounts, Lassen was a pioneer who possessed energy and an enterprising spirit. He became a friend of Isaac Roop in Susanville, and they were at the head of the movement to form a new territory in

Honey Lake Valley. The name of the new territory was to be Nataqua, a local Indian word that is said to mean, "Woman." Out of the "mists of hearsay," comes the story that "Lassen's squaw, when asked her name, replied, 'Me Nataqua.'" *

Fairfield quoted Fariss and Smith:

> *The meeting being organized by the election of Peter Lassen to the chair, and Isaac Roop secretary, the following laws were unanimously adopted by the citizens: 'In as much as Honey Lake valley is not within the limits of California, the same is hereby declared a new territory, and the boundaries thereof shall be as follows, viz.:...'*

The laws were listed, including, "Sec. 19.—That Isaac Roop was elected and qualified a Recorder, and Peter Lassen was elected and qualified a Surveyor, and each shall act in his respective office from this date."

Then Fariss and Smith concluded, "With this meager code of laws, and but the two officers to administer them, the new territory of Nataqua was launched upon the political sea." [2]

Meyerowitz's name was second among signatures to the laws, following that of Lassen. The meeting was concluded sine die, and the record was signed, "Isaac Roop, Sec." and "Peter Lassen, Pres." René Lassen in *Uncle Peter* also wrote that Peter Lassen was president of the new republic, but he pointed out that at a later meeting on August 29, 1857, a document signed by thirty-two men included Lassen's name. He signed that one as a citizen, not as president. [3]

Ironically, the committee of men establishing Nataqua Territory, which was "...240 miles long and 155 miles wide, almost two-thirds the size of the state of Nevada..." [4] proclaimed its location within coordinates that didn't include Susanville or Honey Lake Valley. Since Peter Lassen was voted surveyor, he has often been blamed for this miscalculation, but all should share the blame for the error. The boundaries of the territory were declared and defined by the members present at the meeting. Lassen was only responsible, in the office of surveyor, to survey new land claims within that territory.

---

* The story of Lassen having an Indian wife is commonly told in the Susanville area, but the author has found no published source from Lassen's contemporaries to back this claim. Fred Kingsbury said he was a bachelor.

LEGENDARY TRUTHS

Swartzlow reported that:

Notations in the Roop House Register, August 1856, show that Lassen sustained a keen interest in the new emigrants arriving from the east. He went out to meet some of the emigrant trains. The Woods and Long Train, which arrived at Honey Lake on August 19,...[Lassen] met them at the Humboldt River. Fairfield says that a few days before the train reached Roop's place, a couple of men cut out the brush from here to Big Meadows (Lake Almanor). Fairfield continues, 'When the train left Roop's, Cap Hill and Lassen went with them on horseback as far as Clear Creek. This was the first emigrant train, or any heavy wagons, to go from Honey Lake to Humbug Valley...'[5]

Although the "legendary truths" alleged that in 1849 Lassen met people at the Humboldt to entice them to his rancho, there is no evidence of it, for as we have seen earlier, he was occupied elsewhere. This is the first recorded evidence that he actually went to the Humboldt to meet emigrants. He was probably going to meet someone he knew and expected, and surely was not going to "entice them to come to his place for profit."

A tragedy struck in July of 1856. Meyerowitz, his wife, and three companions went for a sailboat ride on Honey Lake. Meyerowitz had built the sailboat from the bed of a wagon.

When they had reached quite a distance from the shore, a sudden gust of wind upset the boat and threw them all in the water. They all managed to get back to the boat, and some of them clung to it, the others getting up on the bottom of it. The Indian woman kept slipping from the boat, and every time she did this Isadore would put her back. Finally he got tired out, and she drowned. Soon after this, he gave up and let go of the boat.[6]

Ironically, the others who survived discovered—when they were too tired to swim farther—that the lake was only a few feet deep, and they could wade out.

Here again "the Indian woman" appears out of the "mists of hearsay." Stories abounded that she had lived with both Meyerowitz and Lassen, and may have been the "wife" of both. Levenson wrote:

> *According to Amesbury, Lassen lived at Honey Lake Valley*
> *with Meyerowitz and an Indian woman, who had a son*
> *called Isadore Jim Lassen. Amesbury told the story to Larry*
> *Richardson, adding, 'There being a little question as to who*
> *his father was, he covered both bases.'*[7]

The son was said to have worked at the Lassen Honey Lake ranch.

> *The same situation applies to Lassen who also was rumored*
> *to have fathered a son by an Indian woman, according to*
> *Richardson. Lassen lived in both places* [Honey Lake Valley
> and the cabin on Lassen Creek] *during the same years as*
> *Meyerowitz; therefore, any son born during these periods*
> *would not have been old enough to work at his ranch.*[8]

Rosaline Levenson also pointed out that if the rumors of Lassen and Meyerowitz were true, they were never revealed in regional histories or Lassen biographies. Fred Kingsbury, who personally remembered Lassen from childhood, said in one of his recollections, "You know he was a bachelor…" However, the rumors persist; locals still relate the story of an Indian named Isadore Jim Lassen living in the area who claimed to be the son of Peter Lassen, but this man never married nor had children. Tony Jonas, docent at the Lassen Historical Museum in Susanville, claimed to have heard these stories many times, and said that the name of the Indian woman was May Charlie. *

Swartzlow said that Lassen had a blacksmith forge set up in the shade of a tree directly in front of his cabin for his smithy work, and that:

> *…any traveler was welcomed at Lassen's, and he always had*
> *space to bed anyone who wished to spend the night. During*
> *the winter of 1856-1857 Francis Langier and his wife and*
> *two children, together with Epstein, Antone Storff, and*
> *Lynch stayed with Lassen, according to Fairfield's account.*
> *After Lassen's death Lynch continued to live in this same*
> *cabin until his own death in 1885.*[9]

---

* Personal conversation with Tony Jonas on June 23, 2010, at the Lassen Historical Museum in Susanville.

LEGENDARY TRUTHS

1857–1858
Partnership with Kingsbury

Men stumble over the truth from time to time, but most pick
themselves up and hurry off as if nothing happened.

—Winston Churchill

In 1857 Lassen, who had been living and working with Indians
since he arrived in California in 1840 and continued throughout his life
to be a friend to them, was acting as Indian Agent. Fairfield wrote, "…
Mr. Williams had been in San Francisco and laid the case before Col.
Henley, who sent out a quantity of blankets and other Indian goods,
with the view of enabling Mr. Lassen, as agent, to settle all difficulties
without further bloodshed."[1]

Lassen also continued his traveling, and according to Will Bagley,
"He [Lassen] served as a guide for the Pacific Wagon Road Survey
in 1857…"[2] which followed the route of the Nobles Road from the
Humboldt through the Black Rock Desert to Susanville, and on to
the Sacramento River Valley. In addition to farming, blacksmithing,
guiding, and acting as Indian agent, he participated in civic activities,
such as helping in recovering some horses stolen from settlers around
the Clark ranch.

...Peter Lassen raised a party in the upper end of the valley and went in pursuit of the thieves. They followed them over the mountain to the west, and some time in the night found them in a flat on what is now known as Clark's creek, and below where Clark once had a dairy. Lassen told the men they would wait until it was light enough to see the sights of their guns and then they would take in the whole bunch of thieves. So they surrounded their camp and waited, and when it was light enough to see to shoot they fired on the sleeping men. They never hit a man and the thieves jumped out of bed and ran for their lives. In those days of single-barreled, muzzle-loading rifles there was no chance for another shot with their guns, and if they fired their pistols it didn't do any good, and the men got safely away. The Honey Lakers found all of their horses and saddles and returned home with them.

Shortly after this two men came into Indian valley with nothing on but their under-clothes, and they said they had been surprised by the Indians and had to get away as fast as they could, leaving everything behind them. Perhaps they did think it was Indians, for there is nothing on record to show that they stopped long enough to look things over very carefully.[3]

When Lassen had lived in Indian Valley, he had probably known William C. Kingsbury,* who came to the Honey Lake area from the Quincy/Indian Valley area in August of 1857. Fairfield wrote, "William Kingsbury brought in his wife and two boys, Frank and Fred. They came on horseback, each one carrying a child. He soon went into partnership with Lassen." [4]

But, according to Fred Kingsbury, by the time he was born, "on September 27, 1855, his father was a partner of Peter Lassen...in Honey Lake Valley." [5]

In his later life, in 1940, Fred Kingsbury related his fond childhood

---

* William C. Kingsbury, who was Lassen's ranching partner, should not be confused with William V. Kingsbury. William V. Kingsbury was also a prominent citizen in the Quincy/Indian Valley area who later became known as Smoke Creek Sam at a station on the Nobles Trail in the Smoke Creek area east of Susanville.

memories of his family's relationship and dealings with Peter Lassen, and his recollections gave a candid view into the later years of Lassen's life. The *Sacramento Bee* article reported:

Fred's parents, William C. and Sarah Ellen Kingsbury, arrived in California during the gold rush. William arrived in '50, tried mining, became a close friend of Peter Lassen, and then turned his attention to agriculture and ranching. When Sarah Ellen arrived in '52, with an emigrant train which crossed the plains, the couple met and married and settled on a prospective cattle ranch in the mountains. On October 16, 1853, their first son [Frank] was born.[6]

In the article, Fred Kingsbury recalled:

Dad was Lassen's partner in two ranches, one about 7 miles Southeast of Susanville, and the other at Millford, 25 miles away on Honey Lake. The house at the latter ranch was about one mile from the shore. The old fellow was kind of odd. You know he was a bachelor which might account for part of it. He boarded at our place, when not down at the other Honey Lake ranch. He never wanted to bother any one. And never did he hesitate to wait on some one. His kindness and consideration made him that way. But he was so independent he didn't like others to wait on him. For example, if he wanted a piece of bread, and it was on the opposite side of the table, he would get up, walk around in back of everyone, and get it and come back to his place.[7]

Fred fondly related that this was a "peculiarity which always delighted my mother," and he "was a strange individual, with eccentric mannerisms, probably developed and accentuated during his many years in the wilderness."[8] He continued telling about his memories of Lassen up until the time of Lassen's death. Later, after Lassen was killed, Fred would claim to know information about the murder that would add to the mystery, rather than solve it:

One day Frank and I were playing together at the ranch when up rode Peter Lassen on old Wild Tom, the fastest horse, and best horse, and smartest horse that ever was in

California or Nevada. It was Peter's training of him from a colt, that made him smart, kind, and gentle. Mr. Clapper, and Mr. Hyer [Wyatt] *were with Peter, and they were headed for Black Rock Desert. They had seen some good samples of ore that came out of that desolate region, and had planned going over prospecting for some time. They had even talked about it among the neighbors during the winter.*

'Where's your Dad, and your Mother?' he asked. Frank ran to the house to tell them Peter wished to see 'em. He talked over with Dad different things about the ranches, and what should be done during his absence. This was in the Fall of 1859 [Lassen was killed in April 1859]...

An incident that registered, indelibly, upon my youthful mind was Peter picking up Frank and setting him in his saddle. He had tried to pick me up, but I was too scared to get on Wild Tom. Now I was afraid that my brother Frank was going away with him, and I wouldn't have anyone with whom to play. I think I started to bawl. Anyway, he let Frank down, shook hands with Mother, and Dad, said 'Goodbye' and disappeared in a cloud of dust down the road.[9]

Chief Winnemucca was also frequently a guest at the Kingsbury home. Fred recalled Winnemucca's friendship with Lassen and told of him using Masonic signs and handshakes, while saying, "Him alright, he Mason," as he shook Lassen's hand. Fred Kingsbury also inherited Peter Lassen's meerschaum pipe, which he was photographed with in the *Sacramento Bee* article. It is now in the Lassen Historical Museum in Susanville.

Pursuant to the failure to establish Nataqua as a territory, the people of Honey Lake Valley still wanted to avoid being included in California boundaries, so they held another meeting on October 3, 1857, when Lassen was again listed as president.* [10]

A mass meeting of the people of Honey Lake Valley was held in the town of Mataga (probably they got that name from Nataqua, and got it badly mixed)... The meeting was called

---

* This meeting was reported in the October 17, 1857, *Shasta Courier.*

LEGENDARY TRUTHS

to order by Isaac Roop. Peter Lassen was chosen president, C. Arnold, Geo. Purcell, and John A Slater vice-presidents, and L. C. McMurtry and E. Wick, Secretaries...

Resolved, that we endorse what the people have done at Genoa, and we pledge the faith of the people of Honey Lake valley to co-operate with them in this undertaking. That we endorse and approve of the election of James M. Crane as the delegate to Washington for the proposed new territory. That if any attempt is made by the authorities of California to bring the people of Honey Lake valley into subjugation before the line can and shall be made, that we resist all such attempts with all the power we can command...[11]

During the summers of 1857 and 1858, Lassen made several trips to Red Bluff and his old rancho nearby, "where he is allowed to help himself to whatever pleases his fancy."[12] His visits were mentioned in an article in the *Red Bluff Beacon* for October 27, 1858, which said, "Whoever shakes the hand of Peter Lassen shakes the hand of an honest man."[13]

Another of Lassen's trips back to his old rancho at *Bosquejo* was reported by Fairfield, who wrote that in the fall of 1858:

Lassen and Albert A. Smith went to Lassen's old ranch on Deer creek after some millstones. It appears that they allowed him to take anything of that kind any time he wanted it, so he loaded up the millstones and started for home. At the same time Dr. Spalding and Fred Hines went to Red Bluff to get some drugs, the first used by Dr. Spalding in his practice here, and coming back they struck in with Lassen and Smith. Lassen's wagon was heavily loaded and Hines had to help him up the Hat Creek hill. He was up near the leaders driving and Lassen was behind the wagon carrying a big rock to chock the wheel when the team stopped. All at once a chain broke near the wagon which immediately started back down the hill. Lassen was old and clumsy and would have been run over and killed; but in his haste to get out of the way he accidentally dropped the stone where the wheel struck it, and the wagon stopped. It was a close call for Uncle Peter that time.[14]

Fairfield then wrote that after they returned to the Honey Lake Valley:

Lassen rigged up a rude mill near the creek, about half way between where the road runs through Milford and the foothill, or perhaps a little nearer the hill. He ran it with a sort of horsepower; and crushed grain but made no flour. This was the first attempt to build a gristmill in the county. This fall, some say 1857, Lassen and Kingsbury put up a house of hewn logs on the top of the hill west of where the Hulsman residence is now, and it was used as a ranch house for several years. [15]

The Lassen Historical Museum in Susanville has a millstone that was allegedly one of Lassen's, probably brought to the Honey Lake Valley at this time, and maybe even used in Lassen's mill.

Millstone thought to have been quarried near Lassen's *Rancho Bosquejo* and brought to Honey Lake Valley by Peter Lassen. *Photo by Ken Johnston. Courtesy of Lassen Historical Museum, Susanville, California.*

LEGENDARY TRUTHS

1859
Lassen's Final Journey

When a man who is honestly mistaken hears the truth, he will either quit being mistaken, or cease to be honest.

—Unknown

The mysteries of life are not mysteries when truth is sought.—Inscription on Cultural Totem *

In addition to the grist mill Lassen and Kingsbury built in 1857, during the winter of 1858 and 1859 Lassen was, as reported in *The Alta California*, "engaged in the erection of a sawmill, at the time of his death."[1] And he was still ranching and involved in land speculation, because, in March of 1859, Lassen bought out William Kingsbury's interest in their ranch south of Susanville.†[2] However, during this time

---

*   *Wy-Kan-Ush-Pam*, Spirit of Salmon People. Inscription on Cultural Totem by Roslyn Hill and Lillian Pitt, 2003. Alberta Street, Portland, Oregon.

†   In March W. C. Kingsbury sold to Peter Lassen all his interest in the old Lassen Ranch south of Susanville, and in payment received a deed to the west half of the ranch taken by R. J. Scott, May 10, 1856. His witness was Sarah E. Kingsbury and the deed was recorded the 21st of March by H. Crane.

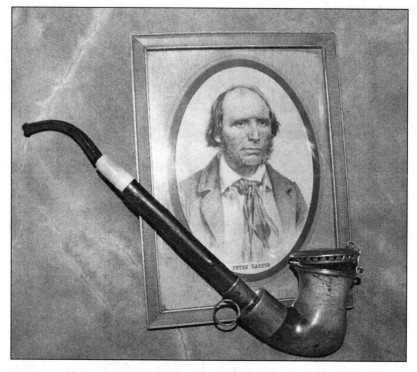

Picture of Peter Lassen and his pipe. *Photo by Ken Johnston.*
Courtesy of Lassen Historical Museum, Susanville, California.

he was still preoccupied with prospecting and pursuing rumors of riches as he had been when searching for "Gold Lake" in 1850.

Fred Kingsbury remembered the day Lassen, Wyatt, and Clapper left, and he said that they "had planned going over prospecting for some time. They had even talked about it among the neighbors during the winter." A few months earlier, in July of 1858:

> ...*James Allen Hardin and a party of men arrived in Honey
> Lake valley from Petaluma, California. They were going to
> the Black Rock range of mountains, which was mentioned in
> the description of the Lassen Trail, in search of a ledge of
> carbonate of lead and silver that Hardin had discovered while
> crossing the plains in 1849. The party went on to Black Rock,
> and although they didn't find the ledge, they started a mining
> excitement that raged with more or less fury for the next ten
> or twelve years.*[3]

286

LEGENDARY TRUTHS

So Lassen was caught up in "mining excitement that raged," and he proceeded to the Black Rock Desert to, again, seek his fortune in prospecting. However, he met his death in a mysterious way that sends the "legendary truths" echoing and resounding from the canyon walls, where they camped, to the historical conjectures of modern trail enthusiasts.

Death of Lassen

The following letter was published in *'The Mountain Messenger'* *of Downieville, Sierra County, California*[4] and quoted in *Fairfield's History of Lassen County* with Fairfield's corrections included in parentheses:

Honey Lake Valley, April 30, 1859.

> *This valley was thrown into great excitement by the arrival on Tuesday morning (it should be Thursday morning) of Mr. Wyatt, one of the Black Rock silver hunters, who narrowly escaped massacre by the Indians.*
>
> *The circumstances are as follows: There has been a party of men stopping in this valley all winter, to be ready as soon as spring opened to prospect Black Rock Canyon for a supposed silver mine. This canyon and watering place is about one hundred and twenty-four miles distant from this valley, towards the Humboldt, on the wagon road. Messrs. Jameson (Probably this was Jenison.), Weatherlow, Lathrop, and Kitts started on Sunday, the 17th inst.; Peter Lassen, Messrs. Wyatt and Clapper, following two days later, and were to rendezvous at Black Rock springs, at which place the prospecting was to commence. Lassen, Wyatt, and Clapper arrived at the appointed place on Sunday, the 24th inst., and not finding the advance party, concluded to await their coming.*
>
> *On Monday Mr. Clapper rode on to Mud lake, eight miles distant, to look for the other party; but not finding them, returned, and during the day found signs of two white men in the vicinity of their camping-ground, and believing them to be those of Captain Weatherlow and Mr. Jameson, one being a large and the other a small track. They also*

saw the tracks of shod horses, which the Indians have not. They then arrived at the conclusion that the advance party were over the mountain at another camping place, and concluded to go there the next morning and see them, having encamped at the mouth of the canyon, within one hundred yards of some projecting rocks. In the evening they saw an Indian, on horseback, making a circuit of their camp, then disappearing. After a while he made his appearance in another direction and dismounted. With much difficulty he was induced to come into camp. He could not speak English, but Lassen said he spoke Piutah. While he was in camp they heard the report of a gun, when the Indian immediately said 'Piutah,' and gave the whites to understand there were six of them.

The Indian then left them, and they retired to rest, supposing themselves safe anywhere in the Piute country. Just at daylight they were fired upon from the rocks near by, killing Mr. Clapper in his bed. Lassen and Wyatt sprang upon their feet and commenced gathering up their things; and not knowing that Clapper was killed, seeing he did not rise, supposed him asleep. Wyatt put his hand on his face to wake him, but found it covered with blood. Turning him over, he saw that he was shot through the head. Lassen said, 'I will watch for the Indians while you (Wyatt) gather up the things.' While doing so the Indians fired on them again, and Lassen fell, to rise no more. He spoke but once. 'They have killed me,' then fell on his face and gasped but once. Thus fell the 'old pioneer' whose whole history and life almost is connected with the exciting and wild scenes of the west; and when this and other generations shall have passed away the traveler will look on the snow-clad buttes, and hear of the fertile meadows that bear his name, and remember with reverence the venerable voyageur.

When Wyatt saw Lassen fall he dropped everything but his rifle, caught his horse and fled with precipitancy. He arrived here on Thursday morning, without having taken food or rest. A party of twenty men started this morning to recover the horses and property, if possible, and ascertain the whereabouts of the other party. Great fears are entertained

LEGENDARY TRUTHS

for their safety. Another party will follow immediately, with a wagon to bring in Lassen's and Clapper's remains. The advance party will proceed, if possible, to trail the Indians to their lurking place and chastise them. Z. N. Spalding.

Fairfield also presented another account of the murder, one repeated often by Wyatt. It is included below for comparison, because Wyatt's personal story, if not just more thorough, may show some embellishments.

In the following story, there is no mention of "signs of two white men in the vicinity of their camping-ground, and believing them to be those of Captain Weatherlow and Mr. Jameson, one being a large and the other a small track." There is no mention, either, of "the tracks of shod horses, which the Indians have not."

Also in the following story, "before he reached the place where they [the horses] were picketed he saw that they had pulled their picket-ropes and stampeded." Then miraculously:

Out of the dust the form of his own fine black pacing horse suddenly appeared. The animal had faced about, apparently struck by some sudden impulse. For a second or two it seemed to take its bearings, and then on a mad gallop retraced its steps until it reached the advancing Wyatt, and invited the old man as plainly as signs could indicate to mount...

Miraculous, whereas, in the first story, he "caught his horse and fled with precipitancy."

The first story made no mention of a bullet tearing through Wyatt's trousers.

The following is an extract from what was published in the San Francisco Chronicle *fifteen or twenty years ago:*[*]

The authority for the following narrative of the killing of Peter Lassen is Ephraim V. Spencer, who has lived in Lassen county for thirty-five years. The story was told to him over and over again by a man named Lemericus Wyatt,

---

[*] *Fairfield's Pioneer History* was published in 1919.

who was in Mr. Spencer's employ for two years, in fact until he died. Though Wyatt was an illiterate man, his story was well worthy of credence. He had the reputation of being both truthful and honest. The reasons for his knowledge of the incidents connected with the killing of Peter Lassen the story itself fully reveals.

Early in the spring of 1859 'Uncle Pete,' with Lemericus Wyatt and a man who went by the name of Clapper and whose Christian name Wyatt never knew, set out on a prospecting trip for silver. They went to what is known as Black rock, in the northwestern part of Nevada and about 140 miles northeast of Susanville. They had three horses, two pack mules and a full prospecting outfit, including rifles. At the Black Rock range they camped one evening beside a small stream ever since known as Clapper creek. The camp was in a nook of the canyon, over-looked by high bluffs on three sides. There was a little feed for the horses, and the place was a very pleasant, if in those times dangerous location for a camp.

While the men were getting supper an Indian came to the camp carrying a good muzzle-loading rifle. He had neither powder, caps nor bullets, and by dumb show made his wants known. Wyatt and Clapper strenuously objected to furnishing the redskin with the ammunition, but Lassen, who, as usual, was friendly with the Indian, said that no harm could come of it; that all the Indians knew Uncle Pete and would never hurt him, especially this Indian, as he was a Pah Ute. Much to the regret of Lassen's companions, the pioneer gave the Indian a good supply of all he asked, and the visitor immediately made off.

They picketed their animals for the night a short distance away and then made a common bed for themselves on the ground, Clapper lying in the middle. Just as day was breaking Wyatt was awakened by the report of a rifle. He sprang to his feet and called to his companions. He jerked the blankets off Clapper and caught him by the shoulder. In so doing he turned the man over. Blood spurted from Clapper's temple, showing that he had been shot clean through the head. Wyatt started to run, calling upon Lassen to do so too. Uncle Pete, however, remained standing by the bed shading his eyes with his hand and holding his rifle easily with the other, trying to discover where the shot came from. While he was still peering into the rocks a second shot rang out and Lassen fell. Wyatt ran back to Lassen and partly raised him from the ground, but life was ebbing fast and nothing could be done. Wyatt looked about for a place of safety, knowing that he was a target for the same murderer. He made for the horses, but before he reached the place where they were picketed he saw that they had pulled their picket-ropes and stampeded. He hurried after them, running for his life toward the mouth of the canyon and the desert beyond. A sharp reminder of the need of haste, in the shape of a bullet, passed through the leg of the fugitive's trousers, but did not draw blood.

Wyatt was then sixty years old, weighed about two hundred pounds, and was both clumsy and slow on his feet. When he reached the entrance to the canyon his courage fell. Stretching from the base of the mountain away over the white alkali plain was a cloud of dust which hid from sight his only hope of safety—the runaway horses.

As he peered hopelessly after the retreating cloud he saw something which made his heart leap into his mouth. Out of the dust the form of his own fine black pacing horse suddenly appeared. The animal had faced about, apparently struck by some sudden impulse. For a second or two it seemed to take its bearings, and then on a mad gallop retraced its steps until it reached the advancing Wyatt, and invited the old man as plainly as signs could indicate to mount.

Wyatt rode the whole one hundred and forty miles to Susanville bareback at breakneck speed, without a mouthful to eat and with nothing but a picket rope to guide his faithful animal.

It must have been a terrible trip. The condition of a man of his age and weight after riding a barebacked horse that distance may be imagined. To the physical suffering add hunger and thirst and the fear of pursuit by the Indians or of meeting an-other band of them, and an idea can be obtained of the horrors of that journey. The fact that Wyatt's saddle horse allowed himself to be caught is one of the strangest things of the whole affair. Wyatt said the horse was always shy and hard to catch, and was the last one of the horses he had any idea of getting hold of. It seemed to him almost like a miracle.

Weatherlow and his party got to Black Rock two days in advance of Lassen and the other two men and camped on the hill seven miles from Mud lake. Lassen and Clapper were killed only a mile from their camp. Weatherlow's party prospected until their provisions were nearly gone and then started for home, thinking Lassen had taken another route and could not find them. On the second day they met the Honey Lakers who were coming out to see what had become of them, and were told of the murder of Lassen and Clapper. The relief party got back to Honey Lake on May the eleventh. Ross Lewers and John H. Neale were the only members of the party whose names could be ascertained. The bodies of the murdered men were in an advanced state of decomposition and were buried where they were found. Everything went to show the truth of Wyatt's statement. The Indians who committed the murder were not pursued as they had eleven days the start.

Captain Weatherlow says: "The killing of Lassen and his companion caused great excitement in the settlement, and much feeling against the Indians. Several of the settlers attributed the murder to the Pah-utes, but from my own knowledge of the friendly relations between the chief Winnemucca and Peter Lassen and the high esteem in which Lassen was held by the Indians and from the fact that there was no apparent change in the conduct of the Pah-utes who continued to visit our houses and exchange civilities and friendship, I did not believe that the Pah-utes had committed the murder nor that they were at all cognizant of the fact. I attributed it entirely to the Pitt river tribe which the whites had fought and defeated and who frequented the Black Rock country in small hunting bands. There had been no difficulty of any kind between the Honey Lake people and the Pah-utes that would have provoked them to so wanton an act of revenge, especially upon Peter Lassen, who had ever been their firm friend. But the Pit river Indians against whom we had fought would certainly have exulted in surprising and cutting off any small party of whites, and to them alone did I attribute the murder of Lassen. "[5]

Fairfield continued with:

The Grizzly Bear *of May, 1912, says that about a month later P. H. Lovell sent the following letter to the Placerville* Semi-Weekly Observer:

Genoa, May 20, 1859.
Editor of Observer:
Our Indian agent, Major F. Dodge, has just returned from Honey and Pyramid Lakes, whither he has been to inquire into the late Indian depredations to the north of Honey lake. The major is not satisfied that the Indians alone are implicated in the matter, from the fact that two sacks of flour, some dried beef, blankets, and part of a keg of whiskey, were found in the camp of the murdered party—a thing unprecedented in Indian depredations. Peter Lassen and Edward Clapper were killed on the spot. Lemarkus Wyatt, one of the survivors of the party, with whom the major had an interview, had returned to Honey Lake. The four others reported killed have also returned to the lake safe, together with the party of twenty who, it was reported, went out to bury the dead. The major held a council with the venerable Piute chief Winnemucca, with about three thousand of his nation, at Pyramid Lake.

'The Grizzly Bear' also says: 'Later, Winnemucca went to Genoa and reported to Major Dodge that he could learn nothing further from the Indians regarding the affair. This leaves one to infer that it was Dodge's opinion that Lassen and Clapper were killed by the other men.'

Weatherlow says: 'Major Dodge, the Indian agent of the Pah-ute tribe, had never visited the valley to my knowledge, but shortly after the killing of Lassen's party he came to Honey Lake, remained but one day, and returned to Carson City without having had an interview with the chief Winnemucca or made any earnest inquiry into the causes or the perpetrators of the murder. Shortly after the departure of Major Dodge there appeared a statement in one of the newspapers (I think the "Sacramento Union") with authority from Major Dodge to the effect that he (Dodge) did not believe that the Indians had killed Lassen at all, but that he was murdered by white men. This was a charge of the most unwarrantable nature against the four white men who were the only ones within hundreds of miles of the place where the massacre took place, and I as their leader and commander called Major Dodge to an account personally for the charge. He retracted his charge and promised to do so publicly through the press. Whether he did so or not I can not say, as I have not heard of Major Dodge visiting our valley since. The suspicion which rested upon the minds of some of the settlers that the Pah-utes had murdered Lassen apparently died away, and the same friendly relations existed as before.'

The report that Lassen had been killed, and by white men, spread rapidly over the country. At first a good many believed it, but in a short time very few put any faith in the story. The writer, however, has met one or two men who believe it to this day and they think they have good reasons for doing so. He has heard these reasons given, but to him they do not warrant any such belief. Bancroft's History says that in the Sacramento valley there was much hard feeling toward him (Lassen) on the part of those who suffered while going over the Lassen Trail. Excepting this, there is nothing to show that he had any enemies among the whites. 'The Red Bluff Beacon' told that he was allowed to go to his old ranch and help himself to whatever pleased his fancy and Fred Hines told the same thing. During a residence of almost fifty years in this county the writer has never heard an old settler say anything against Lassen, or say that he had trouble with any one. That Weatherlow or his party had anything to do with the murder is not even to be thought of. There seems to be absolutely no reason for the belief that Lassen was killed by white men.[6]

Some question this judgment and the mystery of who killed Lassen still remains. Although there is no forensic evidence and the only clues are circumstantial, there are implications, which cause one to question whether a white man and not Indians may have done it.

Fred Kingsbury, the son of Lassen's partner, recalled:

> *Years ago, in Chico I heard an old settler, deep in his cups, boast he knew more concerning the death of Lassen than any living man. I tried to get him to amplify his statement but he would never say anything further.*[7]

In retelling the story of Lassen's murder, Kingsbury said:

> *'Save yourself, I am hit,' shouted Lassen, just before a bullet through the head* laid him low, and the third man sprinted for the picket line, where the frightened horses were snorting and lunging against their picket ropes. He leaped upon Wild Tom* [Lassen's horse, and not his own black one, as reported in the other article] *and, without saddle or bridle rode eighty miles to Susanville with news of the massacre.*[8]

Some people have questioned Wyatt's story, which varies in different reports. Is this because of different reporters, a cover-up, or memory lapse on his part? Why wasn't he killed with the others? Some claim the shots killing Lassen and Clapper were too accurate for an Indian's musket; however, many Indians at the time had good rifles and were accurate marksmen. Why did the accuracy decline and miss Wyatt? And why did his horse that was allegedly difficult to catch return to him?

Fred Kingsbury reported to the *Sacramento Bee* that he heard a redheaded man in a bar boast, "'I know more about the shooting of Peter Lassen than any man alive,' whereupon his buddy grabbed him and pushed him outside silencing him." Fred continued:

> *My folks told me, when I was a young boy, that talk was currently in the Honey Lake region that Lassen was killed by enemies who coveted his enormous land holdings, totaling 23,000 acres which later, in the days of Leland Stanford*

---

*   Most reports say Lassen was shot in the chest; however, no forensic reports have come to light.

became the famous Vina ranch, the world's largest vineyard.[*]

Lassen's camp was not disturbed, as was typical of an Indian raid, nor was anything taken other than Lassen's prized rifle. In a different account, Fred Kingsbury stated:

> *When Indians kill they want something for it. They take anything, and everything in sight. Nothing was disturbed, not even the food in camp, or Peter's pocketbook, containing his money. So, therefore, it wasn't an Indian's job. This red headed white man, and I know his name, showed crude skill in his operation to kill Lassen...*[9]

Weatherlow was incensed to hear that the Indian Agent, Dodge, suggested a white man had done it because nothing had been taken from the camp. He didn't want to be implicated, and he wanted Dodge to retract his supposition.

Weatherlow would later find Lassen's rifle on a dead Indian. But why would the Indian take only the rifle and nothing else from Lassen's camp? (See the story below of the murder of James Bailey and William Cook in 1862.)

According to Sarah Winnemucca of the Paiutes, "As for Agent Dodge, he suspected the Mormons, whom he blamed for most Indian troubles." In addition, her cousin, the Young Chief Winnemucca, "complained that he was accused of killing Pete Lassen, who had been one of the best men he had ever known and with whom he had slept in the same blanket."[10]

Three years later, in the year 1862, Fairfield reported another twist to the story of Lassen's murder:

The Murder of James Bailey and William Cook

> *It has been told that Mr. Bailey went out to the Humboldt mines in April. He settled up his business in Star City and in company with his partner, William Cook, started with five yoke of cattle and a wagon for their homes in Shasta county. On the night of the eighth of July they reached Antelope Springs fifteen miles west of Lassen's Meadows on the*

---

[*]   Lassen had sold the Vina ranch (*Bosquejo*) to Henry Gerke in 1852 for $25,000.

LEGENDARY TRUTHS

Humboldt river. Appearances indicated that they got there late at night, and after turning their cattle loose, they made their bed a short distance from the wagon and went to sleep. Early the next morning Cook took a little keg and a dipper and went to a spring not far away. It looked as though Bailey was rolling up the bed when some one slipped up behind him and struck him on the head with his own ax. This did not kill him and he fought his way to the wagon and tried to get his gun, but he failed to do it and was killed a short distance from the wagon. There were some bushes on the point of a hill between the wagon and the spring and the tracks showed that ten or twelve Indians had been concealed there. When Cook heard the noise of the fighting at the wagon he started to help Bailey, but the Indians who were in the bushes rushed out to meet him and killed him. It is not known whether any Indians were killed or not. Cook had a pistol and probably he gave a good account of himself before he died. Both men were stripped of their clothes and mutilated and left where they fell. The Indians took their weapons and the cattle and everything the wagon contained excepting some ground coffee which they scattered around the ground. They carried away quite a sum of money which the men had with them. They left the yokes and chains and did not burn the wagon. That night John C. Dow and John Prichard, who were coming from the Humboldt mines, reached the scene of the murder. They rolled the bodies of the men in some blankets and buried them where they found them and they still lie there.[*]

When the news reached the Humboldt mines ten men, Captain Weatherlow, William Jackson, and John Pool being among the number, started out on the trail of the Indians and followed them to the northwest into the Queen's river

---

[*] Both graves are near the grave of Susan B. Corrity at Antelope Springs, about a mile above Willow Springs. When the author and Jo Massey visited the gravesite on August 16, 2010 with an OCTA (Oregon California Trails Association) tour led by Chuck Dodd, they heard a story told by one of the members, that one of the murdered men allegedly (legendary truth?) had Peter Lassen's gun when Indians killed him!

country. They found a camp of nine Indians and succeeded in surrounding it and killing eight of them. The ninth one, who was a big fellow, got into the rocks, and thinking himself safe, climbed out onto a point and began to yell and make insulting gestures. Jackson borrowed Weatherlow's gun, a Sharp's rifle, and taking careful aim, shot the Indian through the body killing him instantly. One of the Indians had on a pair of Mr. Bailey's trousers and in one of the pockets was a promissory note for $50, but it was so badly worn out that the name of the maker could not be read. A. L. Harper says that the Indian killed by Jackson had the gun that Peter Lassen was carrying when he was murdered. It was taken to Susanville and the people there recognized it because it had a black walnut stock the whole length of the barrel. It was given to Governor Roop and Mrs. Arnold says that Harper's account is correct.[11]

From this account, new questions arise:

Did the Indians kill Lassen and take his rifle? If so, why didn't they loot the rest of the camp as they did at the Bailey-Cook massacre?

Did the Indian take the rifle from Bailey or Cook, as one "legendary truth" asserts? If so, this would explain why the Lassen camp didn't show evidence of an Indian raid and looting, as the Bailey-Cook site did.

Did Weatherlow, who had been prospecting near the Lassen murder site at the time of the murder, plant the rifle on the dead Indian to frame him and implicate the Indians in Lassen's murder? Perhaps, as Peggy McGuckian questioned:

...However, it was Weatherlow who in 1862 retrieved Lassen's gun, with its handsome walnut stock, from a slain Paiute who had purportedly killed two other prospectors at Antelope Springs in Majuba Mt. How had the Indian come by the gun? Had two men been murdered for an attractive firearm? Was it mere coincidence that Weatherlow had not only the opportunity to kill Lassen but also was the one who had found Lassen's gun in the hands of a dead member

LEGENDARY TRUTHS

of the group toward whom he had attempted to redirect suspicion?[12]

Or could it have been something entirely different, as OCTA member, Jo Massey wondered. "Who was Edward Clapper? What sort of fellow was he (Wyatt claimed he didn't even know Clapper's first name)? Why is it immediately assumed Lassen was the one the murderer(s) was after?" She added, "Lassen may have been just an innocent collateral victim of someone seeking revenge on Clapper for some unknown reason."

So the mystery remains: Who killed Peter Lassen? One of the prospectors in his or Weatherlow's parties? Indians? A white man? Mormons? The only evidence is circumstantial.

Even today, if you go to that canyon in the desert, stand near the murder rock, shade your eyes, as Lassen did, and look up at the ridge from where the shots rang out, you will surely feel the excitement, the haunting mystery, and perhaps even hear the echoes of the shots as they resound through the canyons to the present.

Fred Kingsbury smokes Peter Lassen's Grandfather's meerschaum pipe, which Peter Lassen brought from Denmark more than a score of years before gold was discovered in Coloma. *(Sacramento Bee article November 30, 1940.)*
Photo by Ken Johnston.

John S. Ward, John H. Neale, and Albert A. Smith were the administrators of Lassen's estate, but Fred Kingsbury said, "My father was named as heir to Lassen's property in the old man's will, but he never realized a cent nor a foot of land, from his inheritance." He did inherit Lassen's meerschaum pipe, an heirloom, which Lassen brought from Denmark. It is now housed in the Lassen Historical Museum in Susanville.

In November 1859, Johnson Tutt, Joe Kitts, and perhaps Antone Storff, went to Black Rock and brought Lassen's body to the valley. Edward Clapper's body was left where it was buried in a canyon south of Clapper's Canyon, which was misnamed and mistakenly thought to be the murder site. Much dissatisfaction was expressed throughout the valley because Clapper's body was not brought in when Lassen's body was, and the site was then lost. However, on Memorial Day, 1990, hikers came across human remains eroding out of a streambed wall.

The Humboldt County Sheriff and the Bureau of Land Management were contacted. Forensic work was done on the bones, and it was concluded that they were the remains of Edward Clapper. He was reburied in a grave close to where Lassen had been interred.[13]

On November 27, 1859, Lassen was buried with Masonic honors under the great tree where he camped the first night he stayed in the valley. It was said he often wished that this might be his final resting place.

On June 24, 1862, a monument was erected over his grave. The inscription on the monument said, "In memory of Peter Lassen, the pioneer, who was killed by the Indians, April 26, 1859. Aged 66 years." According to René Lassen in *Uncle Peter,* in 1917 a new monument was placed near the grave and the older monument. The new monument was inscribed: [14]

Peter Lassen
A Native of Denmark
Aged sixty-six
Killed February 26ᵗʰ, 1859

Lassen, born on October 31, 1800, was 58 ½ years old, when he was killed on April 26, 1859 (not February 26). So, even the "legendary truths," followed him to the grave—etched in stone!

LEGENDARY TRUTHS

Lassen grave marker near Janesville, California.   *Photo by Ken Johnston.*

Epilogue

When writing history, I tried to disprove everything, and what was left over was the truth!—John Codd, "the man who found Elisha Stephens."

Although the number of gold-seekers nearly doubled to about 45,000 in the year of 1850, the Lassen route would have again served as a viable alternative. But the fact remained that it was indeed longer, and the rumors and "legendary truths" caused the route to be nearly abandoned in the ensuing years. With the opening of the Nobles Trail in 1852—shortening the distance—the northern route (Applegate/Lassen/Nobles) would have been the much better choice and could have saved lives, property, and suffering that was even more magnified on the more southern routes (Carson and Truckee) by the increased numbers using the same amount of limited grass.

The Nobles Trail began at Black Rock in 1852, by turning off the Applegate/Lassen Trail, and in 1854, it was shortened to begin just past Rabbit Hole Springs. From the Applegate/Lassen Trail, it went west across the playa, through Smoke Creek Desert to Honey Lake, then north and west around the northern base of Mount Lassen, and finally west into the Sacramento Valley. The Honey Lake Road, which later followed the Nobles Route to Susanville, began at Lassen's Meadows.

LEGENDARY TRUTHS

It was much shorter and easier than the Lassen Trail, which technically began just south of Goose Lake, and should have become the route of choice.

Tolsten Kittelsen Stabaek was traveling to California in 1852 via Black Rock when he wrote, "In the evening we arrived in good condition at Black Rock Spring." He then followed the Nobles Trail and added:

> *Remains could still be seen of oxen and horses lying in pairs and partly covered with sand; of wagons nothing was left but wheel rims and other iron work. The hides and hair of the five yoke of oxen and of several teams of horses lying there in the sand were surprisingly well preserved. The sight I saw there made so deep an impression on me that I can never forget it.*[1]

James Cowden, who later followed the same route to Yreka, summed up the 1853 experience thus:

> *An overland trip to California or Oregon is not difficult or dangerous. I really enjoyed it and could spend several years very pleasantly traveling through the hills and mountains of the western country, it[s] wild scenery is very interesting to me and I do not see how any person can help enjoying it.*[2]

Both of these testimonies showed that the routes pioneered by Levi Scott, Jesse Applegate, Peter Lassen, and William Nobles weren't inherently bad or the source of suffering, if approached early in the season. Continued use of them could have alleviated much suffering and loss of equipment and livestock; however, the Carson Route remained the route of choice, and continued to cause suffering and hardship, even to those approaching it early in the season.

Following the Carson Route in 1850, Dr. J. S. Shepherd explained that the desert crossing "...would not be as bad as it is, did it not follow close after the Humboldt River, the water of which has such a weakening influence on the stock that is next to a miracle to get over without leaving some, if not all of them behind. [3]

John Wood also noted the Carson Route difficulties as he crossed the desert in 1850:

We now begin to meet with the destruction of property and stock; the road being almost lined with wagons, the dead and dying horses, mules and cattle...They were left, and we went to victory, stalking our way through indescribable scenes of suffering and want...hundreds of horses, mules and cattle dead, dying and suffering, are laying thick around, and wagons, carts, and carriages line both sides of the road; also, property of all kinds lying in large heaps, such as harness, clothing, tools and chains. This man who has been selling water here for several weeks, told me that it was estimated by all that there had been left on this plain or desert, this season at least 3,000 wagons and at a low estimate of $3,000,000 worth of property and thousands will yet be left. [4]

Wood then went on to predict:

But the destruction of property and stock is and will not be all. Hundreds will toil on this far, and then leave their bones to bleach on the Great American Desert, and the worst of it all now is to see, every few hundred yards, the grave of some kind brother, father or mother, and even some who have not been buried, but have probably been forsaken when sick or faint, and left to die and waste away in the winds and rains of heaven.... But the sight of the dead is not so fearful as the living dying. God of heaven! Could human suffering appease thy wrath, the world would soon be forgiven. [5]

Several years later, in 1858, William A. Wallace traveled across the Forty Mile Desert on the Carson Route. He was a correspondent for the San Francisco *Alta California* newspaper, and he wrote:

...And here, too, over this whole forty miles, are the signs of wrack and ruin which has fallen upon unfortunate emigrants in past years. Heaps of bones lie everywhere, and everywhere are the iron remnants of wagons. It is estimated that ten thousands tons of wagon irons are lying in the sands of that desert; and there are ox chains enough unbroken, to form a continuous line to Salt Lake. This forty miles is the terror of the whole route, and no wonder. These

LEGENDARY TRUTHS

bleaching bones and rusty irons are evidences the sight of which makes one wish to hurry on, and not feel safe until they no longer greet the eye. I never saw a desert before, and I do not wish to see another.[6]

During the ensuing years, the railroad surveys of Warner, Williamson, and Lyon, following in Lassen's wake, would be lost in the sands of time and the routes would remain remote in the developing West. Political pressures and the proximity to Sacramento and San Francisco would force the Transcontinental Railroad to cross Donner Pass at the cost of many lives—mostly Chinese laborers—a cost that arguably could have been prevented if the railroad had followed a more northerly route, such as the Nobles Trail. In the 1950s, a "Winnemucca to the Sea" highway was proposed, which would have taken traffic north and west from Winnemucca to Lakeview and Medford, Oregon, and then to the coast. But this proposal never reached fruition.

Interstate 80 now follows the railroad over Donner Summit and past Donner Memorial State Park, where tourists can learn about the Donner Tragedy, and a smidgeon about the California trails. But the epic stories of the development of the California Trail and its various alternate routes, the explorations, hardships, and sufferings of those pioneering and using those trails, are slipping into the legends of the past.

It is hoped that the contributions of those pioneers—like Peter Lassen—whose lives and endeavors helped to open the West, will not be forgotten.

After Lassen's death, the August 4, 1859 edition of *The Alta California*, printed this tribute to him:

The poor, sick and unfortunate, who formed so large a class of the immigration of that year, found, in the worthy old Dane, a warm-hearted and true friend, ever ready to alleviate their sufferings and provide for their wants, to the fullest possible extent. It may be easily imagined that a man possessed of so generous a heart would soonest become a victim to the wiles of speculators, who thronged the land in those days. Lassen was eventually deprived of nearly all his property, and, finally, settled down at Honey Lake in Plumas county, where he was engaged in the erection of a sawmill, at the time of his death.[7]

Author with Peter Lassen's pipe at Lassen Historical Museum in Susanville, California. *Courtesy of Lassen Historical Museum. Photo by Jo Massey*

LEGENDARY TRUTHS

Endnotes

Preface and Prologue

1   Scott, 207.
2   Ibid., 195; Read &
    Gaines, xxxviii-xxxix.
3   Ibid., p. 213.
4   Curran, 92-93.
5   Osborne, 127.

1829–1838 Denmark to Missouri

1   Lassen, *Uncle Peter*
2   Ibid., 28.
3   Ibid., 36.
4   Fischer, *Longing For Frontiers.*
5   Ibid., 49.
6   Swartzlow, Lassen, *His Life and
    Legacy*, 12, and Peninou, Leland
    Stanford's *Great Vina Ranch*, 1.
7   Stewart, *The California Trail*, 196.
8   Lassen, 46.
9   *History of Howard And
    Chariton Counties*, 424-425.
10 Chariton County, Missouri,
    Records and Abstracts.
11 Ibid., E-17.
12 Swartzlow, *Trail Blazer*, 291.

1839–1845 Moving West to Oregon

1   Wislizenus, *A Journey*, 28.
2   Wislizenus Journal
3   *The Pioneer*, April 6, 1878.
4   Ibid.
5   Dutton.
6   Ibid., 4.
7   Wiggins, *Reminiscences.*
8   Dutton, 6.
9   *The Pioneer*, April 6, 1878.
10 Wislizenus, *A Journey*, 74.
11 *The Pioneer*. April 6, 1878.
12 Wislizenus Journal
13 Burton.
14 Irving, 29.
15 Wislizenus, *A Journey.*

16 Irving, 30.
17 Ibid., 32.
18 Ibid., 33.
19 Wislizenus, *A Journey*, 76.
20 Ibid., 82-84.
21 Ibid., 88.
22 Ibid., 92.
23 Swartzlow, *Trail Blazer*
24 Williams of Monterey
25 Lassen, 56.
26 Williams.
27 Ibid.
28 Swartzlow, *Trail Blazer*, 294.
29 Fischer, Ch 3.
30 *Pioneer*, April 6, 1878.
31 Jorgensen.
32 Lassen, 61.
33 Ibid., 61.
34 Jorgensen, 19.
35 Scott, 190; Jorgensen, 19.
36 Swartzlow, *Lassen: His Life*, 13.
37 Jorgensen, 19.
38 Lassen, 62.
39 Parmeter, 8.
40 Rogers, Ch 3.
41 Fischer; Cook, 7.
42 Lassen, 62.
43 *Hutchings' California
    Magazine*, 352.
44 Jorgensen, 43; Lassen, 80.
45 Dillon, *Siskiyou Trail*, 21.
46 Scott, 191.
47 Fischer.

Fremont's Trip to Klamath from *Rancho Bosquejo*

1   Southern, *Our Stories
    Landmarks*, 11-12.
2   Fremont, *Geographical
    Memoir*, 149.
3   Warner, *The Bear Flag Revolt*, 115.
4   Martin, *With Fremont
    To California*, 7.
5   Ibid., 7.

6 Southern, 11.
7 Ibid.
8 Martin, *With Fremont*, 8.
9 Ibid., 335.
10 Ibid., 335.
11 Fremont, *Memoirs of My Life*, 486.
12 Swartzlow, *Lassen*, 23.
13 Davis, *Exploring Oregon*, 337.
14 Fremont, *Memoirs*, 486.
15 Ibid., 491-492.
16 Egan, *Fremont, Explorer*, 329.
17 Ibid., 330.
18 Bancroft, *Works of*, Vol. 1, 546-547.
19 Fremont, *Memoirs*, 495.
20 Davis, 340.
21 Swartzlow, *Lassen*, 23; Scott, 193.
22 Lassen, 73.
23 Fremont, *Memoirs*, 404.
24 Ibid., 405.
25 Ibid., 406-407.
26 Ibid., 408.
27 Court Martial Proceedings, 118.
28 Ibid., 175-176.
29 Ibid., 5.

1846 Trail Development and the Donner Tragedy

1 Stewart, *California Trail*, 12.
2 Ibid., 20.
3 Ibid., 41.
4 Stewart, *California Trail*, 99.
5 Ibid., 143.
6 Helfrich, 2.
7 Bancroft, *Works*, 546-547.
8 Stewart, *California Trail*, 167.
9 Ibid., 168.
10 Morgan, 750-751.

1847 Donner Fallout and Lassen's Trip East

1 Blackburn, 103.
2 Lassen, 73; Fairfield, 169.
3 Scott, 193.
4 Ibid., 193; Read & Gaines, *Gold Rush*, 634.
5 McKinstry, *Overland Letters*, 206.
6 Newell, 158.

7 Ibid., 159.
8 Ibid., 159.
9 Ibid., 159.
10 Fremont, *Memoirs*, 553-554.
11 Helfrich & Ackerman, *Schreek of Wagons*, 19.
12 Morgan.
13 Stewart, *California Trail*, 192.
14 Ibid., 190-191.
15 Gray, Journal, 1849.
16 Helfrich, *Klamath Echoes*, V. 9, 8-9.
17 Stewart, *California Trail*, 191.
18 Ibid., 192.
19 Helfrich, *Klamath Echoes*, V. 9, 8-9.
20 Calhoun, 11.
21 Bagley, *So Rugged*, 369-370.
22 Davis, *South Road*.
23 Burnett, *Reflections and Opinions*, Mar 1904, 64-99, and Dec 1904, 370-401.
24 Lavender, *The Great West*, 306.
25 Egan, 554.
26 Blackburn.
27 Swartzlow, *Lassen: His Life*, 23.
28 Huffman, *Lassen Thread*.
29 Dutton, 3.
30 Scott, 193; Read & Gaines, *Gold Rush*, 634.
31 Dutton, 3.

1848 Lassen's Return and News of Gold

1 Helfrich/Ackerman, 70-71.
2 Stewart, *California Trail*, 198.
3 Fariss & Smith, 145.
4 Lavender, 306.
5 Howard, 78.
6 Calhoun, 12-14.
7 Stewart, *California Trail*, 196-197.
8 Helfrich/Ackerman, 22 & 86.
9 Huffman; also Fairfield, 3.
10 Ibid.
11 Bagley, *Lassen Thread*.
12 Lassen.
13 Helfrich/Ackerman.
14 Ibid., 22-23.
15 Ibid., 32.
16 Ibid., June 12, 1848 entry.

17 Mattes, 423.
18 Helfrich/Ackerman, 38.
19 Dunlop, 88.
20 Read & Gaines, *Gold Rush*, 62.
21 Helfrich/Ackerman, 70-71.
22 Bagley, *So Rugged*,
    footnote #92, 380.
23 Ibid., 84.
24 Helfrich/Ackerman, footnote, 90.
25 Ibid., 92-93.
26 Ibid., 92-93.
27 Stewart, *California Trail*, 203.
28 Ibid., 203.
29 Helfrich/Ackerman, 96.
30 Ibid., 102.

Trail Beginnings: Lassen's Meadows to *Rancho Bosquejo*

1   Stewart, *California Trail*, 211.
2   Ibid., 207.
3   Read & Gaines, *Gold
    Rush*, 314, 683, 697.
4   Ibid., 345.
5   Helfrich/Ackerman, 48.
6   Howell, Diary, Aug 23, 1849.
7   Applegate, Mar, 1921.
8   Tiffany, Sep 14, 1849.
9   Fairfield, 4.
10 Bagley, *Lassen Thread* #02,
    November 11, 2005.
11 Fairfield, 7-8.
12 Stewart, 211.
13 Ibid., 211.
14 King, 187.
15 Stewart, 211.
16 Lavender, 306.
17 Swartzlow, *Peter Lassen,
    Trail Blazer,* 301.
18 Ibid., 301.
19 Fairfield, 7-8.
20 Burnett, 373.
21 Lovejoy.
22 Burnett, 375.
23 Ibid., 376.
24 Ibid., 379.
25 Ibid., 370-401.
26 Ibid., 157-158.
27 Kirov, 18.
28 Lovejoy, 270.

29 Ibid., 270.
30 Bagley, *Lassen Thread.*
31 Burnett, 266.
32 Ibid., 270.
33 Swartzlow, 59.

Easterners Respond to News of Gold Discovery

1   Mattes, 15.
2   Stewart, *California Trail*, 229.
3   Mattes, 54.
4   Read & Gaines, 567.
5   Ibid., xvi.
6   Mattes, 52.
7   Ibid., 46.
8   Haun, Henry Peter,
    Overland Guide.
9   Unruh, 132-133.
10 Read & Gaines, Vol. I, 350.
11 Ibid., 123-125.
12 Middleton, Sept 20, 1849.
13 Fischer.
14 Stewart, *California Trail*, 270.

Beginning Use of the Lassen Route

1   Curran, 42.
2   Hale, Aug 21, 1849.
3   Davis, *The South Road,* 108.
4   Webster, 82-83.
5   Ibid., 83.
6   DeWolf, 25.
7   Tiffany, Sept 12, 1849.
8   Booth, Aug 18, 1850.
9   Minges.
10 Stewart. *California Trail,* 269.
11 Ibid., 269.
12 Reading, 187-188.
13 Stewart, *California Trail,* 269.
14 Read & Gaines, 1201.
15 Ibid.
16 Van Dorn.
17 Hoffman, 24.
18 Unruh, 132-133.
19 Read & Gaines, xxxviii & xxxix.

LEGENDARY TRUTHS

Misconceptions of the Trail

1 Bagley, *Lassen Thread # 8.*
2 Davis, *Exploring Oregon,* 182.
3 Fremont, *Expeditions of, Vol. I,* 590.
4 Davis, *Exploring Oregon,* 321.

The Cherokee Cutoff

1 Lord, Doctor's *Gold Rush,* 108.
2 Tiffany, Sept 14, 1849.
3 Webster, Sept 14, 1849.
4 Fletcher, Fletcher, Whitley, *Cherokee Trail Diaries,* Vol. 1, 13..
5 Bancroft, *History of California, Vol.19,* 732-33.
6 Fletcher, 161-168.
7 Ibid., 184.
8 Read & Gaines, 642.
9 Fletcher, 173.
10 Ibid., 173.
11 Read & Gaines, 642.
12 Fletcher, 187.

Responsibility for the Trail

1 Delano, *Across the Plains,* 86.
2 Fletcher, 186.
3 Stewart, 291.
4 Read & Gaines, xxxviii & xxxix.

Lassen's Meadow to Black Rock

1 Helfrich, *Applegate Trail,* 23.
2 Read & Gaines, 146.
3 Buck, 18.
4 Howell, *1849 California Trail,* 103.
5 Read & Gaines, 146.
6 Middleton.
7 Sprague.
8 Delano, *Across The Plains,* 78.
9 Lord, *Doctor's Gold Rush,* 115.
10 Read & Gaines, Vol. I, 336.
11 Ibid., 151.
12 Lord, 117.
13 Ibid., 118.
14 Tiffany, Sept 14, 1849.
15 Staebeck.

Black Rock to Mud Lake

1 Delano, *Across the Plains,* 82.
2 Foster, 51.
3 Delano, *Across the Plains,* 82
4 Bachelder, Sept 18, 1849.
5 Hale, June 30, 1926.
6 Read & Gaines, 157.
7 Tiffany, Sept 10, 12, 14, 1849.
8 Delano, 83.

Mud Lake to High Rock Canyon

1 Biddle.
2 Delano, *Across the Plains,* 84.
3 Howell, Diary, ms.
4 Read & Gaines, 160.
5 Farnham.
6 Hale, 121.
7 Read & Gaines, 162.
8 Lord, 127-128.
9 Biddle, Aug 18, 1849.
10 Read & Gaines, 166.
11 Ibid., 166.
12 Doyle, Sept 13, 1849.
13 Castleman, Sept 17, 1849.
14 Gray, *Off at Sunrise,* 93.

High Rock Canyon to Fandango Pass

1 Delano, 26.
2 Middleton, Aug 4, 1849.
3 Lord, *Doctors Gold Rush,* 130.
4 Middleton, Oct 6, 1849.
5 Ibid., Oct 6, 1849.
6 Read & Gaines, 170.
7 Delano, 86.
8 Doyle, Sept 14, 1849.
9 Read & Gaines, 170.
10 Lord, 130.
11 Read & Gaines, 170.
12 Middleton, Oct 7, 1849.
13 Lord, *Doctor's Gold Rush,* 130.
14 Hale.
15 Holliday, 281.
16 Tiffany.
17 Delano, *Across the Plains*, 88.
18 Ibid.,
19 Hale, II, 2.
20 Read & Gaines, 174.

Fandango Pass to Pit River
& Hanging Rock Canyon

1   Read & Gaines, 140, 692.
2   Helfrich, Helfrich, Hunt, 141-142.
3   Castleman.
4   Austin.
5   Read & Gaines, 177-178.
6   Ibid., 178, 653.
7   Delano, *Across the Plains,* 92.
8   Holliday, 279.
9   Delano, *Across the Plains,* 92.
10 Read & Gaines, 180-181.
11 Lord, *Doctor's Gold Rush,* 146-147.
12 Doyle.

Hanging Rock Canyon
to Big Valley

1   Foster, 54.
2   Josselyn, *Overland Journal,* 47.
3   Delano, *Across the Plains,* 93-94.
4   Lord, *Doctor's Gold Rush,* 150.
5   Castleman, 99.
6   Middleton.
7   Gray, *Off at Sunrise,* 99-100.
8   Ibid., 99-100.
9   Ibid., 99-100.

Big Valley Road Forks
to Road Junction

1   Burnett, 157.
2   Doyle.
3   Jewett, Sept 13, 1849.
4   Doyle.
5   Helfrich, Helfrich, Hunt, 151.
6   Read & Gaines, 185.
7   Pratt.
8   Delano, *Across the Plains,* 96.
9   Lord, *Doctor's Gold Rush,* 151-152.
10 Read & Gaines, 187.
11 Howell, *1849 California Trail.*
12 Read & Gaines, 186-187.
13 Howell, *1849 California Trail.* 190.
14 Ibid., 136-137.
15 Read & Gaines, 648.
16 Ibid., 379, 704.

17 Ibid., 646.
18 Ibid., 701.
19 Ibid., 648.

Road Junction to Feather River

1   Doyle, Sept 30 and Oct 3, 1849.
2   Gray, *Off at Sunrise,* 102.
3   Castleman, Oct 8, 1849.
4   Read & Gaines, 194.

Feather River
to Deer Creek Crossing

1   Delano, *Across the Plains,* 98.
2   Castleman, Oct 10, 1849.
3   Austin, Oct 16, 1849.
4   Read & Gaines, 198-199.
5   Ibid., 199.
6   Lord, *Doctor's Gold Rush,* 158.
7   Ibid., 159.
8   Doyle, Oct 5, 1849.
9   Delano, *Across the Plains,* 98.
10 Gray, 104.
11 Doyle, Oct 6, 1849.
12 Read & Gaines, 201.

Deer Creek Crossing
to Bruff's Camp

1   Doyle, Oct 8, 1849.
2   Read & Gaines, 202.
3   Pratt.
4   Doyle, Oct 12, 1849.
5   Delano, *Across the Plains,* 108.
6   Gray, *Off at Sunrise,* 111.
7   Lord, *Doctor's Gold Rush,* 164.

Bruff's Camp
to Lassen's *Rancho Bosquejo*

1   Read & Gaines, 663.
2   Ibid., 206.
3   Lovejoy.
4   Ibid., 206.
5   Werner, 63.
6   Read & Gaines, 223-224.
7   Ibid., 341, 343.

LEGENDARY TRUTHS

8 Lord, *Doctor's Gold Rush*, 164.
9 Gray, *Off at Sunrise*, 111-112.
10 Pratt, Nov 6, 1849.
11 Gray, *Off at Sunrise*, 112.

At Lassen's *Rancho Bosquejo*

1 Lord, *Doctor's Gold Rush*, 165-166.
2 Ibid., 166.
3 Delano, *Across The Plains*, 102.
4 Castleman, 110.
5 Jewett, Oct 8, 1849
6 Castleman, 111-112.
7 Holliday, J.S. 291.
8 Rucker, 68.
9 Werner, 67.
10 Rucker, 55.
11 Doyle, Oct 14, 1849.
12 Read & Gaines, 706.
13 Unruh, 354.
14 Ibid., 504.

Forty Mile Desert and the Other Routes

1 Geiger, 170.
2 Levy, 19.
3 Hurlbert, 244.
4 Ibid., 185.
5 Johnston, July 15.
6 Harris, 61.
7 Scamehorn, 78.
8 Ingalls.
9 Kelly.
10 Breyfogle, July 22, 1849.
11 Ibid., 18.
12 Ibid., 19.
13 Harrow, 56-57.
14 Ibid., 56-57.
15 Harris, 80.
16 Clark, 3-43.
17 Lavender, 306.
18 Langworthy.
19 Frink, 88.
20 Bennett, 75.
21 Perkins, 121-122.
22 Johnston, 153.
23 Perkins, 130.
24 Ibid., 131-132.

25 Hurlbert, 252.
26 Bennett, 76.
27 Ibid., 79.

The 1849 Rescue Party

1 *The Nevada Observer*, 18.
2 Ibid., 28.
3 Ibid., 21.
4 Ibid., 23.
5 Stewart, *California Trail*, 288.
6 Werner, 57.
7 Ibid., 58.
8 Doyle, Oct 12, 1849.
9 *The Nevada Observer*, 28.
10 Pratt.
11 *The Nevada Observer*, 55.

Dealing With the Wilsons

1 Read & Gaines, 585.
2 Culmer, *General John Wilson*.
3 Read & Gaines, 586.
4 *The Nevada Observer*, 32.
5 Court Transcripts, Exhibit F.
6 Read & Gaines, 674.
7 Ibid., 232.
8 Ibid., 676.
9 Court Transcripts, Lassen's defense testimony.
10 Read & Gaines, 677.
11 Ibid., 237.
12 Culmer, *California Letter*, 200.
13 Court Transcripts, Peter Lassen testimony.
14 Ibid., William Myer's testimony.
15 Ibid., Lassen's Defense Testimony.
16 Ibid.
17 Fairfield, 170.
18 Scott, 199.
19 Court Transcripts, Exhibit F.
20 Read & Gaines, 360.
21 Swartzlow, *Lassen:, His Life*, 34.
22 Read & Gaines, 687.
23 Ibid., 687.
24 Court Transcripts, Witness Testimonies.
25 Ibid.
26 Ibid., Peter Lassen Defense.

27   Swartzlow, *Lassen: His Life*, 35.
28   Fischer.
29   Lassen, 85.
30   Read & Gaines, 725-726.
31   Ibid., 695.
32   Swartzlow, *Lassen: His Life*, 32.
33   Read & Gaines, 366.
34   Ibid., 469.

1850 Prospecting in the Mountains & Discovery of Honey Lake

 1   Read & Gaines, 381.
 2   Ibid., 388-389.
 3   Ibid., 392.
 4   Ibid., 410.
 5   Ibid., 422.
 6   Ibid., 715.
 7   Ibid., 446.
 8   Ibid., 450-451.
 9   Ibid., 453.
10   Ibid., 455.

1851-1852 Nobles Emigrant Trail

 1   Amesbury, 4.
 2   Purdy, 7-8.
 3   Swartzlow, *Lassen: His Life* 72.
 4   Read & Gaines, 382.
 5   Swartzlow, *Lassen: His Life*, 76.
 6   Ibid., 76.
 7   Fairfield, 18.
 8   Hunt, 5.
 9   Brock, et. al., 5.
10   Ibid., 7
11   Nobles, 1.
12   Ibid., 2.
13   Brock, et. al., 4.
14   Ibid.,7.
15   Jackson, 190.
16   Hunt, 5.
17   Swartzlow, *Lassen: His Life*, 44.
18   Ibid., 79, 9.
19   Ibid., 74.
20   Hunt, 5.
21   Hunt, 6.
22   Court Transcripts, California Witness Testimonies, 70-71.

23   Hunt, 6-7.
24   Court Transcripts, California Witness Testimonies, 66-67.
25   Ibid., 68.
26   www.blm.gov/ca/st/en/fo/ eaglelake/nobles.html

1851-1854 Indian Valley

1   Levenson, 24.
2   Court Transcripts.
3   Levenson, 25.
4   Swartzlow, *Lassen: His Life*, 42.
5   Fariss & Smith, 179, 204.

1855-Finding Gold in Honey Lake Valley

1   Fairfield, 25.
2   Ibid., 26.
3   Ibid., 27.
4   Ibid., 27.
5   Ibid., 28.
6   Levenson, 27.
7   *The Sacramento Bee*, 3.

1856 Honey Lake Politics

1   Levenson, 29.
2   Fairfield, 47, 49.
3   Lassen, 95, 101.
4   Purdy, 10.
5   Swartzlow, *Lassen: His Life*, 73.
6   Fairfield, 35.
7   Levenson, 35.
8   Ibid., 35.
9   Swartzlow, *Lassen: His Life*, 54.

1857-1858 Partnership With Kingsbury

1   Fairfield, 88.
2   Bagley, *So Rugged*, 386.
3   Fairfield, 145-146.
4   Ibid., 63.
5   *The Sacramento Bee*, 3.
6   Ibid., 3.
7   *Pony Express Courier*, 6.
8   *The Sacramento Bee*, 3.

LEGENDARY TRUTHS

9   *Pony Express Courier*, 6.
10 Fairfield, 81.
11 Ibid., 81.
12 *The Red Bluff Beacon.*
13 Swartzlow, *Lassen: His Life*, 44.
14 Fairfield, 100-101.
15 Ibid., 100-101.

1859 Lassen's Final Journey

1   *The Alta California,*
    August 4, 1859.
2   Fairfield, 150.
3   Ibid., 145.
4   Ibid., 171-172.
5   Ibid., 172-175.
6   Ibid., 175-177.
7   *The Sacramento Bee,* 3.
8   *Pony Express Courier,* 6.
9   Ibid., 6.
10 Canfield, 19, 27.
11 Fairfield, 187-288.
12 McGuckian & Dansie, and personal
    interview with Peggy McGuckian,
    Jan.19, 2011. Winnemucca, NV.
13 Ibid.
14 Lassen, 107.

Epilogue

1   Staebeck.
2   Cowden, 141.
3   Shepherd.
4   Curran, 182-183.
5   Ibid., 183.
6   Wheeler, 54.
7   *The Alta California*, Aug 4, 1859.

Bibliography

Alta California, a 19th century San Francisco newspaper. Microfiche, California State Library, Sacramento

Amesbury, Robert. Nobles' Emigrant Trail. 1967, S.P., printed by Lassen Litho, Susanville, CA.

Applegate, Lindsey. "Notes and Reminiscences of Laying Out and Establishing the Old Emigrant Road into Southern Oregon in the Year 1846." *Oregon Historical Quarterly*. Vol. 22, No. 1, March 1921.

Austin, Dr. Henry. Diary,1849. Ms. Berkeley, CA: Bancroft Library.

Bachelder, Amos. *Journal of a Trip*. Ms. Berkeley, CA: Bancroft Library,1849.

Bagley, Will. *So Rugged And Mountainous: Blazing The Trails To Oregon And California 1812-1848*. Norman, OK: University of Oklahoma Press, 2010.

———. *Lassen Thread* #02, November 11, 2005.

Bancroft, Hubert Howe. *History of California* with an introduction by Edmund G. Brown. San Rafael: Bancroft Press, 1990.

———. *The Works of Herbert Howe Bancroft*, Vol. XXIX, History of Oregon, Vol. I 1834-1848. San Francisco: The History Company, 1886-88.

Banks, Edwin P. and Lytle-Webb, Jamie. *The Buckeye Rovers in the Gold Rush*, An Edition of Two Diaries, Athens, OH, 1965

Bennett, James. *Overland Journey to California: Journal of James Bennett Whose Party Left New Harmony in 1850 and Crossed the Plains and Mountains until the Golden West was Reached.* Fairfield, WA: Ye Galleon Press 1987.

Biddle, B.R. "Letters of May 13, 20, and 24 and June 17, 1849." *Illinois State Journal.* 1849. Springfield: Illinois Historical Library.

Bidwell, John, see Rogers.

Blackburn, Abner. *Frontiersman: Abner Blackburn's Narrative*. Will Bagley, ed. Salt Lake City: University of Utah Press, 1992.

Booth, Edmund. *Edmund Booth (1810-1905), Forty-niner: the Life Story of a Deaf Pioneer.* Stockton, CA: San Joaquin Pioneer and Historical Society, 1953.

Breyfogle, Joshua D. *Diary of J.D. Breyfogle, Sr. : Covering his Experiences During his Overland Trip to California During the Gold Rush in 1849.* Hanover, NH: Dartmouth College Library.

Brock, Richard K., et al. *A Guide to the Nobles Trail: An Emigrant Trails West Series Guidebook* . Reno, NV: Trails West, Inc., 2008.

Brown, John Henry. *Early Days of San Francisco, California.* Oakland, CA: Biobooks, 1949.

Bruff, J. Goldsborough. See Read & Gaines.

LEGENDARY TRUTHS

Brunswicker, the newspaper of Brunswick, Chariton County, Missouri, began publication in 1847.

Buck, Donald. Essay in *Emigrant Trails West: A Guide to the Applegate Trail, The South Road to Oregon.* Brock, Richard, ed.

Burnett, Peter H. *Recollections and Opinions of an Old Pioneer.* New York: 1880.

———. "Recollections and Opinions of an Old Pioneer." *Oregon Historical Society Quarterly,* Mar. 1904 and Dec.1904.

Burton, Richard. *Mileposts Along The Oregon Trail—Nebraska.* 1860 Prof. Jim Tompkins, compiler. www.oregonpioneers.com

Calhoun, F. D. *The Lassen Trail.* Sacramento, CA: Cal-Con Press, 1987.

Canfield, Gae Whitney. *Sarah Winnemucca of the Northern Paiutes.* Norman, OK: University of Oklahoma Press,1983.

Carroll, John Alexander, et al, eds. *Probing the American West: Papers from the Santa Fe Conference.* Santa Fe 1962.

Case, Chester H. Jr. *The Development of Roads Between Oregon and California.* University of California, 1955 (Thesis). Source: Early Exploration: Historical Interpretations and Reviews.

Castleman, P.F. *Diary While Crossing the Plains.* 1849. Microfilm of ms. Bancroft Library, Berkeley, CA.

Chariton County Records and Abstracts. Keytesville, MO.

Clark, Bennett, Journal. "Diary of a Journey from Missouri to California in 1849." Ralph P. Bieber, ed. *Missouri Historical Review, XXIII* (October 1928). Columbus, MO: Missouri Historical Society.

Cook, Fred S. "Father of the County, Peter Lassen." *Legends of Lassen County.* Volcano, CA: California Traveler, 1970.

Court Transcripts of Charles L. Wilson & John Wilson vs. Peter Lassen & Henry Gerke. Sacramento, CA: California State Archives, October 5, 1853.

Cowden, James. *1853 Journal.* Ms. in archives San Francisco, CA: California Historical Society.

Culmer, Frederic A. "General John Wilson Signer of the Deseret Petition, Including Letters from the Leonard Collection." *California Historical Society Quarterly,* 1947. Columbia, MO: Missouri State Historical Society.

———. "California Letter of John Wilson, 1850." *Missouri Historical Review.* Vol. 24, No. 2 January1930.

Curran, Harold. *Fearful Crossing: The Central Overland Trail Through Nevada.* Las Vegas: Nevada Publications, 1982.

Davis, Charles George. *Exploring Oregon—California Trails.* North Plains, Oregon: EmigrantsWest.com. 2003.

———. *The South Road and the Route Across Southern Oregon.* North Plains, Oregon: EmigrantsWest.com, 2000.

Delano, Alanzo. *Across The Plains and Among the Diggings.* A reprint of the original edition, first published in 1853. New York: Wilson-Erickson, Inc. 1936.

————. "California Correspondence." Sacramento: *Sacramento Book Collectors Club*, 1952.

De Wolf, Captain David. *Diary of the Overland Trail 1849 and Letters 1849-50 of Captain David De Wolf.* Independence, MO: Merrill J. Mattes Research Library, National Frontier Trails Museum.

Dillon, Richard. *Fool's Gold: A Biography of John Sutter.* New York: Coward-McCann, Inc., 1967.

————. *Siskiyou Trail: The Hudson's Bay Company Route to California.* New York: McGraw-Hill Book Company, 1975

Dorin, May. *The Emigrant Trails into California.* Masters Thesis, 1922. Bancroft Library, Berkeley, CA. mf593 D68.

Doyle, Simon. Journal, Microfilm. New Haven, CT: Yale University. 1849-1854.

Dunlop, Richard. *Wheels West.* San Francisco: Rand McNally & Co., 1977

Dutton, Edward W. "Pioneer Peter Lassen 1793 [sic] -1859." *The Pony Express, Stories of Pioneers and Old Trails.* Vol. XXV. No. 1. No. 289. Sonora, CA. June 1958.

Egan, Ferol. *Frémont: Explorer For a Restless Nation.* Reno: University of Nevada Press, 1977, 1985.

Emerson, William. *Applegate Trail of 1846.* Ashland, OR: Ember Enterprises, 1996.

Fairfield, Asa Merrill. *Fairfield's Pioneer History of Lassen County California.* San Francisco: H. S. Crocker Company, 1916.

Fariss and Smith. *History of Plumas County, California.* (Reproduction of Fariss and Smith's *History of Plumas, Lassen &Sierra Counties, 1882.*) Burbank, CA: Howell-North Books, 1971.

Farnham, Elijah Bryan. "From Ohio to California..." Mattes, Merrill J. and Esley J. Kirk, eds. *Indiana Magazine of History, XLVI* (September 1950), and (December, 1950).

Fischer, Flemming. *Longing For Frontiers, Dramas and Adventures in the Life of Peter Lassen.* Dissertation, 1986. Sacramento, CA: California State Library, .

Fletcher, Patricia K. A., Dr. Jack Earl Fletcher, Lee Whitley. *Cherokee Trail Diaries.* Sequim, WA: Fletcher Family Foundation, n.d.

Foster, Rev. Isaac, et al. *The Foster Family; California Pioneers 1849.* Santa Barbara, CA: Press of The Schauer Printing Studio, Inc. 1925. Diary is entitled, *"A Journal of the Route to Alta California and Letters Enroute.* Santa Barbara, CA: R.C. Foster, 1889.

Fremont, John C. *The Expeditions of John Charles Fremont.* Jackson, Donald and Mary Lee Spence, eds. Four volumes and map portfolio. Urbana, Chicago: University of Illinois Press, 1970.*Geographical Memoir Upon Upper California, In Illustration Of His Map Of Oregon And California.* San Francisco, Book Club of California, 1964.

————. *Memoirs of My Life.* Chicago: Belford, Clark, 1887, c 1886.

Frink, Mrs. Margaret A., *Journal of the Adventures of a Party of California Gold Seekers.* Addenda by Ledyard Frink. Fairfield, WA: Ye Galleon Press, 1987.

LEGENDARY TRUTHS

Originally published: Oakland, CA, 1897

Geiger, Vincent, et al. *The Trail to California: The Overland Journal of Vincent Geiger and Wakeman Bryarly.* David M. Potter, ed. New Haven: Yale University Press, 1945 and 1962.

Gillespie, Archibald H. *Personal Papers of Archibald H. Gillespie 1847-1860.* Special Collections, 133. University of California at Los Angeles Library.

Gray, Charles Glass. *Off at Sunrise: The Overland Journal of Charles Glass Gray.* Thomas D. Clark, ed. San Marino, CA: Huntington Library, 1976

————. *Journal of an Overland Passage from Independence to San Francisco.* Diary ms. San Marino, CA: Huntington Library, 1849.

Gronfeldt, Henry. "The Dane Who Became the Uncrowned King Of the California Pioneers." *Vejle District News.* May 30, 1958, Vejle, Denmark.

Hafen, Leroy. *Trappers of the Far West.* Lincoln: University of Nebraska Press,1972

Hafen, Leroy R. and Francis Marion Young. *Fort Laramie and the Pageant of the West.* Glendale, CA: Arthur H. Clark Co, 1938.

Hale, Israel. "Diary of a Trip to California, 1849." *Quarterly, Society of California Pioneers,* v. II, no.2, June 30, 1926. California State Library, Sacramento.

Harris, Everett W. *The Emigrants Passed This Way.* Reno, NV: Department 13 Designs, 2002.

Harrow, Edward C. *The Gold Rush Overland Journal of Edward C. Harrow, 1849.* Austin, TX: Michael Vinson Publishing, 1993.

Haun, Henry Peter (aka "Major Horn"), *Overland Guide, 1849.*

Hays, Lorena. *To The Land Of Gold and Wickedness: The 1848-59 Diary of Lorena L. Hays.* Jeanne Hamilton Watson, ed. St. Louis: The Patrice Press. 1988.

Helfrich, Devere. "The Applegate Trail." *Klamath Echoes,* no. 9 (1971). pp.1-106.

Helfrich, Devere and Trudy Ackerman, eds. *The Schreek Of Wagons:1848 Diary of Richard M. May, A Sketch of a Migrating Family to California.* Hopkinton, MA: Rigel Publications, 1993.

Helfrich, Devere, Helen Helfrich and Thomas Hunt. *Emigrant Trails West: A Guide to Trail Markers Placed by Trails West, Inc.* Reno, NV: Trails West, Inc. 1984.

————. *History of Howard and Chariton Counties, Missouri.* St Louis: National Historic Company, 1883.

Hoffman, Wilhelm. Journal, 1849-50. New Haven, CT: Rare Book and Manuscript Library, Yale University.

Holliday, Geo. H. *On the Plains in '65.* 1865 N.p.: 1883. San Marino, CA: Huntington Library.

Holliday, J[aquelin] S[mith]. *The World Rushed In, The California Gold Rush Experience.* Norman, OK: University of Oklahoma Press, 2002.

————. "The California Gold Rush Reconsidered." *Probing the American West: Papers from the Santa Fe Conference.* Santa Fe, 1962.

Howard, Thomas. *Sierra Crossing: First Roads to California.* Berkeley, CA: University of California Press, 1998

Howell, Elijah Preston. Diary, microfilm. 1849. Columbia, MO: State Historical Society of Missouri.

————. *The 1849 California Trail Diaries of Elijah Preston Howell.* Susan Badger Doyle and Donald E. Buck, eds. Independence, MO: Oregon-California Trails Association, c1995.

Huffman, Wendell. "What Did Lassen Know When He Turned North on the Applegate Trail in 1848?" *Lassen Thread* Message # 01, November 11, 2005. http://canvocta.org/lassenthread01.html

Hunt, Tom. Essay. *A Guide to the Nobles Trail.* Brock, Richard K., Robert S. Black, and Donald E. Buck, eds. Reno, NV: Trails West, Inc., 2008.

Hurlbert, Archer Butler. *Forty-Niners: The Chronicle of the California Trail.* Boston: Little, Brown and Company, 1940.

Hutchings California Magazine. "Peter Lassen, with portrait of Peter Lassen." No.32. February, 1859. San Francisco: Published by Hutchings & Rosenfield.

Hutchings, James Mason. Diary, 1849, microfilm of ms. Berkeley: Bancroft Library.

Ingalls, E[leazer] S[tillman]. *Journal of a Trip to California by the Overland Route Across the Plains in 1850-51* The Project Gutenberg eBook, 2010. http://www. gutenberg.org/

Irving, Washington. *Adventures of Captain Bonneville.* 1837. Republished Portland, OR: Binfords and Mort, Publishers 1954.

Jackson, W. Turrentine. Foreword by William H. Goetzmann. *Wagon Roads West: A Study of Federal Road Surveys and Construction in the Trans-Mississippi West, 1846-1869.* Lincoln: University of Nebraska Press 1964. The first Bison Book Printing, 1979.

Jewett, George E. Diary, microfilm of ms. 1849. San Mateo County Historical Society. Berkeley: Bancroft Library.

Johnston, Wm. G. *Overland to California.* Foreword by Jos. A. Sullivan. Oakland, CA: Biobooks, Centennial Edition, 1948

Jorgensen, T. Vogel. *Peter Lassen of California.* Translated by Helge Norrung. Red Bluff, CA: Red Bluff Union High School.

Josselyn, Amos P. *The Overland Journal of Amos Piatt Josselyn, Zanesville to Sacramento.* ms. J. William Barrett II, ed. Baltimore: Gateway Press, Inc. 1978.

————. *Zanesville to Sacramento* ms. Sacramento, CA: California State Library.

Keller, George, *Crossing the Plains to California in 1849-1850.* Fairfield, WA: YE Galleon Press, 1983.

Kelly, William. *Across the Rocky Mountains from New York to California with a Visit to the Celebrated Mormon Colony at the Great Salt Lake.* London: Simms & McIntyre, 1852.

Kilgore, William H. *The Kilgore Journal of an Overland Journey to California in the Year 1850.* Joyce Rockwood Muench, ed. From the original journal of William H. Kilgore. New York: Hastings House, 1949.

King, Joseph A. *Winter of Entrapment*. Toronto: P.D. Maury Publishers, 1992

Kingsbury, Fred. *Reminiscences of Mr. Kingsbury* as told to Harry Peterson at Roops Fort, April 20, 1940. Pioneer Manuscript Collection 346 I-R. Sacramento State Historic Library.

Kirov, George. *Peter Lassen: Highlights of his Life and Achievements*. Sacramento, CA: Senate of the State of California, 1940.

Langworthy, Franklin. *Scenery of the Plains, Mountains, and Mines*. 1850. Paul C. Phillips, ed. From 1855 edition. Princeton, NJ. 1932.

Lassen, René Weybye. *Uncle Peter: The Story of Peter Lassen and the Lassen Trail*. Paradise, CA: Ox Shoe Publications, 1990.

Lathrop, Gerald Richard. *The Life of Peter Lassen*. A thesis presented to the Department of History, California State University, Long Beach. 1974.

Lavender, David. *The Great West*. Boston, New York: Houghton Mifflin Co. 1965.

Levenson, Rosaline. *The Short-Lived Explorations of Isadore Meyerowitz, Gold Prospecting in Northeastern California with Peter Lassen*. Janesville, CA: High Desert Press, 1994 A Lassen County Historical Society Book.

Levy, Jo Ann. *They Saw The Elephant: Women In The California Gold Rush*. Hamden, CT: Archon Books, an imprint of The Shoe String Press, 1990.

Lewis, Oscar. *Sutter's Fort: Gateway to the Gold Fields*. Englewood Cliffs, NJ: Prentice Hall, Inc., 1966.

Lord, Israel Shipman Pelton. *A Doctor's Gold Rush Journey To California*. Necia Dixon Liles, ed. Lincoln and London: University of Nebraska Press, 1995. First Bison Books printing, 1999.

———. Diary, 1849-51. Ms and clippings from Elgin, IL, *Western Christian*. San Marino, CA: Huntington Library.

Lorton, William B. Diary and Letters, 1848-50. Microfilm of typescripts. Berkeley: Bancroft Library.

Lovejoy, Peter J. "Lovejoy's Pioneer Narrative, 1842-1848." Recorded by Henry E. Reed. *Oregon Historical Society Quarterly*. 81 No. 3. September 1930.

Martin, Thomas Salathiel. *Narrative of John C. Frémont's expedition to California in 1845-6 and Subsequent Events in California Down to 1853 Including Frémont's Exploring Expedition of 1848*. Taken down by E. F. Murray for Bancroft Library, 1878. Microfilm ms. P. 3 & 13.

Martin, Thomas S. *With Fremont to California and The Southwest 1845-1849*. Ferol Egan, ed , Ashland: Lewis Osborne, 1975. Sacramento CA: California State Library.

Mattes, Merrill J. *The Great Platte River Road: the Covered Wagon Mainline via Fort Kearny to Fort Laramie*. Lincoln: University of Nebraska Press, 1987. Reprinted Nebraska State Historical Society, c1969.

May, Richard M[artin]. See Helfrich/Ackerman, *The Schreek of Wagons*.

———. *A Sketch of a Migrating Family to California in 1848*. Fairfield, WA: Ye Galleon Press, 1991.

McGuckian, Peggy, and Dansie, Amy. *Edward Clapper's Grave and the Peter Lassen Murder Mystery.* Program and Abstracts presented at the 23rd Great Basin Anthropological Conference. Boise, Idaho. October 8-10, 1992.

McKinstry, George. *Overland Letters* to *California Star.* New Helvetia (Sacramento), CA. Feb. 13, 1847.

Middleton, Joseph. *Joseph Middleton 1849 Diary.* New Haven, CT: Yale University, Beinecke Library, WA Mss S-39

Minges, Abram. *Journal May 8, 1849 to June 12, 1851.* Portion transcribed by Richard L. Reick. Bentley Historical Library, University Of Michigan.

Mitchell, Lyman. *Journal from Lyons, Iowa to Lassen's Ranch in 1849.* Microfilm of Diaries of Overland Journeys to California. C-F50 Pt. I Reel 1 #1-10 Berkeley, CA: Bancroft Library.

Morgan, Dale ed. *Overland in 1846 Diaries and Letters of the California-Oregon Trail.* Georgetown, CA: Talisman Press, 1963.

National League of Pen Women, Butte County Branch. *Butte Remembers.* Chico(?) CA, 1973. Lassen Library, Susanville, CA

Neasham, Ernest R. *Fall River Valley: An Examination of Historical Sources*; Sacramento, CA: Citadel Press, Inc.1957-renewed in 1985.

Nelsen, Lawrence. *Peter Lassen, Called the Cecil Rhodes of Northern California.* Peter Guldbrandsen, trans. 1947. Berkeley CA: Gift to Bancroft Library.

Newell, Olive. *Tail of the Elephant: The Emigrant Experience on the Truckee Route of the California Trail, 1844-1852.* Cedar Ridge, CA: Nevada County Historical Society (California Sesquicentennial Publication), 1997.

Nevada Observer, The (TND). Web-based news magazine. Publisher, David Thompson.

Nobles, William. "William Nobles' Letter to Jacob Thompson, Secretary of the Interior April 16, 1857." Washington D.C.: National Archives and Records Administration, Interior Department Records, RG 48, Entry 624, Box 5.

Parmeter, Chris. "Staying Found And Safe In The Mountains." *International Hunter Education Association Journal.* Vol. 11. No. 4, p. 8 – Winter 2011. Burien, WA: Focus Group, Inc.

Peninou, Ernest P. *Peter Lassen's Bosquejo Rancho, 1844-1851.* Red Bluff, CA 1965.

———. *Leland Stanford's Great Vina Ranch 1881-1919.* San Francisco: Research Paper. Yolo Hills Viticultural Society, 1991.

Perkins, Elisha Douglass. *Gold Rush Diary, Being the Journal of Elisha Douglass Perkins on the Overland Trail in the Spring and Summer of 1849.* Thomas D. Clark, ed. Lexington: University of Kentucky Press, 1967.

Peters, De Witt C[linton]. *The Life and Adventures of Kit Carson; the Nestor of the Rocky Mountains–from Facts Narrated by Himself.* New York: W.R.C. Clark & Co. 1858. Republished Freeport, NY: Books for Libraries Press, 1970

Pioneer, The. "The Pacific Coast in 1839," Williams of Monterey Recollections. San Jose, California, Saturday April 6, 1878.

LEGENDARY TRUTHS

Pleasants, William J. *Twice Across the Plains—1849 & 1856.* Fairfield, WA: Ye Galleon Press, 1981.

Pony Express Courier. "Highlights of Lassen County and Susanville, an interview of Fred Kingsbury as told to W. F. Skyhawk." July, 1941.

Pratt, Orson. Journal. *Latter Day Saints' Millennial Star*, XI (1849), 362-70 and XII (1850), 1-180. Council Bluffs 1846-1849. Lincoln: Nebraska State Historical Society.

Purdy, Tim. *At a Glance: A Susanville History.* Susanville, CA: Lahonton Images, 2005.

Rahm, Louisa M[oeller]. Diary, photographic facsimile of ms, 1862. Berkley, CA: Bancroft Library.

Read, Georgia Willis and Ruth Gaines, eds. *Gold Rush: The Journals, Drawings, & Other Papers of J. Goldsborough Bruff. Vol. I & Vol. II.* New York: Columbia University Press, 1944.

———. *Gold Rush: The Journals, Drawings, & Other Papers of J. Goldsborough Bruff, April 2, 1849 - July 20, 1851,* Single Volume, California Centennial Edition. New York: Columbia University Press, 1944, 1949.

Reading, Pierson Barton. "Journal of Pierson Barton Reading....1843." Edited by Helen Putnam Van Sicklen. *Quarterly of the Society of California Pioneers*, Vol. VII, No. 3, San Francisco, 1930.

Red Bluff Beacon, Vol. II, No. 46, February 2, 1859 and Vol. I, No. 33, November 4, 1857.

Rogers, Justus H. "Earliest Explorations of Colusa County." *Colusa County: Its History Traced from a State of Nature Through the Early Period of Settlement and Development, to the Present Day.* Orland, CA, 1891.

Royce, Sarah. *A Frontier Lady; Recollections of the Gold Rush and Early California.* Ralph Henry Gabriel, ed. New Haven, CT: Yale University Press. 1932 and 1933).

Rucker, D. H. "Report to Major General P. F. Smith: September 2-December 3." 1849 Under "Nevada History: The Emigrant Relief Expedition of 1849." *Nevada Observer*, Nevada's Online State News Journal. June 4, 2006. [From Senate Executive Document No. 52, 31st Congress, 1st Session, Serial 561, pp. 96-152]

Russell, Osborne and Aubrey L. Haines. *Journal of a Trapper: In the Rocky Mountains Between 1834 and 1843; Comprising a General Description of the Country, Climate, Rivers, Lakes.* Boise, Idaho: Symes-York Company, 1921

Sacramento Bee. November 30, 1940. Magazine Section. p. 3.

Scamehorn, H. Lee. *The Buckeye Rovers in the Gold Rush: An Edition of Two Diaries.* From journals of John Edwin Banks and J. Elza Armstrong. Edwin P. Banks, and Jamie Lytle-Webb eds. Athens, OH: Ohio University Press, 1965, 1989.

Schallenberger, Moses. *Opening of the California Trail: The Story of the Stevens Party from Reminiscences of Moses Schallenberger...about 1885.* G. R. Stewart, ed. Berkeley: University of California Press, 1953.

Scott, Franklin D. *Peter Lassen: Danish Pioneer of California, 1800-1859.* 1980. Susanville, CA: Lassen Library District.

Shepherd, Dr. J. S. *Journal of Travel Across the Plains to California and a Guide to the Future Emigrant.* Racine, WI: 1851. Reprinted Jan. 1945.

Smith, Harriet A. L. *A Sketch of My Trip Across the Plains in 1849.* A dictation in 1917, transcribed and read to Mrs. Smith by H. C. Readex in 1921. No.: CASLOO18 cf 593 S55. Sacramento: California State Historical Library.

Southern, May Hazel. *Our Stories*[Storied] *Landmarks: Shasta County California.* San Francisco: P. Balakshin Print. Co., 1942.

Sprague, Royal Tyler. *Royal T. Sprague journals: holographs, 1835-1852.* Berkeley, CA: Bancroft Library. BANC MSS 2002/79 cz.

Staebeck, Tosten Kittelsen. *"An Account of a Journey to California in 1852."* Publication of the Norwegian-American Historical Association. Vol. IV, Northfield, MN, 1929

Stewart, George R. *Ordeal by Hunger: The Story of the Donner Party.* Boston and New York: Houghton Mifflin Company, 1936, 1960 and renewed 1963.

———. *The California Trail.* New York: McGraw-Hill, 1962.

Stillson, Richard T. *Spreading the Word: A History of Information in the California Gold Rush.* Lincoln: University of Nebraska Press, 2006.

Swartzlow, Ruby Johnson. *Lassen: His Life and Legacy.* Mineral, CA: Loomis Museum Association, Lassen Volcanic National Park, 1964, reissued 1982.

———. "Peter Lassen, Northern California's Trail-Blazer." San Francisco: *California Historical Society Quarterly.* Vol. XVIII, No. 4, December 1939.

Tiffany, Pardon. Tiffany Diary, September 10, 12, & 14, 1849. *Mississippi Valley Historical Review.* Vol. 42, no.3, Dec. 1955. Missouri Historical Society, Threlkeld Typescript, 117-19.

Trash Guide XXV. "Truckee River Route." July 17, 18, 19, 1998. Sacramento: California State Historical Library.

———. XXVIII: "To the Carson River Route." July 20, 21, 22, 2001. Sacramento: California State Historical Library.

Unruh, John D. Jr. *The Plains Across: The Overland Emigrants and the Trans-Mississippi West, 1840-60.* Urbana and Chicago: University of Illinois Press, 1979.

Van Dorn, T.J. *Diary, 14, 15 August 1849.* New Haven, CT: Yale University, Beinecke Rare Book and Manuscript Library.

Vogel-Jørgensen, T[heodore]. *Peter Lassen of California.* Copenhagen: Berlingske Forlag, 1937. Loomis Museum Association, 1946.

Warner, Barbara R. *The Men of the Bear Flag Revolt and Their Heritage.* Arthur H. Clark Publishing Company for the Sonoma Valley Historical Society, 1996.

Webster, Kimball. *The Gold Seekers of '49: A Personal Narrative of the Overland Trail and Adventures in California and Oregon from 1849 to 1852.* Manchester, NH: Standard Book Company, 1917.

LEGENDARY TRUTHS

Werner, Emmy E. *Pioneer Children on the Journey West.* Boulder, CO: Westview Press, 1995.

Wheeler, Sessions S. *The Nevada Desert.* Caldwell, ID: The Caxton Printers, Ltd., 1989.

Wiggins, William. *Reminiscences of William Wiggins, who Came to California in 1840 on the 'Lausanné'.* Dictated to Thos. Savage for the Bancroft Library, MS 1877 pp. 1-3.

———. Letter of April 23, 1844. In the Thomas O[liver] Larkin Papers, Berkeley: Bancroft Library. C-B 38:1-139, CB 38-80

Williams of Monterey. Recollections. An article titled, "The Pacific Coast in 1839, credited to the "pen of Williams of Monterey." San Jose, CA: *The Pioneer,* Saturday April 6, 1878. Note: This is possibly William Wiggins.

Williamson, R[obert] S[tockton]. "Report of a Reconnaissance and Survey in California: In Connexion [sic] With Explorations for a Practical Railway Route from the Mississippi River to the Pacific Ocean, in 1853." Washington, D.C. 1854 Bound in *Pamphlets on California's Railroads,* Bancroft Library.

Wislizenus, Fredrick A. M.D. *A Journey to The Rocky Mountains in The Year 1839.* Translated from German by Frederick A Wislizenus, Esq. St. Louis: Missouri Historical Society, 1912.

———. Journal on line. Library of Western Fur Trade Historical Source Documents, Diaries, Narratives, and Letters of the Mountain Men.— http://www.xmission. com/~drudy/mtman/html/wislizenus/#_Toc504985229 ch. 4.

Wood, John. *Journal of John Wood: as Kept by Him While Traveling from Cincinnati to the Gold Diggings in California, in the Spring and Summer of 1850....* Columbus, Ohio: Nevins & Meyers, 1871. Lincoln: Nebraska State Historical Society.

Wyeth, Nathaniel J., Capt. *The Correspondence and Journals of Captain Nathaniel J. Wyeth, 1831-6: a Record of Two Expeditions for the Occupation of the Oregon Country....* F.G. Young, ed. Eugene, OR: University Press, 1899.

CPSIA information can be obtained
at www.ICGtesting.com
Printed in the USA
FFOW01n1649191114
8823FF